BREAD FOR THE DAY

DAILY BIBLE READINGS AND PRAYERS

2018

 AUGSBURG FORTRESS

Minneapolis

BREAD FOR THE DAY 2018
Daily Bible Readings and Prayers

Editors: Dennis Bushkofsky, Suzanne Burke
Cover design: Laurie Ingram
Interior design: Becky Lowe-Weyand
Cover art: Christina Saj
Interior art: Gertrud Mueller Nelson

Contributors to the weekday prayers: Kristin Berkey-Abbott, Hollywood, Florida (January); Sarah Carson, Chicago, Illinois (February); Amy White, Grand Rapids, Michigan (March); Laurel Hensel, Park Ridge, Illinois (April); Meghan Johnston Aelabouni, Fort Collins, Colorado (May); Michael Tassler, Colorado Springs, Colorado (June); Julie A. Kanarr, Belfair, Washington (July); Robin McCullough-Bade, Baton Rouge, Louisiana (August); Rebecca Eve Schweitzer, Sterling Heights, Michigan (September); Will Storm, Houston, Texas (October); Sue Edison-Swift, Decorah, Iowa (November); Christine Therriault-Merkel, Bristol, Connecticut (December)

ACKNOWLEDGMENTS
Scripture quotations are from the New Revised Standard Version Bible © 1989 Division of Christian Education of the National Council of the Churches of Christ in the United States of America. Used by permission.

Hymn suggestions and prayers of the day for Sundays and festivals are from *Evangelical Lutheran Worship,* copyright © 2006 Evangelical Lutheran Church in America.

Materials prepared by the Consultation on Common Texts (CCT), published in *Revised Common Lectionary* © 1992 and *Revised Common Lectionary Daily Readings* © 2005. Used by permission.

"Table prayer for the season of Lent," "Table prayer for Summer," "A prayer to begin the work day," "A prayer to begin the school day," "Morning blessing," and "Evening blessing" are from *Reformation 500 Sourcebook: Anniversary Resources for Congregations,* © 2016 Augsburg Fortress.

Materials prepared by the English Language Liturgical Consultation (ELLC), published in *Praying Together* © 1988: "Blessed are you, Lord" and "My soul proclaims the greatness of the Lord." Used by permission.

ISBN 978-1-4514-9611-6
Manufactured in the U.S.A.

Contents

September

October

November

December

Additional Resources

Foreword

Beloved of God,

For generations, the living word has sustained God's people. In times of prosperity and turmoil, joy and sorrow, the church has found hope and consolation in scripture.

The Evangelical Lutheran Church in America has embraced the initiative called Book of Faith. In it we have committed ourselves to deepening our fluency in the first language of faith, holy scripture. Bread for the Day is a wonderful resource for your daily encounter with the word. You will be nourished, encouraged, and sustained, as have the saints before you.

As the Conference of Bishops, we invite you to join us, and this whole church in persistent attentiveness to the word. Your faith will be deepened, your witness empowered, and your church enriched. God bless your journey in faith.

Conference of Bishops
Evangelical Lutheran Church in America

For more about Book of Faith, visit www.bookoffaith.org.

Introduction

Daily prayer is an essential practice for those who seek to hear God's voice and cultivate an inner life. Whether you pray alone or with others, with brevity or sustained meditation, the rhythm of daily prayer reveals the life-sustaining communion to which God invites all human beings. Such prayer is a serene power silently at work, drawing us into the ancient yet vital sources of faith, hope, and love.

The guiding principle of the selection of daily readings in *Bread for the Day* is their relationship to the Sunday readings as presented in the Revised Common Lectionary (a system of readings in widespread use across denominations). The readings are chosen so that the days leading up to Sunday (Thursday through Saturday) prepare for the Sunday readings. The days flowing out from Sunday (Monday through Wednesday) reflect on the Sunday readings.

How this book is organized

- Each day's page is dated and named in relationship to the church's year. Lesser festivals are listed along with the date as part of the day heading. Commemorations are listed just below in smaller type. Notes on those commemorated can be found on pages 407–415.
- Several verses of one of the appointed scripture texts are printed. The full text citation is provided for those who would like to reflect on the entire text. In addition, two or three additional reading citations with short descriptions are provided.
- Two psalms are appointed for each week; one psalm for Monday through Wednesday and a second psalm for Thursday through Saturday. In this way the days leading up to Sunday or flowing out from Sunday have a distinct relationship with one another in addition to their relationship with the Sunday readings.

- Following the printed scripture text is a hymn suggestion from *Evangelical Lutheran Worship* and a prayer that incorporates a theme present in one or more of the readings.
- Household prayers and blessings appropriate to the changing seasons are placed throughout the book. Simplified forms of morning and evening prayer, morning and evening blessings, and prayers with children can be found on pages 424–431.

How to use this book

- Use the weekday readings to prepare for and reflect on the Sunday readings.
- Use the questions printed on page 431 to guide your reflection on the scripture texts.
- Use the resources for household prayer placed throughout the book. See the Contents on pages 3–4 for a complete list.
- Use the page at the beginning of each month to record prayer requests.
- In addition to being used to guide individual prayer, this book may also be used to guide family prayer, prayer in congregational or other settings during the week, prayer with those who are sick or homebound, or with other groups.

Even though Christians gather on the Lord's day, Sunday, for public worship, much of our time is spent in the home. We first learn the words, gestures, and songs of faith in the home. We discover our essential identity as a community of faith and mark significant transitions of life in the home. To surround and infuse the daily rhythm of sleeping and waking, working, resting, and eating with the words and gestures of Christian prayer is to discover the ancient truth of the gospel: the ordinary and the human can reveal the mystery of God and divine grace. Like planets around the sun, our daily prayer draws us to the Sunday assembly where we gather for the word and the breaking of the bread in the changing seasons of the year. From the Sunday assembly, our daily prayer flows into the week.

Prayer List for January

_____

_____

_____

_____

_____

_____

_____

_____

_____

_____

Monday, January 1, 2018
Name of Jesus

Numbers 6:22-27
The Aaronic blessing

The LORD spoke to Moses, saying: Speak to Aaron and his sons, saying,
Thus you shall bless the Israelites: You shall say to them,

> The LORD bless you and keep you;
> the LORD make his face to shine upon you, and be gracious to you;
> the LORD lift up his countenance upon you, and give you peace.

So they shall put my name on the Israelites, and I will bless them.
(Num. 6:22-27)

Psalm
Psalm 8
How exalted is your name

Additional Readings
Galatians 4:4-7
We are no longer slaves

Luke 2:15-21
The child is named Jesus

Hymn: Jesus, the Very Thought of You, ELW 754

Eternal Father, you gave your incarnate Son the holy name of Jesus to be a sign of our salvation. Plant in every heart the love of the Savior of the world, Jesus Christ our Lord, who lives and reigns with you and the Holy Spirit, one God, now and forever.

Tuesday, January 2, 2018
Week of Christmas 1

Johann Konrad Wilhelm Loehe, renewer of the church, died 1872

Psalm 148

God's splendor is over earth and heaven

Kings of the earth and all peoples,
    princes and all rulers of the earth!
Young men and women alike,
    old and young together!
Let them praise the name of the LORD,
    for his name alone is exalted;
    his glory is above earth and heaven.
He has raised up a horn for his people,
    praise for all his faithful,
    for the people of Israel who are close to him.
Praise the LORD! (Ps. 148:11-14)

Additional Readings

Proverbs 1:1-7
Grow in wisdom and knowledge

James 3:13-18
The wisdom from above

Hymn: Where Charity and Love Prevail, ELW 359

Praise to you, God of all creation and of all peoples across the earth. We praise you for your protection. We praise you for your bountiful blessings. We exalt your name forever.

Wednesday, January 3, 2018
Week of Christmas 1

James 4:1-10
Humble yourselves before God

Those conflicts and disputes among you, where do they come from? Do they not come from your cravings that are at war within you? You want something and do not have it; so you commit murder. And you covet something and cannot obtain it; so you engage in disputes and conflicts. You do not have, because you do not ask. You ask and do not receive, because you ask wrongly, in order to spend what you get on your pleasures. Adulterers! Do you not know that friendship with the world is enmity with God? Therefore whoever wishes to be a friend of the world becomes an enemy of God. (James 4:1-4)

Psalm
Psalm 110
Prayers for the king

Additional Reading
Proverbs 1:20-33
Give heed to Wisdom, live without dread

Hymn: Oh, That the Lord Would Guide My Ways, ELW 772

God of generosity, you give us so much before we even think to ask. You know what we crave. Help us to ask for what we need and open our hearts to share with others.

Thursday, January 4, 2018
Week of Christmas 1

Psalm 110
Prayers for the king

The Lord says to my lord,
    "Sit at my right hand
until I make your enemies your footstool."

The Lord sends out from Zion
    your mighty scepter.
    Rule in the midst of your foes.
Your people will offer themselves willingly
    on the day you lead your forces
    on the holy mountains.
From the womb of the morning,
    like dew, your youth will come to you.
The Lord has sworn and will not change his mind,
    "You are a priest forever according to the order of Melchizedek."
(Ps. 110:1-4)

Additional Readings
Proverbs 3:1-12
Trust in God with all your heart

James 4:11-17
Our plans for our time are in God's hands

Hymn: Abide, O Dearest Jesus, ELW 539

God who rules over all, though many people seek positions of leadership, fewer of them are attuned to your guidance and counsel. Help us to fulfill our duties with wisdom and compassion.

Friday, January 5, 2018
Week of Christmas 1

Luke 6:27-31

Do to others as you would have them do to you

"But I say to you that listen, Love your enemies, do good to those who hate you, bless those who curse you, pray for those who abuse you. If anyone strikes you on the cheek, offer the other also; and from anyone who takes away your coat do not withhold even your shirt. Give to everyone who begs from you; and if anyone takes away your goods, do not ask for them again. Do to others as you would have them do to you." (Luke 6:27-31)

Psalm

Psalm 110
Prayers for the king

Additional Reading

Proverbs 22:1-9
The generous are blessed

Hymn: Angels, from the Realms of Glory, ELW 275

Peace-creating God, you know how hard it is for us to love our enemies and to bless those who would oppress us. Help us to live as peacemakers, treating others in ways we yearn to be treated.

Blessing for a Home at Epiphany

Matthew writes that when the magi saw the shining star stop overhead, they were filled with joy. "On entering the house, they saw the child with Mary his mother" (Matt. 2:10-11). In the home, Christ is met in family and friends, in visitors and strangers. In the home, faith is shared, nurtured, and put into action. In the home, Christ is welcome.

Twelfth Night (January 5), Epiphany of Our Lord (January 6), or another day during the time after Epiphany offers an occasion for gathering with friends and family members for a blessing for the home. Someone may lead the greeting and blessing, while another person may read the scripture passage. Following an eastern European tradition, a visual blessing may be inscribed with white chalk above the main door; for example, 20 + CMB + 18. The numbers change with each new year. The three letters stand for either the ancient Latin blessing Christe mansionem benedicat, which means, "Christ, bless this house," or the legendary names of the magi (Caspar, Melchior, and Balthasar).

Greeting
Peace to this house and to all who enter here.
By wisdom a house is built,
and through understanding it is established;
through knowledge its rooms are filled
with rare and beautiful treasures. *(Prov. 24:3-4)*

Reading
As we prepare to ask God's blessing on this household,
let us listen to the words of scripture.
In the beginning was the Word,
and the Word was with God, and the Word was God.
He was in the beginning with God.
All things came into being through him,
and without him not one thing came into being.

What has come into being in him was life,
and the life was the light of all people.
The Word became flesh and lived among us, and we have seen his glory,
the glory as of a father's only son, full of grace and truth.
From his fullness we have all received, grace upon grace.
(John 1:1-4, 14, 16)

Inscription

This inscription may be made with chalk above the entrance:

20 + C M B + 18

Write the appropriate character (left) while speaking the text (right).

The magi of old, known as

C   Caspar,

M   Melchior, and

B   Balthasar

followed the star of God's Son who came to dwell among us

20   two thousand

18   and eighteen years ago.

+   Christ, bless this house,

+   and remain with us throughout the new year.

Prayer of Blessing

O God,
you revealed your Son to all people by the shining light of a star.
We pray that you bless this home and all who live here
with your gracious presence.
May your love be our inspiration, your wisdom our guide,
your truth our light, and your peace our benediction;
through Christ our Lord. Amen.

*Then everyone may walk from room to room, blessing the house with incense or by
sprinkling with water, perhaps using a branch from the Christmas tree.*

Saturday, January 6, 2018
Epiphany of Our Lord

Matthew 2:1-12
Christ revealed to the nations

In the time of King Herod, after Jesus was born in Bethlehem of Judea, wise men from the East came to Jerusalem, asking, "Where is the child who has been born king of the Jews? For we observed his star at its rising, and have come to pay him homage." When King Herod heard this, he was frightened, and all Jerusalem with him; and calling together all the chief priests and scribes of the people, he inquired of them where the Messiah was to be born. They told him, "In Bethlehem of Judea; for so it has been written by the prophet." (Matt. 2:1-5)

Psalm
Psalm 72:1-7, 10-14
All shall bow down

Additional Readings
Isaiah 60:1-6
Nations come to the light

Ephesians 3:1-12
The gospel's promise for all

Hymn: Brightest and Best of the Stars, ELW 303

Everlasting God, the radiance of all faithful people, you brought the nations to the brightness of your rising. Fill the world with your glory, and show yourself to all the world through him who is the true light and the bright morning star, your Son, Jesus Christ, our Savior and Lord, who lives and reigns with you and the Holy Spirit, one God, now and forever.

Time after Epiphany

On the Epiphany of Our Lord (January 6), the household joins the church throughout the world in celebrating the manifestation, the "epiphany," of Christ to the world. The festival of Christmas is thus set within the context of outreach to the larger community; it possesses an outward movement. The festival of the Epiphany asks the Christian household: How might our faith in Christ the Light be shared with friends and family, with our neighbors, with the poor and needy in our land, with those who live in other nations?

Table Prayer for Epiphany and the Time after Epiphany (January 6–February 13)

Generous God,
you have made yourself known in Jesus, the light of the world.
As this food and drink give us refreshment,
so strengthen us by your Spirit,
that as your baptized sons and daughters
we may share your light with all the world.
Grant this through Christ our Lord.
Amen.

Sunday, January 7, 2018
Baptism of Our Lord

Mark 1:4-11

Jesus revealed as God's servant

John the baptizer appeared in the wilderness, proclaiming a baptism of repentance for the forgiveness of sins. And people from the whole Judean countryside and all the people of Jerusalem were going out to him, and were baptized by him in the river Jordan, confessing their sins. Now John was clothed with camel's hair, with a leather belt around his waist, and he ate locusts and wild honey. He proclaimed, "The one who is more powerful than I is coming after me; I am not worthy to stoop down and untie the thong of his sandals. I have baptized you with water; but he will baptize you with the Holy Spirit." (Mark 1:4-8)

Psalm

Psalm 29
The voice of God upon the waters

Additional Readings

Acts 19:1-7
Baptized in the name of Jesus

Genesis 1:1-5
God creates light

Hymn: When Jesus Came to Jordan, ELW 305

Holy God, creator of light and giver of goodness, your voice moves over the waters. Immerse us in your grace, and transform us by your Spirit, that we may follow after your Son, Jesus Christ, our Savior and Lord, who lives and reigns with you and the Holy Spirit, one God, now and forever.

Monday, January 8, 2018
Time after Epiphany

Psalm 69:1-5, 30-36
God will save through water

Save me, O God,
>for the waters have come up to my neck.

I sink in deep mire,
>where there is no foothold;

I have come into deep waters,
>and the flood sweeps over me.

I am weary with my crying;
>my throat is parched.

My eyes grow dim
>with waiting for my God. (Ps. 69:1-3)

Additional Readings
Genesis 17:1-13
Circumcision a covenant sign

Romans 4:1-12
God makes righteous apart from works

Hymn: Rock of Ages, Cleft for Me, ELW 623

Rescuer God, you know how often we battle against forces that threaten to separate us from you. As we wait for deliverance, sustain our faith that you will come to our aid.

Tuesday, January 9, 2018
Time after Epiphany

Acts 22:2-16

Paul describes his own baptism

"A certain Ananias, who was a devout man according to the law and well spoken of by all the Jews living there, came to me; and standing beside me, he said, 'Brother Saul, regain your sight!' In that very hour I regained my sight and saw him. Then he said, 'The God of our ancestors has chosen you to know his will, to see the Righteous One and to hear his own voice; for you will be his witness to all the world of what you have seen and heard. And now why do you delay? Get up, be baptized, and have your sins washed away, calling on his name.'" (Acts 22:12-16)

Psalm
Psalm 69:1-5, 30-36
God will save through water

Additional Reading
Exodus 30:22-38
Anointing a sign of holiness

Hymn: All Who Believe and Are Baptized, ELW 442

God of kept promises, you see how forces of this world can blind us to all wonders. Let us hear your voice. Give us the courage to follow you without delay.

Wednesday, January 10, 2018
Time after Epiphany

Isaiah 41:14-20
God gives water in the desert

When the poor and needy seek water,
   and there is none,
   and their tongue is parched with thirst,
I the Lord will answer them,
   I the God of Israel will not forsake them.
I will open rivers on the bare heights,
   and fountains in the midst of the valleys;
I will make the wilderness a pool of water,
   and the dry land springs of water. . . .
so that all may see and know,
   all may consider and understand,
that the hand of the Lord has done this,
   the Holy One of Israel has created it. (Isa. 41:17-18, 20)

Psalm
Psalm 69:1-5, 30-36
God will save through water

Additional Reading
John 1:29-34
John's account of Jesus' baptism

Hymn: Crashing Waters at Creation, ELW 455

God of restoration, you know how many of us live in wilderness spaces. You hear our parched cells crying out for the water that only you can give. Bring us nourishment and let every desert bloom.

Thursday, January 11, 2018
Time after Epiphany

Psalm 139:1-6, 13-18
You have searched me out

O LORD, you have searched me and known me.
You know when I sit down and when I rise up;
    you discern my thoughts from far away.
You search out my path and my lying down,
    and are acquainted with all my ways.
Even before a word is on my tongue,
    O LORD, you know it completely. (Ps. 139:1-4)

Additional Readings
Judges 2:6-15
Uncertain times after Joshua's death

2 Corinthians 10:1-11
Corinthian behavior during Paul's absence

Hymn: Borning Cry, ELW 732

Ever-present God, we thank you for keeping watch over us. You are the one who knows our most secret spaces. We are grateful that you know us so completely and that you still love us so fully.

Friday, January 12, 2018
Time after Epiphany

Acts 13:16-25

Leaders prior to Christ's coming

Paul spoke: "... God has brought to Israel a Savior, Jesus, as he promised; before his coming John had already proclaimed a baptism of repentance to all the people of Israel. And as John was finishing his work, he said, 'What do you suppose that I am? I am not he. No, but one is coming after me; I am not worthy to untie the thong of the sandals on his feet.'" (Acts 13:23-25)

Psalm
Psalm 139:1-6, 13-18
You have searched me out

Additional Reading
Judges 2:16-23
God calls forth the judges

Hymn: Soli Deo Gloria, ELW 878

God, we praise you as a keeper of promises. In this world of desperation, may we look to you for our salvation. Help us to remember that your Messiah has already come to us in the person of Jesus.

Saturday, January 13, 2018
Time after Epiphany

1 Samuel 2:21-25

Eli's sons sin

And the Lord took note of Hannah; she conceived and bore three sons and two daughters. And the boy Samuel grew up in the presence of the Lord.

Now Eli was very old. He heard all that his sons were doing to all Israel, and how they lay with the women who served at the entrance to the tent of meeting. He said to them, "Why do you do such things? For I hear of your evil dealings from all these people. No, my sons; it is not a good report that I hear the people of the Lord spreading abroad. If one person sins against another, someone can intercede for the sinner with the Lord; but if someone sins against the Lord, who can make intercession?" But they would not listen to the voice of their father; for it was the will of the Lord to kill them. (1 Sam. 2:21-25)

Psalm
Psalm 139:1-6, 13-18
You have searched me out

Additional Reading
Matthew 25:1-13
Wise and foolish bridesmaids

Hymn: Lord Jesus, Think on Me, ELW 599

Thanks, God, for taking notice of us. We bless you for the voices of our elders who have sought wisdom from you. Open our ears to their voices that we might also take notice of your desires for us.

Sunday, January 14, 2018
Second Sunday after Epiphany

John 1:43-51

The calling of the first disciples

The next day Jesus decided to go to Galilee. He found Philip and said to him, "Follow me." Now Philip was from Bethsaida, the city of Andrew and Peter. Philip found Nathanael and said to him, "We have found him about whom Moses in the law and also the prophets wrote, Jesus son of Joseph from Nazareth." Nathanael said to him, "Can anything good come out of Nazareth?" Philip said to him, "Come and see." (John 1:43-46)

Psalm

Psalm 139:1-6, 13-18
You have searched me out

Additional Readings

1 Samuel 3:1-10
[11-20]
The calling of Samuel

1 Corinthians 6:12-20
Glorify God in your body

Hymn: The Son of God, Our Christ, ELW 584

Thanks be to you, Lord Jesus Christ, most merciful redeemer, for the countless blessings and benefits you give. May we know you more clearly, love you more dearly, and follow you more nearly, day by day praising you, with the Father and the Holy Spirit, one God, now and forever.

Monday, January 15, 2018
Time after Epiphany

Martin Luther King Jr., renewer of society, martyr, died 1968

Psalm 86
Walking in God's way

Teach me your way, O Lord,
>that I may walk in your truth;
>give me an undivided heart to revere your name.
I give thanks to you, O Lord my God, with my whole heart,
>and I will glorify your name forever.
For great is your steadfast love toward me;
>you have delivered my soul from the depths of Sheol. (Ps. 86:11-13)

Additional Readings
1 Samuel 9:27—10:8
Samuel anoints Saul king

2 Corinthians 6:14—7:1
Believers are called out

Hymn: You Are the Way, ELW 758

God, we give you thanks for all the wonders large and small that surround us every day. Continue to school us in all that is true. Unite our hearts together so that we can glorify your name forever.

Tuesday, January 16, 2018
Time after Epiphany

Acts 5:1-11

Ananias and Sapphira judged

But a man named Ananias, with the consent of his wife Sapphira, sold a piece of property; with his wife's knowledge, he kept back some of the proceeds, and brought only a part and laid it at the apostles' feet. "Ananias," Peter asked, "why has Satan filled your heart to lie to the Holy Spirit and to keep back part of the proceeds of the land? While it remained unsold, did it not remain your own? And after it was sold, were not the proceeds at your disposal? How is it that you have contrived this deed in your heart? You did not lie to us but to God!" Now when Ananias heard these words, he fell down and died. And great fear seized all who heard of it. (Acts 5:1-5)

Psalm
Psalm 86
Walking in God's way

Additional Readings
1 Samuel 15:10-31
Samuel rebukes King Saul

Hymn: I Want to Walk as a Child of the Light, ELW 815

Glorious God, we repent of our greedy natures and grasping hands. Reform us yet again. Fashion us new hearts so full of your love that we withhold nothing from anyone in need.

Wednesday, January 17, 2018
Time after Epiphany

Antony of Egypt, renewer of the church, died around 356
Pachomius, renewer of the church, died 346

Luke 18:15-17
Jesus blesses little children

People were bringing even infants to Jesus that he might touch them; and when the disciples saw it, they sternly ordered them not to do it. But Jesus called for them and said, "Let the little children come to me, and do not stop them; for it is to such as these that the kingdom of God belongs. Truly I tell you, whoever does not receive the kingdom of God as a little child will never enter it." (Luke 18:15-17)

Psalm
Psalm 86
Walking in God's way

Additional Reading
Genesis 16:1-14
Hagar sees God and is blessed

Hymn: Cradling Children in His Arm, ELW 444

Caregiver God, give us the faith of little children. Restore to us the ability to see the wonders of the world that we perceived so clearly when we were younger. Help us to approach you and be received.

Thursday, January 18, 2018
Confession of Peter

Week of Prayer for Christian Unity begins

Matthew 16:13-19

Peter confesses, You are the Messiah

[Jesus] said to [his disciples,] "But who do you say that I am?" Simon Peter answered, "You are the Messiah, the Son of the living God." And Jesus answered him, "Blessed are you, Simon son of Jonah! For flesh and blood has not revealed this to you, but my Father in heaven. And I tell you, you are Peter, and on this rock I will build my church, and the gates of Hades will not prevail against it. I will give you the keys of the kingdom of heaven, and whatever you bind on earth will be bound in heaven, and whatever you loose on earth will be loosed in heaven." (Matt. 16:15-19)

Psalm

Psalm 18:1-6, 16-19
My God, my rock, worthy of praise

Additional Readings

Acts 4:8-13
Salvation is in no one other than Jesus

1 Corinthians 10:1-5
Drinking from the spiritual rock of Christ

Hymn: Oh, Praise the Gracious Power, ELW 651

Almighty God, you inspired Simon Peter to confess Jesus as the Messiah and Son of the living God. Keep your church firm on the rock of this faith, so that in unity and peace it may proclaim one truth and follow one Lord, your Son, Jesus Christ our Savior, who lives and reigns with you and the Holy Spirit, one God, now and forever.

Friday, January 19, 2018
Time after Epiphany

Henry, Bishop of Uppsala, martyr, died 1156

Psalm 62:5-12
In God is my safety and my honor

For God alone my soul waits in silence,
    for my hope is from him.
He alone is my rock and my salvation,
    my fortress; I shall not be shaken.
On God rests my deliverance and my honor;
    my mighty rock, my refuge is in God. (Ps. 62:5-7)

Additional Readings
Jeremiah 20:7-13
Jeremiah denounces his persecutors

2 Peter 3:1-7
Scoffers doubt God's message

Hymn: O God of Light, ELW 507

Centering God, silence our noisy world that we may hear your voice. Help us to abandon fortresses of our own making to seek shelter on your firm rock and refuge.

Saturday, January 20, 2018
Time after Epiphany

Luke 10:13-16

Woe to those who reject God's messengers

[The Lord said,] "Woe to you, Chorazin! Woe to you, Bethsaida! For if the deeds of power done in you had been done in Tyre and Sidon, they would have repented long ago, sitting in sackcloth and ashes. But at the judgment it will be more tolerable for Tyre and Sidon than for you. And you, Capernaum,

> will you be exalted to heaven?
>> No, you will be brought down to Hades.

"Whoever listens to you listens to me, and whoever rejects you rejects me, and whoever rejects me rejects the one who sent me." (Luke 10:13-16)

Psalm
Psalm 62:5-12
In God is my safety and my honor

Additional Reading
Jeremiah 20:14-18
Jeremiah curses the day of his birth

Hymn: Listen, God Is Calling, ELW 513

O God, you have sent many prophets through the ages. Train our ears to hear you and not to reject the people you have sent. Give us open hearts and ears so that we can listen.

Sunday, January 21, 2018
Third Sunday after Epiphany

Agnes, martyr, died around 304

Mark 1:14-20

The calling of the disciples at the sea

Now after John was arrested, Jesus came to Galilee, proclaiming the good news of God, and saying, "The time is fulfilled, and the kingdom of God has come near; repent, and believe in the good news."

As Jesus passed along the Sea of Galilee, he saw Simon and his brother Andrew casting a net into the sea—for they were fishermen. And Jesus said to them, "Follow me and I will make you fish for people." And immediately they left their nets and followed him. As he went a little farther, he saw James son of Zebedee and his brother John, who were in their boat mending the nets. Immediately he called them; and they left their father Zebedee in the boat with the hired men, and followed him. (Mark 1:14-20)

Psalm

Psalm 62:5-12
In God is my safety and my honor

Additional Readings

Jonah 3:1-5, 10
Repentance at Nineveh

1 Corinthians 7:29-31
Living in the end times

Hymn: You Have Come Down to the Lakeshore, ELW 817

Almighty God, by grace alone you call us and accept us in your service. Strengthen us by your Spirit, and make us worthy of your call, through Jesus Christ, our Savior and Lord.

Monday, January 22, 2018
Time after Epiphany

Psalm 46
The God of Jacob is our stronghold

Come, behold the works of the LORD;
>   see what desolations he has brought on the earth.
He makes wars cease to the end of the earth;
>   he breaks the bow, and shatters the spear;
>   he burns the shields with fire.
"Be still, and know that I am God!
>   I am exalted among the nations,
>   I am exalted in the earth."
The LORD of hosts is with us;
>   the God of Jacob is our refuge. (Ps. 46:8-11)

Additional Readings

Genesis 12:1-9
God calls Abram to go to Canaan

1 Corinthians 7:17-24
Live the life assigned

Hymn: O God of Love, O King of Peace, ELW 749

Healer of divisions, we live in a world of conflicts and deep separations. Bring us your guidance and give us the tools we need to patch a peaceful world together again.

Tuesday, January 23, 2018
Time after Epiphany

Genesis 45:25—46:7
God calls Jacob to go to Egypt

When Israel set out on his journey with all that he had and came to Beer-sheba, he offered sacrifices to the God of his father Isaac. God spoke to Israel in visions of the night, and said, "Jacob, Jacob." And he said, "Here I am." Then he said, "I am God, the God of your father; do not be afraid to go down to Egypt, for I will make of you a great nation there. I myself will go down with you to Egypt, and I will also bring you up again; and Joseph's own hand shall close your eyes." (Gen. 46:1-4)

Psalm
Psalm 46
The God of Jacob is our stronghold

Additional Reading
Acts 5:33-42
The apostles are tried and flogged

Hymn: O God of Every Nation, ELW 713

God of visions and journeys, help us never to shirk the tasks you have for us. Lead us where you need us to go. Help us trust that you will be forever at our sides.

Wednesday, January 24, 2018
Time after Epiphany

Proverbs 8:1-21
Wisdom calls the people

Does not wisdom call,
    and does not understanding raise her voice?
On the heights, beside the way,
    at the crossroads she takes her stand;
beside the gates in front of the town,
    at the entrance of the portals she cries out:
"To you, O people, I call,
    and my cry is to all that live.
O simple ones, learn prudence;
    acquire intelligence, you who lack it. " (Prov. 8:1-5)

Psalm
Psalm 46
The God of Jacob is our stronghold

Additional Reading
Mark 3:13-19a
Jesus appoints the Twelve

Hymn: O Holy Spirit, Root of Life, ELW 399

God of every intelligence, help us listen for voices of wisdom among us. Give us courage to join those who stand ground in desolate places. Let us not be lacking in understanding the needs around us.

Thursday, January 25, 2018
Conversion of Paul

Week of Prayer for Christian Unity ends

Galatians 1:11-24
Paul receives a revelation of Christ

You have heard, no doubt, of my earlier life in Judaism. I was violently persecuting the church of God and was trying to destroy it. I advanced in Judaism beyond many among my people of the same age, for I was far more zealous for the traditions of my ancestors. But when God, who had set me apart before I was born and called me through his grace, was pleased to reveal his Son to me, so that I might proclaim him among the Gentiles, I did not confer with any human being, nor did I go up to Jerusalem to those who were already apostles before me, but I went away at once into Arabia, and afterwards I returned to Damascus. (Gal. 1:13-17)

Psalm

Psalm 67
Let all the peoples praise you, O God

Additional Readings

Acts 9:1-22
Saul is converted to Christ

Luke 21:10-19
The end times will require endurance

Hymn: For by Grace You Have Been Saved, ELW 598

O God, by the preaching of your apostle Paul you have caused the light of the gospel to shine throughout the world. Grant that we may follow his example and be witnesses to the truth of your Son, Jesus Christ, our Savior and Lord, who lives and reigns with you and the Holy Spirit, one God, now and forever.

Friday, January 26, 2018
Time after Epiphany

Timothy, Titus, and Silas, missionaries

Psalm 111

The beginning of wisdom

Praise the LORD!
I will give thanks to the LORD with my whole heart,
    in the company of the upright, in the congregation.
Great are the works of the LORD,
    studied by all who delight in them.
Full of honor and majesty is his work,
    and his righteousness endures forever. (Ps. 111:1-3)

Additional Readings

Deuteronomy 12:28-32
Warnings against idolatry

Revelation 2:12-17
Idolatrous behavior is condemned

Hymn: Baptized and Set Free, ELW 453

O God, we spend too much time in pursuit of things that do not ultimately nourish or satisfy. Help us to see the great works you are accomplishing in our world today that we might lend our support to them.

Saturday, January 27, 2018
Time after Epiphany

Lydia, Dorcas, and Phoebe, witnesses to the faith

Deuteronomy 13:1-5
Beware of false prophets

If prophets or those who divine by dreams appear among you and promise you omens or portents, and the omens or the portents declared by them take place, and they say, "Let us follow other gods" (whom you have not known) "and let us serve them," you must not heed the words of those prophets or those who divine by dreams; for the LORD your God is testing you, to know whether you indeed love the LORD your God with all your heart and soul. The LORD your God you shall follow, him alone you shall fear, his commandments you shall keep, his voice you shall obey, him you shall serve, and to him you shall hold fast. But those prophets or those who divine by dreams shall be put to death for having spoken treason against the LORD your God—who brought you out of the land of Egypt and redeemed you from the house of slavery—to turn you from the way in which the LORD your God commanded you to walk. So you shall purge the evil from your midst. (Deut. 13:1-5)

Psalm
Psalm 111
The beginning of wisdom

Additional Reading
Matthew 8:28—9:1
Jesus heals the Gadarene demoniacs

Hymn: O Jesus, I Have Promised, ELW 810

God, you know how we face temptations to create many false idols. Keep our hearts in tune with you and help us walk in the ways that you desire.

Sunday, January 28, 2018
Fourth Sunday after Epiphany

Thomas Aquinas, teacher, died 1274

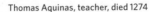

Mark 1:21-28
The healing of one with an unclean spirit

[Jesus' disciples] went to Capernaum; and when the sabbath came, [Jesus] entered the synagogue and taught. They were astounded at his teaching, for he taught them as one having authority, and not as the scribes. Just then there was in their synagogue a man with an unclean spirit, and he cried out, "What have you to do with us, Jesus of Nazareth? Have you come to destroy us? I know who you are, the Holy One of God." But Jesus rebuked him, saying, "Be silent, and come out of him!" (Mark 1:21-25)

Psalm

Psalm 111
The beginning of wisdom

Additional Readings

Deuteronomy 18:15-20
The prophet speaks with God's authority

1 Corinthians 8:1-13
Limits to liberty

Hymn: O Christ, Our Light, O Radiance True, ELW 675

Compassionate God, you gather the whole universe into your radiant presence and continually reveal your Son as our Savior. Bring wholeness to all that is broken and speak truth to us in our confusion, that all creation will see and know your Son, Jesus Christ, our Savior and Lord.

Monday, January 29, 2018
Time after Epiphany

Psalm 35:1-10
God is our salvation

Contend, O Lord, with those who contend with me;
  fight against those who fight against me!
Take hold of shield and buckler,
  and rise up to help me!
Draw the spear and javelin
  against my pursuers;
say to my soul,
  "I am your salvation." (Ps. 35:1-3)

Additional Readings
Numbers 22:1-21
King Balak asks Balaam to curse Israel

Acts 21:17-26
Rules for Gentile converts

Hymn: A Mighty Fortress Is Our God, ELW 503/504/505

Protector God, keep us from every threat that pursues us. Help us to trust that with you beside us we need no other defense. May we see you as the true source of our salvation.

Tuesday, January 30, 2018
Time after Epiphany

1 Corinthians 7:32-40
Paul on marriage

I want you to be free from anxieties. The unmarried man is anxious about the affairs of the Lord, how to please the Lord; but the married man is anxious about the affairs of the world, how to please his wife, and his interests are divided. And the unmarried woman and the virgin are anxious about the affairs of the Lord, so that they may be holy in body and spirit; but the married woman is anxious about the affairs of the world, how to please her husband. I say this for your own benefit, not to put any restraint upon you, but to promote good order and unhindered devotion to the Lord. (1 Cor. 7:32-35)

Psalm
Psalm 35:1-10
God is our salvation

Additional Reading
Numbers 22:22-28
An angel speaks God's word to Balaam

Hymn: Jesus Lives, My Sure Defense, ELW 621

Comforter God, so many things make us anxious. Free us from our most debilitating fears that we might channel our energy toward transforming the world into your vision of wholeness.

Wednesday, January 31, 2018
Time after Epiphany

Jeremiah 29:1-14
Jeremiah speaks God's word

Thus says the LORD of hosts, the God of Israel, to all the exiles whom I have sent into exile from Jerusalem to Babylon: Build houses and live in them; plant gardens and eat what they produce. Take wives and have sons and daughters; take wives for your sons, and give your daughters in marriage, that they may bear sons and daughters; multiply there, and do not decrease. But seek the welfare of the city where I have sent you into exile, and pray to the LORD on its behalf, for in its welfare you will find your welfare. For thus says the LORD of hosts, the God of Israel: Do not let the prophets and the diviners who are among you deceive you, and do not listen to the dreams that they dream, for it is a lie that they are prophesying to you in my name; I did not send them, says the LORD. (Jer. 29:4-9)

Psalm
Psalm 35:1-10
God is our salvation

Additional Reading
Mark 5:1-20
Jesus heals a man with a demon

Hymn: Let the Whole Creation Cry, ELW 876

God of movement, we are a people of refugees and exiles. Give us comfort as we mourn for what we've lost. Help us to create a homeland, a garden in which to root new lives.

Prayer List for February

_____

_____

_____

_____

_____

_____

_____

_____

_____

Thursday, February 1, 2018
Time after Epiphany

Psalm 147:1-11, 20c
The Lord heals the brokenhearted

Praise the LORD!
How good it is to sing praises to our God;
> for he is gracious, and a song of praise is fitting.
The LORD builds up Jerusalem;
> he gathers the outcasts of Israel.
He heals the brokenhearted,
> and binds up their wounds.
He determines the number of the stars;
> he gives to all of them their names.
Great is our LORD, and abundant in power;
> his understanding is beyond measure. (Ps. 147:1-5)

Additional Readings
Proverbs 12:10-21
The tongue of the wise brings healing

Galatians 5:2-15
The nature of Christian freedom

Hymn: Come, Ye Disconsolate, ELW 607

Creator God, you have numbered the stars, set the earth in its orbit, and named all creatures; still in your vastness you know us by name. Before you may we be both humbled and called as your beloved sons and daughters in the world.

Friday, February 2, 2018
Presentation of Our Lord

Luke 2:22-40
The child is brought to the temple

Simeon took [Jesus] in his arms and praised God, saying,
> "Master, now you are dismissing your servant in peace,
>> according to your word;
> for my eyes have seen your salvation,
>> which you have prepared in the presence of all peoples,
> a light for revelation to the Gentiles
>> and for glory to your people Israel." (Luke 2:28-32)

Psalm

Psalm 84
How dear to me is your dwelling, O God

Additional Readings

Malachi 3:1-4
My messenger, a refiner and purifier

Hebrews 2:14-18
Jesus shares human flesh and sufferings

Hymn: In His Temple Now Behold Him, ELW 417

Almighty and ever-living God, your only-begotten Son was presented this day in the temple. May we be presented to you with clean and pure hearts by the same Jesus Christ, our great high priest, who lives and reigns with you and the Holy Spirit, one God, now and forever.

Saturday, February 3, 2018
Time after Epiphany

Ansgar, Bishop of Hamburg, missionary to Denmark and Sweden, died 865

Isaiah 46:1-13
Who is equal to God?

Listen to me, O house of Jacob,
    all the remnant of the house of Israel,
who have been borne by me from your birth,
    carried from the womb;
even to your old age I am he,
    even when you turn gray I will carry you.
I have made, and I will bear;
    I will carry and will save.

To whom will you liken me and make me equal,
    and compare me, as though we were alike?
Those who lavish gold from the purse,
    and weigh out silver in the scales—
they hire a goldsmith, who makes it into a god;
    then they fall down and worship! (Isa. 46:3-6)

Psalm
Psalm 147:1-11, 20c
The Lord heals the brokenhearted

Additional Reading
Matthew 12:9-14
A healing on the sabbath

Hymn: Be Thou My Vision, ELW 793

Lord, from the house of Jacob to our own houses today, there has been none like you. Like Isaiah's goldsmith, may we also fall down and worship, never forgetting your boundless, steadfast love.

Sunday, February 4, 2018
Fifth Sunday after Epiphany

Mark 1:29-39

The healing of Peter's mother-in-law

As soon as [Jesus and the disciples] left the synagogue, they entered the house of Simon and Andrew, with James and John. Now Simon's mother-in-law was in bed with a fever, and they told him about her at once. He came and took her by the hand and lifted her up. Then the fever left her, and she began to serve them. (Mark 1:29-31)

Psalm

Psalm 147:1-11, 20c
The Lord heals the brokenhearted

Additional Readings

Isaiah 40:21-31
The Creator cares for the powerless

1 Corinthians 9:16-23
A servant of the gospel

Hymn: God, Whose Almighty Word, ELW 673

Everlasting God, you give strength to the weak and power to the faint. Make us agents of your healing and wholeness, that your good news may be made known to the ends of your creation, through Jesus Christ, our Savior and Lord.

Monday, February 5, 2018
Time after Epiphany

The Martyrs of Japan, died 1597

Psalm 102:12-28

Prayer for healing

Let this be recorded for a generation to come,
     so that a people yet unborn may praise the LORD:
that he looked down from his holy height,
     from heaven the LORD looked at the earth,
to hear the groans of the prisoners,
     to set free those who were doomed to die;
so that the name of the LORD may be declared in Zion,
     and his praise in Jerusalem,
when peoples gather together,
     and kingdoms, to worship the LORD. (Ps. 102:18-22)

Additional Readings
2 Kings 4:8-17, 32-37
Elisha raises the Shunammite child

Acts 14:1-7
Resistance to the message of the apostles

Hymn: I'm So Glad Jesus Lifted Me, ELW 860

God, just as you heard the groans of prisoners in Jerusalem, you hear our cries today. Help us to listen for the voices of those who are weary, that we will walk with the broken-hearted, the lonely, and those who grieve.

Tuesday, February 6, 2018
Time after Epiphany

2 Kings 8:1-6
The Shunammite widow's land restored

Now the king was talking with Gehazi the servant of the man of God, saying, "Tell me all the great things that Elisha has done." While he was telling the king how Elisha had restored a dead person to life, the woman whose son he had restored to life appealed to the king for her house and her land. Gehazi said, "My lord king, here is the woman, and here is her son whom Elisha restored to life." When the king questioned the woman, she told him. So the king appointed an official for her, saying, "Restore all that was hers, together with all the revenue of the fields from the day that she left the land until now." (2 Kings 8:4-6)

Psalm
Psalm 102:12-28
Prayer for healing

Additional Reading
Acts 15:36-41
Paul and Barnabas separate

Hymn: By Gracious Powers, ELW 626

Almighty God, just as you entrusted your servant Elisha to restore that which was lost, you entrust us to restore our relationships and your creation. Guide us in your work of healing and wholeness every day of our lives.

Wednesday, February 7, 2018
Time after Epiphany

Mark 3:7-12

Jesus heals many people

Jesus departed with his disciples to the sea, and a great multitude from Galilee followed him; hearing all that he was doing, they came to him in great numbers from Judea, Jerusalem, Idumea, beyond the Jordan, and the region around Tyre and Sidon. He told his disciples to have a boat ready for him because of the crowd, so that they would not crush him; for he had cured many, so that all who had diseases pressed upon him to touch him. Whenever the unclean spirits saw him, they fell down before him and shouted, "You are the Son of God!" But he sternly ordered them not to make him known. (Mark 3:7-12)

Psalm

Psalm 102:12-28
Prayer for healing

Additional Reading

Job 6:1-13
Job's lament at misfortune

Hymn: O Christ, What Can It Mean for Us, ELW 431

You are a God to whom even the unclean spirits bow. As Jesus' disciples made a boat ready for him, may we prepare places where you continue your faithful work in the world.

Thursday, February 8, 2018
Time after Epiphany

Psalm 50:1-6
God shines forth in glory

Our God comes and does not keep silence,
    before him is a devouring fire,
    and a mighty tempest all around him.
He calls to the heavens above
    and to the earth, that he may judge his people:
"Gather to me my faithful ones,
    who made a covenant with me by sacrifice!"
The heavens declare his righteousness,
    for God himself is judge. (Ps. 50:3-6)

Additional Readings
1 Kings 11:26-40
Ahijah prophesies to Jereboam

2 Corinthians 2:12-17
God spreads the fragrance of life in Christ

Hymn: Blessing and Honor, ELW 854

God of heaven and earth, wind and flame, help us never forget to whom we and this world belong, that you are judge and ruler of all, and that all we do is in your service.

Friday, February 9, 2018
Time after Epiphany

1 Timothy 1:12-20
Gratitude for mercy

I am grateful to Christ Jesus our Lord, who has strengthened me, because he judged me faithful and appointed me to his service, even though I was formerly a blasphemer, a persecutor, and a man of violence. But I received mercy because I had acted ignorantly in unbelief, and the grace of our Lord overflowed for me with the faith and love that are in Christ Jesus. The saying is sure and worthy of full acceptance, that Christ Jesus came into the world to save sinners—of whom I am the foremost. But for that very reason I received mercy, so that in me, as the foremost, Jesus Christ might display the utmost patience, making me an example to those who would come to believe in him for eternal life. (1 Tim. 1:12-16)

Psalm
Psalm 50:1-6
God shines forth in glory

Additional Reading
1 Kings 14:1-18
Ahijah receives Jereboam's wife

Hymn: Amazing Grace, How Sweet the Sound, ELW 779

Lord of all, it is only in the cleansing waters of your forgiveness that we are made whole. Thank you for your unending willingness to forgive us and for your constant reminder of that need.

Saturday, February 10, 2018
Time after Epiphany

Luke 19:41-44
The time of God's visitation

As [Jesus] came near and saw the city, he wept over it, saying, "If you, even you, had only recognized on this day the things that make for peace! But now they are hidden from your eyes. Indeed, the days will come upon you, when your enemies will set up ramparts around you and surround you, and hem you in on every side. They will crush you to the ground, you and your children within you, and they will not leave within you one stone upon another; because you did not recognize the time of your visitation from God." (Luke 19:41-44)

Psalm
Psalm 50:1-6
God shines forth in glory

Additional Reading
1 Kings 16:1-7
Jehu warns King Baasha

Hymn: Lord Christ, When First You Came to Earth, ELW 727

God, even when we fail to see signs of your peace, your mercy for us does not end. Thank you for staying with us even when we refuse to recognize your presence. Help us every day to acknowledge your ways.

Sunday, February 11, 2018
Transfiguration of Our Lord

Mark 9:2-9

Christ revealed as God's beloved Son

Six days later, Jesus took with him Peter and James and John, and led them up a high mountain apart, by themselves. And he was transfigured before them, and his clothes became dazzling white, such as no one on earth could bleach them. And there appeared to them Elijah with Moses, who were talking with Jesus. Then Peter said to Jesus, "Rabbi, it is good for us to be here; let us make three dwellings, one for you, one for Moses, and one for Elijah." He did not know what to say, for they were terrified. (Mark 9:2-6)

Psalm

Psalm 50:1-6
God shines forth in glory

Additional Readings

2 Kings 2:1-12
Elijah taken up to heaven

2 Corinthians 4:3-6
God's light seen in Christ

Hymn: Jesus on the Mountain Peak, ELW 317

Almighty God, the resplendent light of your truth shines from the mountaintop into our hearts. Transfigure us by your beloved Son, and illumine the world with your image, through Jesus Christ, our Savior and Lord, who lives and reigns with you and the Holy Spirit, one God, now and forever.

Monday, February 12, 2018
Time after Epiphany

Psalm 110:1-4
A priest forever

The LORD says to my lord,
    "Sit at my right hand
until I make your enemies your footstool."

The LORD sends out from Zion
    your mighty scepter.
    Rule in the midst of your foes.
Your people will offer themselves willingly
    on the day you lead your forces
    on the holy mountains.
From the womb of the morning,
    like dew, your youth will come to you.
The LORD has sworn and will not change his mind,
    "You are a priest forever according to the order of Melchizedek."
(Ps. 110:1-4)

Additional Readings
Exodus 19:7-25
Moses meets God on the mountain

Hebrews 2:1-4
Do not neglect so great a salvation

Hymn: Oh, Wondrous Image, Vision Fair, ELW 316

Creator of mountains and rulers, creator of our enemies and friends, your promises never fail us. In you we can be secure that whatever the future holds, you will be with us, and that by your grace we will endure.

Tuesday, February 13, 2018
Time after Epiphany

Job 19:23-27
Job will see God

"O that my words were written down!
    O that they were inscribed in a book!
O that with an iron pen and with lead
    they were engraved on a rock forever!
For I know that my Redeemer lives,
    and that at the last he will stand upon the earth;
and after my skin has been thus destroyed,
    then in my flesh I shall see God,
whom I shall see on my side,
    and my eyes shall behold, and not another.
    My heart faints within me!" (Job 19:23-27)

Psalm
Psalm 110:1-4
A priest forever

Additional Reading
1 Timothy 3:14-16
The mystery of our religion

Hymn: I Know That My Redeemer Lives! ELW 619

You are the God to whom Job cried out with unfailing faith. Like Job, may we also trust in your unending faithfulness. When we feel alone, help us to know that you are always with us.

Lent

Lent is a forty-day journey to Easter. Christians keep company with Noah and his family, who were in the ark for forty days; with the Hebrews, who journeyed through the desert for forty years; and with Moses, Elijah, and Jesus, who fasted for forty days before they embarked on the tasks God had prepared for them.

During Lent Christians journey with those who are making final preparations for baptism at Easter. Together, Christians struggle with the meaning of their baptismal promises: Do you reject evil? Do you believe in God the Father, the Son, and the Holy Spirit? Do you believe in the church, the forgiveness of sins, the resurrection of the dead?

The disciples of the Lord Jesus are called to contend against everything that leads them away from love of God and neighbor. Fasting, prayer, and works of love—the disciplines of Lent—help the household rejoice in the gifts of baptism: God's forgiveness and mercy.

Table Prayer for the Season of Lent

Blessed are you, O God, giver of all.
You adorn our tables with food
and give companionship for our journeys.
Be present with us as we are fed in body and spirit
that our sharing this meal is a sign of your life
broken and shared for the world.
In Jesus' name we pray.
Amen.

Wednesday, February 14, 2018
Ash Wednesday

Cyril, monk, died 869; Methodius, bishop, died 885; missionaries to the Slavs

Matthew 6:1-6, 16-21
The practice of faith

[Jesus said,] "Do not store up for yourselves treasures on earth, where moth and rust consume and where thieves break in and steal; but store up for yourselves treasures in heaven, where neither moth nor rust consumes and where thieves do not break in and steal. For where your treasure is, there your heart will be also." (Matt. 6:19-21)

Psalm
Psalm 51:1-17
Plea for mercy

Additional Readings
Joel 2:1-2, 12-17
Return to God

2 Corinthians
5:20b—6:10
Now is the day of salvation

Hymn: Savior, When in Dust to You, ELW 601

Almighty and ever-living God, you hate nothing you have made, and you forgive the sins of all who are penitent. Create in us new and honest hearts, so that, truly repenting of our sins, we may receive from you, the God of all mercy, full pardon and forgiveness through your Son, Jesus Christ, our Savior and Lord, who lives and reigns with you and the Holy Spirit, one God, now and forever.

Thursday, February 15, 2018
Week before Lent 1

Psalm 25:1-10
Your paths are love and faithfulness

To you, O LORD, I lift up my soul.
O my God, in you I trust;
> do not let me be put to shame;
> do not let my enemies exult over me.
Do not let those who wait for you be put to shame;
> let them be ashamed who are wantonly treacherous.

Make me to know your ways, O LORD;
> teach me your paths.
Lead me in your truth, and teach me,
> for you are the God of my salvation;
> for you I wait all day long. (Ps. 25:1-5)

Additional Readings
Daniel 9:1-14
Daniel prays for the people's forgiveness

1 John 1:3-10
The apostolic message of forgiveness

Hymn: O Master, Let Me Walk with You, ELW 818

Holy God, you have led people in your ways of righteousness in the past, and you continue to guide us as well. Be with us as we follow your paths and return us to you when we stray from them.

Friday, February 16, 2018
Week before Lent 1

2 Timothy 4:1-5
Apostolic and pastoral advice for Timothy

In the presence of God and of Christ Jesus, who is to judge the living and the dead, and in view of his appearing and his kingdom, I solemnly urge you: proclaim the message; be persistent whether the time is favorable or unfavorable; convince, rebuke, and encourage, with the utmost patience in teaching. For the time is coming when people will not put up with sound doctrine, but having itching ears, they will accumulate for themselves teachers to suit their own desires, and will turn away from listening to the truth and wander away to myths. As for you, always be sober, endure suffering, do the work of an evangelist, carry out your ministry fully. (2 Tim. 4:1-5)

Psalm
Psalm 25:1-10
Your paths are love and faithfulness

Additional Reading
Daniel 9:15-25a
An angel speaks to Daniel

Hymn: How Clear Is Our Vocation, Lord, ELW 580

Almighty God, you are always speaking, even when we are too busy or the chaos of our lives drowns out your voice. When we have lost our way, help us to listen and to turn back to you.

Saturday, February 17, 2018
Week before Lent 1

Matthew 9:2-13

Jesus forgives sin and calls sinners to service

And as [Jesus] sat at dinner in the house, many tax collectors and sinners came and were sitting with him and his disciples. When the Pharisees saw this, they said to his disciples, "Why does your teacher eat with tax collectors and sinners?" But when he heard this, he said, "Those who are well have no need of a physician, but those who are sick. Go and learn what this means, 'I desire mercy, not sacrifice.' For I have come to call not the righteous but sinners." (Matt. 9:10-13)

Psalm
Psalm 25:1-10
Your paths are love and faithfulness

Additional Reading
Psalm 32
God forgives sin

Hymn: Lord, Whose Love in Humble Service, ELW 712

Lord, just as your Son ate with tax collectors and sinners, you meet us even in the most hidden and ugly spaces of our lives. Help us to accompany those who are most in need of your love.

Sunday, February 18, 2018
First Sunday in Lent

Martin Luther, renewer of the church, died 1546

Mark 1:9-15

The temptation of Jesus

In those days Jesus came from Nazareth of Galilee and was baptized by John in the Jordan. And just as he was coming up out of the water, he saw the heavens torn apart and the Spirit descending like a dove on him. And a voice came from heaven, "You are my Son, the Beloved; with you I am well pleased."

And the Spirit immediately drove him out into the wilderness. He was in the wilderness forty days, tempted by Satan; and he was with the wild beasts; and the angels waited on him.

Now after John was arrested, Jesus came to Galilee, proclaiming the good news of God, and saying, "The time is fulfilled, and the kingdom of God has come near; repent, and believe in the good news." (Mark 1:9-15)

Psalm

Psalm 25:1-10
Your paths are love and faithfulness

Additional Readings

Genesis 9:8-17
The rainbow, sign of God's covenant

1 Peter 3:18-22
Saved through water

Hymn: O Lord, throughout These Forty Days, ELW 319

Holy God, heavenly Father, in the waters of the flood you saved the chosen, and in the wilderness of temptation you protected your Son from sin. Renew us in the gift of baptism. May your holy angels be with us, that the wicked foe may have no power over us, through Jesus Christ, our Savior and Lord, who lives and reigns with you and the Holy Spirit, one God, now and forever.

Monday, February 19, 2018
Week of Lent 1

Psalm 77
Prayer for God to remember us

I cry aloud to God,
>   aloud to God, that he may hear me.
In the day of my trouble I seek the Lord;
>   in the night my hand is stretched out without wearying;
>   my soul refuses to be comforted.
I think of God, and I moan;
>   I meditate, and my spirit faints. (Ps. 77:1-3)

Additional Readings

Job 4:1-21
Eliphaz speaks of sin

Ephesians 2:1-10
The death of sin, the gift of grace

Hymn: What a Friend We Have in Jesus, ELW 742

Everlasting God, in both light and darkness, joy and despair, you are with us. There is nothing that you cannot overcome, and for that we give you our unending praise.

Tuesday, February 20, 2018
Week of Lent 1

1 Peter 3:8-18a
About suffering

Now who will harm you if you are eager to do what is good? But even if you do suffer for doing what is right, you are blessed. Do not fear what they fear, and do not be intimidated, but in your hearts sanctify Christ as Lord. Always be ready to make your defense to anyone who demands from you an accounting for the hope that is in you; yet do it with gentleness and reverence. Keep your conscience clear, so that, when you are maligned, those who abuse you for your good conduct in Christ may be put to shame. For it is better to suffer for doing good, if suffering should be God's will, than to suffer for doing evil. For Christ also suffered for sins once for all, the righteous for the unrighteous, in order to bring you to God. (1 Peter 3:13-18a)

Psalm
Psalm 77
Prayer for God to remember us

Additional Reading
Job 5:8-27
Seek God

Hymn: When We Are Living, ELW 639

Lord of all, throughout the ages your servants have suffered in service to your unending hope and love for all of humanity. May we have the courage and the desire to work for the glory of your name.

Wednesday, February 21, 2018
Week of Lent 1

Proverbs 30:1-9
Plea to be safe from temptation

Two things I ask of you;
> do not deny them to me before I die:
Remove far from me falsehood and lying;
> give me neither poverty nor riches;
> feed me with the food that I need,
or I shall be full, and deny you,
> and say, "Who is the LORD?"
or I shall be poor, and steal,
> and profane the name of my God. (Prov. 30:7-9)

Psalm
Psalm 77
Prayer for God to remember us

Additional Reading
Matthew 4:1-11
Matthew's account of Jesus' temptation

Hymn: If You But Trust in God to Guide You, ELW 769

Holy Lord, in Jesus Christ you overcame the temptations of this world to free humanity from its most destructive pursuits. Grant us wisdom to be fully satisfied by walking in your ways.

Thursday, February 22, 2018
Week of Lent 1

Psalm 22:23-31
All the earth shall turn to God

All the ends of the earth shall remember
   and turn to the LORD;
and all the families of the nations
   shall worship before him.
For dominion belongs to the LORD,
   and he rules over the nations.

To him, indeed, shall all who sleep in the earth bow down;
   before him shall bow all who go down to the dust,
   and I shall live for him.
Posterity will serve him;
   future generations will be told about the Lord,
and proclaim his deliverance to a people yet unborn,
   saying that he has done it. (Ps. 22:27-31)

Additional Readings
Genesis 15:1-6, 12-18
God covenants with Abraham

Romans 3:21-31
Righteousness through faith

Hymn: Shout to the Lord, ELW 821

Dear God, only you know the future that lies ahead of us. When we are afraid or uncertain, may we find comfort in the knowledge that you go before us, calling us to walk boldly in love and peace.

Friday, February 23, 2018
Week of Lent 1

Polycarp, Bishop of Smyrna, martyr, died 156

Genesis 16:1-6
Ishmael born to Abram and Hagar

Now Sarai, Abram's wife, bore him no children. She had an Egyptian slave-girl whose name was Hagar, and Sarai said to Abram, "You see that the LORD has prevented me from bearing children; go in to my slave-girl; it may be that I shall obtain children by her." And Abram listened to the voice of Sarai. So, after Abram had lived ten years in the land of Canaan, Sarai, Abram's wife, took Hagar the Egyptian, her slave-girl, and gave her to her husband Abram as a wife. He went in to Hagar, and she conceived; and when she saw that she had conceived, she looked with contempt on her mistress. Then Sarai said to Abram, "May the wrong done to me be on you! I gave my slave-girl to your embrace, and when she saw that she had conceived, she looked on me with contempt. May the LORD judge between you and me!" But Abram said to Sarai, "Your slave-girl is in your power; do to her as you please." Then Sarai dealt harshly with her, and she ran away from her. (Gen. 16:1-6)

Psalm
Psalm 22:23-31
All the earth shall turn to God

Additional Reading
Romans 4:1-12
Abraham counted righteous by God for his faith

Hymn: The God of Abraham Praise, ELW 831

Lord, in the same ways that you blessed our ancestors in the faith, you have blessed us today. Though we may be quick to anger or to judge, your patience is unending. Give us courage and strength to change our ways.

Saturday, February 24, 2018
Week of Lent 1

Mark 8:27-30

Peter's confession

Jesus went on with his disciples to the villages of Caesarea Philippi; and on the way he asked his disciples, "Who do people say that I am?" And they answered him, "John the Baptist; and others, Elijah; and still others, one of the prophets." He asked them, "But who do you say that I am?" Peter answered him, "You are the Messiah." And he sternly ordered them not to tell anyone about him. (Mark 8:27-30)

Psalm
Psalm 22:23-31
All the earth shall turn to God

Additional Reading
Genesis 16:7-15
An angel comforts Hagar at a spring of water

Hymn: O Christ the Same, ELW 760

Holy Lord, as you sent Jesus into a world needing redemption, you also send us to do your work of restoring justice and truth. May we trust in your word, steadfast in knowing that our hope is in you.

Sunday, February 25, 2018
Second Sunday in Lent

Elizabeth Fedde, deaconess, died 1921

Mark 8:31-38

The passion prediction

[Jesus] called the crowd with his disciples, and said to them, "If any want to become my followers, let them deny themselves and take up their cross and follow me. For those who want to save their life will lose it, and those who lose their life for my sake, and for the sake of the gospel, will save it. For what will it profit them to gain the whole world and forfeit their life? Indeed, what can they give in return for their life? Those who are ashamed of me and of my words in this adulterous and sinful generation, of them the Son of Man will also be ashamed when he comes in the glory of his Father with the holy angels." (Mark 8:34-38)

Psalm

Psalm 22:23-31
All the earth shall turn to God

Additional Readings

Genesis 17:1-7, 15-16
God blesses Abraham and Sarah

Romans 4:13-25
The promise to those of Abraham's faith

Hymn: Come, Follow Me, the Savior Spake, ELW 799

O God, by the passion of your blessed Son you made an instrument of shameful death to be for us the means of life. Grant us so to glory in the cross of Christ that we may gladly suffer shame and loss for the sake of your Son, Jesus Christ, our Savior and Lord, who lives and reigns with you and the Holy Spirit, one God, now and forever.

Monday, February 26, 2018
Week of Lent 2

Psalm 105:1-11, 37-45
God promises life to Abraham

O give thanks to the LORD, call on his name,
    make known his deeds among the peoples.
Sing to him, sing praises to him;
    tell of all his wonderful works.
Glory in his holy name;
    let the hearts of those who seek the LORD rejoice.
Seek the LORD and his strength;
    seek his presence continually.
Remember the wonderful works he has done,
    his miracles, and the judgments he uttered,
O offspring of his servant Abraham,
    children of Jacob, his chosen ones. (Ps. 105:1-6)

Additional Readings
Genesis 21:1-7
God gives Abraham and Sarah a son

Hebrews 1:8-12
The Son whose years will never end

Hymn: My God, How Wonderful Thou Art, ELW 863

O God of Abraham and Jacob, for generations your promise of new life has endured for those who seek you. May we never cease to rejoice in those promises and to sing your praises with every breath.

Tuesday, February 27, 2018
Week of Lent 2

Hebrews 11:1-3, 13-19
By faith Abraham obeyed God

By faith Abraham, when put to the test, offered up Isaac. He who had received the promises was ready to offer up his only son, of whom he had been told, "It is through Isaac that descendants shall be named for you." He considered the fact that God is able even to raise someone from the dead—and figuratively speaking, he did receive him back. (Heb. 11:17-19)

Psalm
Psalm 105:1-11, 37-45
God promises life to Abraham

Additional Reading
Genesis 22:1-19
God asks Abraham to sacrifice Isaac

Hymn: Give Thanks for Saints, ELW 428

Lord God, you are ever-present, never failing to offer us exactly what we need. May we also be ready to offer our best to you when you require it of us, and may we be ready to recognize your call when the time comes.

Wednesday, February 28, 2018
Week of Lent 2

Jeremiah 30:12-22
God will restore Israel

Thus says the LORD:
I am going to restore the fortunes of the tents of Jacob,
  and have compassion on his dwellings;
the city shall be rebuilt upon its mound,
  and the citadel set on its rightful site.
Out of them shall come thanksgiving,
  and the sound of merrymakers.
I will make them many, and they shall not be few;
  I will make them honored, and they shall not be disdained.
Their children shall be as of old,
  their congregation shall be established before me;
  and I will punish all who oppress them. . . .
And you shall be my people,
  and I will be your God. (Jer. 30:18-20, 22)

Psalm
Psalm 105:1-11, 37-45
God promises life to Abraham

Additional Reading
John 12:36-43
The unbelief of the people

Hymn: Oh, Happy Day When We Shall Stand, ELW 441

Almighty God, what song could we sing or monument could we build that would be sufficient to thank you for your grace and love? Help us never to forget the hope we have in you.

Prayer List for March

_____

_____

_____

_____

_____

_____

_____

_____

_____

Thursday, March 1, 2018
Week of Lent 2

George Herbert, hymnwriter, died 1633

Psalm 19

The commandments give light to the eyes

The law of the LORD is perfect,
    reviving the soul;
the decrees of the LORD are sure,
    making wise the simple;
the precepts of the LORD are right,
    rejoicing the heart;
the commandment of the LORD is clear,
    enlightening the eyes;
the fear of the LORD is pure,
    enduring forever;
the ordinances of the LORD are true
    and righteous altogether.
More to be desired are they than gold,
    even much fine gold;
sweeter also than honey,
    and drippings of the honeycomb. (Ps. 19:7-10)

Additional Readings

Exodus 19:1-9a
Preparation for the giving of the commandments

1 Peter 2:4-10
You are God's own people

Hymn: O Christ, Your Heart, Compassionate, ELW 722

Lord eternal, you are our comfort and guide. May our eyes be ever widening to your perfect, restorative law. Teach us to desire your works and your ways now and forever.

Friday, March 2, 2018
Week of Lent 2

John Wesley, died 1791; Charles Wesley, died 1788; renewers of the church

Exodus 19:9b-15
Preparation for the giving of the commandments

When Moses had told the words of the people to the LORD, the LORD said to Moses: "Go to the people and consecrate them today and tomorrow. Have them wash their clothes and prepare for the third day, because on the third day the LORD will come down upon Mount Sinai in the sight of all the people. You shall set limits for the people all around, saying, 'Be careful not to go up the mountain or to touch the edge of it. Any who touch the mountain shall be put to death. No hand shall touch them, but they shall be stoned or shot with arrows; whether animal or human being, they shall not live.' When the trumpet sounds a long blast, they may go up on the mountain." So Moses went down from the mountain to the people. He consecrated the people, and they washed their clothes. And he said to the people, "Prepare for the third day; do not go near a woman." (Exod. 19:9b-15)

Psalm
Psalm 19
The commandments give light to the eyes

Additional Reading
Acts 7:30-40
God spoke to Moses at Mount Sinai

Hymn: Lord Jesus, Think on Me, ELW 599

God on high, we come to you open and ready to receive your eternal plan. We long to live with the awareness that we are on holy ground. When we fail to notice, call us back to you. Raise us up in your forgiveness and grace.

Saturday, March 3, 2018
Week of Lent 2

Exodus 19:16-25

Preparation for the giving of the commandments

Then the LORD said to Moses, "Go down and warn the people not to break through to the LORD to look; otherwise many of them will perish. Even the priests who approach the LORD must consecrate themselves or the LORD will break out against them." Moses said to the LORD, "The people are not permitted to come up to Mount Sinai; for you yourself warned us, saying, 'Set limits around the mountain and keep it holy.'" The LORD said to him, "Go down, and come up bringing Aaron with you; but do not let either the priests or the people break through to come up to the LORD; otherwise he will break out against them." So Moses went down to the people and told them. (Exod. 19:21-25)

Psalm
Psalm 19
The commandments give light to the eyes

Additional Reading
Mark 9:2-8
Moses with Elijah and Jesus on a mountain

Hymn: Before You, Lord, We Bow, ELW 893

Holy God, we know we need you and desire to be close to you. We acknowledge how far we have to go and how much we have yet to understand. Consecrate your people, God, that we may persist in seeking you.

Sunday, March 4, 2018
Third Sunday in Lent

John 2:13-22

The cleansing of the temple

The Passover of the Jews was near, and Jesus went up to Jerusalem. In the temple he found people selling cattle, sheep, and doves, and the money changers seated at their tables. Making a whip of cords, he drove all of them out of the temple, both the sheep and the cattle. He also poured out the coins of the money changers and overturned their tables. He told those who were selling the doves, "Take these things out of here! Stop making my Father's house a marketplace!" (John 2:13-16)

Psalm

Psalm 19
The commandments give light to the eyes

Additional Readings

Exodus 20:1-17
The commandments given at Sinai

1 Corinthians 1:18-25
Christ crucified, the wisdom of God

Hymn: Holy God, Holy and Glorious, ELW 637

Holy God, through your Son you have called us to live faithfully and act courageously. Keep us steadfast in your covenant of grace, and teach us the wisdom that comes only through Jesus Christ, our Savior and Lord, who lives and reigns with you and the Holy Spirit, one God, now and forever.

Monday, March 5, 2018
Week of Lent 3

Psalm 84
How lovely is God's dwelling place

How lovely is your dwelling place,
    O LORD of hosts!
My soul longs, indeed it faints
    for the courts of the LORD;
my heart and my flesh sing for joy
    to the living God.

Even the sparrow finds a home,
    and the swallow a nest for herself,
    where she may lay her young,
at your altars, O LORD of hosts,
    my King and my God.
Happy are those who live in your house,
    ever singing your praise. (Ps. 84:1-4)

Additional Readings
1 Kings 6:1-4, 21-22
Solomon builds the temple

1 Corinthians 3:10-23
You are God's temple

Hymn: In Heaven Above, ELW 630

God who is in our midst, you are our strength and our joy. Lead us into your presence. When we wander into the desert, draw us back to you. Hear us raise our collective voice for your glory.

Tuesday, March 6, 2018
Week of Lent 3

Hebrews 9:23-28
Christ as priest and once-for-all sacrifice

Thus it was necessary for the sketches of the heavenly things to be purified with these rites, but the heavenly things themselves need better sacrifices than these. For Christ did not enter a sanctuary made by human hands, a mere copy of the true one, but he entered into heaven itself, now to appear in the presence of God on our behalf. Nor was it to offer himself again and again, as the high priest enters the Holy Place year after year with blood that is not his own; for then he would have had to suffer again and again since the foundation of the world. But as it is, he has appeared once for all at the end of the age to remove sin by the sacrifice of himself. And just as it is appointed for mortals to die once, and after that the judgment, so Christ, having been offered once to bear the sins of many, will appear a second time, not to deal with sin, but to save those who are eagerly waiting for him. (Heb. 9:23-28)

Psalm
Psalm 84
How lovely is God's dwelling place

Additional Reading
2 Chronicles 29:1-11, 16-19
Hezekiah cleanses the temple

Hymn: Lord of Glory, You Have Bought Us, ELW 707

Life-giving God, you sent your Son to enter the pain of sin and the process of redemption, and he willingly gave himself so we could be drawn back to you. Teach us to continuously stand in awe of his sacrifice as we yearn to live like him.

Wednesday, March 7, 2018
Week of Lent 3

Perpetua and Felicity and companions, martyrs at Carthage, died 202

Mark 11:15-19
Jesus cleanses the temple

Then [Jesus and his disciples] came to Jerusalem. And he entered the temple and began to drive out those who were selling and those who were buying in the temple, and he overturned the tables of the money changers and the seats of those who sold doves; and he would not allow anyone to carry anything through the temple. He was teaching and saying, "Is it not written,

> 'My house shall be called a house of prayer for all the nations'?
> But you have made it a den of robbers."

And when the chief priests and the scribes heard it, they kept looking for a way to kill him; for they were afraid of him, because the whole crowd was spellbound by his teaching. And when evening came, Jesus and his disciples went out of the city. (Mark 11:15-19)

Psalm
Psalm 84
How lovely is God's dwelling place

Additional Reading
Ezra 6:1-16
King Darius orders the temple rebuilt

Hymn: Open Now Thy Gates of Beauty, ELW 533

God, you are a generous father. Drive out our pride and overwhelm our greed. Purify our thoughts, words, and actions. Show us how to live in light of the calling you have given us that we may dwell in your house and live in your presence forever.

Thursday, March 8, 2018
Week of Lent 3

Psalm 107:1-3, 17-22
God delivers from distress

Some were sick through their sinful ways,
> and because of their iniquities endured affliction;
they loathed any kind of food,
> and they drew near to the gates of death.
Then they cried to the Lord in their trouble,
> and he saved them from their distress;
he sent out his word and healed them,
> and delivered them from destruction.
Let them thank the Lord for his steadfast love,
> for his wonderful works to humankind. (Ps. 107:17-21)

Additional Readings
Genesis 9:8-17
The covenant with Noah

Ephesians 1:3-6
Blessed be God, who chose us in Christ

Hymn: O God, My Faithful God, ELW 806

Sustainer of life, we know how desperately we need you. We cry out for your help and your healing. We thank you that you know our needs and hear us, and that you respond in love and grace.

Friday, March 9, 2018
Week of Lent 3

Ephesians 1:7-14

We live to the praise of God's glory

In Christ we have also obtained an inheritance, having been destined according to the purpose of him who accomplishes all things according to his counsel and will, so that we, who were the first to set our hope on Christ, might live for the praise of his glory. In him you also, when you had heard the word of truth, the gospel of your salvation, and had believed in him, were marked with the seal of the promised Holy Spirit; this is the pledge of our inheritance toward redemption as God's own people, to the praise of his glory. (Eph. 1:11-14)

Psalm

Psalm 107:1-3, 17-22
God delivers from distress

Additional Reading

Daniel 12:5-13
The people will be purified

Hymn: How Great Thou Art, ELW 856

Consume us with your holy presence, God. May we live lives worthy of the inheritance you have bestowed upon us in Christ Jesus.

Saturday, March 10, 2018
Week of Lent 3

Harriet Tubman, died 1913; Sojourner Truth, died 1883; renewers of society

Numbers 20:22-29
The death of Aaron

Then the LORD said to Moses and Aaron at Mount Hor, on the border of the land of Edom, "Let Aaron be gathered to his people. For he shall not enter the land that I have given to the Israelites, because you rebelled against my command at the waters of Meribah. Take Aaron and his son Eleazar, and bring them up Mount Hor; strip Aaron of his vestments, and put them on his son Eleazar. But Aaron shall be gathered to his people, and shall die there." (Num. 20:23-26)

Psalm
Psalm 107:1-3, 17-22
God delivers from distress

Additional Reading
John 3:1-13
Jesus and Nicodemus

Hymn: Guide Me Ever, Great Redeemer, ELW 618

We are dust, Lord. And yet we rejoice at what you can do with dust. Pour your blessings on us as we make our way through a dry and weary land. We long to be restored by you, our living water.

Sunday, March 11, 2018
Fourth Sunday in Lent

John 3:14-21
The lifting up of the Son of Man

[Jesus said to Nicodemus,] ". . . as Moses lifted up the serpent in the wilderness, so must the Son of Man be lifted up, that whoever believes in him may have eternal life.

"For God so loved the world that he gave his only Son, so that everyone who believes in him may not perish but may have eternal life." (John 3:14-16)

Psalm
Psalm 107:1-3, 17-22
God delivers from distress

Additional Readings
Numbers 21:4-9
The lifting up of the serpent

Ephesians 2:1-10
Alive in Christ

Hymn: God Loved the World, ELW 323

O God, rich in mercy, by the humiliation of your Son you lifted up this fallen world and rescued us from the hopelessness of death. Lead us into your light, that all our deeds may reflect your love, through Jesus Christ, our Savior and Lord, who lives and reigns with you and the Holy Spirit, one God, now and forever.

Monday, March 12, 2018
Week of Lent 4

Gregory the Great, Bishop of Rome, died 604

Psalm 107:1-16
God gives food and light

Some wandered in desert wastes,
> finding no way to an inhabited town;
hungry and thirsty,
> their soul fainted within them.
Then they cried to the LORD in their trouble,
> and he delivered them from their distress;
he led them by a straight way,
> until they reached an inhabited town.
Let them thank the LORD for his steadfast love,
> for his wonderful works to humankind.
For he satisfies the thirsty,
> and the hungry he fills with good things. (Ps. 107:4-9)

Additional Readings

Exodus 15:22-27
God gives the people water

Hebrews 3:1-6
The faithfulness of Moses

Hymn: All Who Hunger, Gather Gladly, ELW 461

You are the Lord who provides. While we are prone to seeking food that ultimately does not satisfy, guide us to what is good. Remind us to cry out to you in our joys and sorrows so we can receive your love and mercy.

Tuesday, March 13, 2018
Week of Lent 4

1 Corinthians 10:6-13
God is faithful

Now these things occurred as examples for us, so that we might not desire evil as they did. Do not become idolaters as some of them did; as it is written, "The people sat down to eat and drink, and they rose up to play." We must not indulge in sexual immorality as some of them did, and twenty-three thousand fell in a single day. We must not put Christ to the test, as some of them did, and were destroyed by serpents. And do not complain as some of them did, and were destroyed by the destroyer. These things happened to them to serve as an example, and they were written down to instruct us, on whom the ends of the ages have come. (1 Cor. 10:6-11)

Psalm
Psalm 107:1-16
God gives food and light

Additional Reading
Numbers 20:1-13
God gives water from the rock

Hymn: Goodness Is Stronger than Evil, ELW 721

God who sees the thoughtlessness of your people and yet chooses to see the goodness of your Son instead, teach us to remember your faithfulness through the generations as we share your light and your love with your world.

Wednesday, March 14, 2018
Week of Lent 4

Isaiah 60:15-22
God is our light

The sun shall no longer be
>your light by day,
nor for brightness shall the moon
>give light to you by night;
but the LORD will be your everlasting light,
>and your God will be your glory.
Your sun shall no more go down,
>or your moon withdraw itself;
for the LORD will be your everlasting light,
>and your days of mourning shall be ended.
Your people shall all be righteous;
>they shall possess the land forever.
They are the shoot that I planted, the work of my hands,
>so that I might be glorified. (Isa. 60:19-21)

Psalm
Psalm 107:1-16
God gives food and light

Additional Reading
John 8:12-20
Christ the light of the world

Hymn: Glorious Things of You Are Spoken, ELW 647

Mighty God of Israel, be our compassionate guide. It is your light that directs our lives, and we want to reflect it into every corner of your creation. May Jesus shine through our words and deeds.

Thursday, March 15, 2018
Week of Lent 4

Psalm 51:1-12
Create in me a clean heart

Create in me a clean heart, O God,
    and put a new and right spirit within me.
Do not cast me away from your presence,
    and do not take your holy spirit from me.
Restore to me the joy of your salvation,
    and sustain in me a willing spirit. (Ps. 51:10-12)

Additional Readings
Isaiah 30:15-18
God's gifts of returning and rest

Hebrews 4:1-13
God promises an eternal sabbath rest

Hymn: Change My Heart, O God, ELW 801

Eternal father, we are made in your image. We claim our inheritance as your children. Draw us closer so we can know you more. Draw us closer to your restorative presence. Transform our hearts and minds.

Friday, March 16, 2018
Week of Lent 4

Exodus 30:1-10
Aaron's responsibility for altar and atonement

Aaron shall offer fragrant incense on [an altar;] every morning when he dresses the lamps he shall offer it, and when Aaron sets up the lamps in the evening, he shall offer it, a regular incense offering before the LORD throughout your generations. You shall not offer unholy incense on it, or a burnt offering, or a grain offering; and you shall not pour a drink offering on it. Once a year Aaron shall perform the rite of atonement on its horns. Throughout your generations he shall perform the atonement for it once a year with the blood of the atoning sin offering. It is most holy to the LORD. (Exod. 30:7-10)

Psalm
Psalm 51:1-12
Create in me a clean heart

Additional Reading
Hebrews 4:14—5:4
Jesus' priesthood surpasses Aaron's

Hymn: How Sweet the Name of Jesus Sounds, ELW 620

Everlasting God, we approach you confidently because of your unending grace. While we were lost in transgression you sought us out and sent your Son as a redeeming sacrifice. Sanctify us in our weakness that your love will be known.

Saturday, March 17, 2018
Week of Lent 4

Patrick, bishop, missionary to Ireland, died 461

John 12:1-11
Jesus is anointed for his coming death

Mary took a pound of costly perfume made of pure nard, anointed Jesus' feet, and wiped them with her hair. The house was filled with the fragrance of the perfume. But Judas Iscariot, one of his disciples (the one who was about to betray him), said, "Why was this perfume not sold for three hundred denarii and the money given to the poor?" (He said this not because he cared about the poor, but because he was a thief; he kept the common purse and used to steal what was put into it.) Jesus said, "Leave her alone. She bought it so that she might keep it for the day of my burial. You always have the poor with you, but you do not always have me." (John 12:3-8)

Psalm
Psalm 51:1-12
Create in me a clean heart

Additional Reading
Habakkuk 3:2-13
God will save the anointed

Hymn: Tree of Life and Awesome Mystery, ELW 334

Open our hands, our hearts, and our minds so we will freely offer our gifts of gratitude to you, O gracious Lord. May we breathe so deeply of your love that our lives will be an aroma pleasing to you.

Sunday, March 18, 2018
Fifth Sunday in Lent

John 12:20-33

The grain of wheat dying in the earth

Jesus answered [the Greeks who came to see him,] "The hour has come for the Son of Man to be glorified. Very truly, I tell you, unless a grain of wheat falls into the earth and dies, it remains just a single grain; but if it dies, it bears much fruit. Those who love their life lose it, and those who hate their life in this world will keep it for eternal life. Whoever serves me must follow me, and where I am, there will my servant be also. Whoever serves me, the Father will honor." (John 12:23-26)

Psalm

Psalm 51:1-12
Create in me a clean heart

Additional Readings

Jeremiah 31:31-34
A new covenant written on the heart

Hebrews 5:5-10
Through suffering Christ saves

Hymn: As the Sun with Longer Journey, ELW 329

O God, with steadfast love you draw us to yourself, and in mercy you receive our prayers. Strengthen us to bring forth the fruits of the Spirit, that through life and death we may live in your Son, Jesus Christ, our Savior and Lord, who lives and reigns with you and the Holy Spirit, one God, now and forever.

Monday, March 19, 2018
Joseph, Guardian of Jesus

Matthew 1:16, 18-21, 24a

The Lord appears to Joseph in a dream

Now the birth of Jesus the Messiah took place in this way. When his mother Mary had been engaged to Joseph, but before they lived together, she was found to be with child from the Holy Spirit. Her husband Joseph, being a righteous man and unwilling to expose her to public disgrace, planned to dismiss her quietly. But just when he had resolved to do this, an angel of the Lord appeared to him in a dream and said, "Joseph, son of David, do not be afraid to take Mary as your wife, for the child conceived in her is from the Holy Spirit. She will bear a son, and you are to name him Jesus, for he will save his people from their sins." (Matt. 1:18-21)

Psalm

Psalm 89:1-29
The Lord's steadfast love is established forever

Additional Readings

2 Samuel 7:4, 8-16
God makes a covenant with David

Romans 4:13-18
The promise to those who share Abraham's faith

Hymn: Our Father, by Whose Name, ELW 640

O God, from the family of your servant David you raised up Joseph to be the guardian of your incarnate Son and the husband of his blessed mother. Give us grace to imitate his uprightness of life and his obedience to your commands, through Jesus Christ, our Savior and Lord, who lives and reigns with you and the Holy Spirit, one God, now and forever.

Tuesday, March 20, 2018
Week of Lent 5

Psalm 119:9-16
I treasure your promise in my heart

How can young people keep their way pure?
>By guarding it according to your word.
With my whole heart I seek you;
>do not let me stray from your commandments.
I treasure your word in my heart,
>so that I may not sin against you. (Ps. 119:9-11)

Additional Readings
Isaiah 44:1-8
God gives life to the people

Acts 2:14-24
Peter proclaims the crucified Christ to be alive

Hymn: Come to Me, All Pilgrims Thirsty, ELW 777

Righteous Lord, we long to hear your voice and know your ways. Your Son willingly gave his life to make our way straight. Bind us together in his love as we seek always to follow him.

Wednesday, March 21, 2018
Week of Lent 5

Thomas Cranmer, Bishop of Canterbury, martyr, died 1556

Haggai 2:1-9, 20-23

God promises future blessings

The word of the LORD came a second time to Haggai on the twenty-fourth day of the month: Speak to Zerubbabel, governor of Judah, saying, I am about to shake the heavens and the earth, and to overthrow the throne of kingdoms; I am about to destroy the strength of the kingdoms of the nations, and overthrow the chariots and their riders; and the horses and their riders shall fall, every one by the sword of a comrade. On that day, says the LORD of hosts, I will take you, O Zerubbabel my servant, son of Shealtiel, says the LORD, and make you like a signet ring; for I have chosen you, says the LORD of hosts. (Hag. 2:20-23)

Psalm

Psalm 119:9-16
I treasure your promise in my heart

Additional Reading

John 12:34-50
God gives eternal life

Hymn: If God My Lord Be for Me, ELW 788

King of the ages, we long for your righteous, never-ending reign. You are a strong tower, and we turn to you, relying on your sovereignty and holding fast to the promises you have given your people now and forever.

Thursday, March 22, 2018
Week of Lent 5

Jonathan Edwards, teacher, missionary to American Indians, died 1758

Psalm 118:1-2, 19-29
Blessed is the one who comes

Blessed is the one who comes in the name of the LORD.
> We bless you from the house of the LORD.
The LORD is God,
> and he has given us light.
Bind the festal procession with branches,
> up to the horns of the altar.

You are my God, and I will give thanks to you;
> you are my God, I will extol you.

O give thanks to the LORD, for he is good,
> for his steadfast love endures forever. (Ps. 118:26-29)

Additional Readings
Deuteronomy 16:1-8
The feast of unleavened bread

Philippians 2:1-11
Paul's plea for Christ-like humility

Hymn: Rejoice, Ye Pure in Heart! ELW 873/874

You are the Lord who saves. You humble the proud and strengthen the weak and we rejoice in your steadfast love. We bless you for revealing your Son— the one closest to your heart—so your people could be redeemed.

Friday, March 23, 2018
Week of Lent 5

Philippians 2:12-18

Shine like stars in the world

Do all things without murmuring and arguing, so that you may be blameless and innocent, children of God without blemish in the midst of a crooked and perverse generation, in which you shine like stars in the world. It is by your holding fast to the word of life that I can boast on the day of Christ that I did not run in vain or labor in vain. But even if I am being poured out as a libation over the sacrifice and the offering of your faith, I am glad and rejoice with all of you—and in the same way you also must be glad and rejoice with me. (Phil. 2:14-18)

Psalm

Psalm 118:1-2, 19-29
Blessed is the one who comes

Additional Reading

Jeremiah 33:1-9
God will restore and cleanse from sin

Hymn: Day by Day, ELW 790

Most high God, we long to be your light. We long to shine the love and grace of your Son, Jesus Christ, into every corner of your creation. Help us walk in your ways forever.

Saturday, March 24, 2018
Week of Lent 5

Oscar Arnulfo Romero, Bishop of El Salvador, martyr, died 1980

Jeremiah 33:10-16

In a place of desolation, God will bring gladness

Thus says the LORD of hosts: In this place that is waste, without human beings or animals, and in all its towns there shall again be pasture for shepherds resting their flocks. In the towns of the hill country, of the Shephelah, and of the Negeb, in the land of Benjamin, the places around Jerusalem, and in the towns of Judah, flocks shall again pass under the hands of the one who counts them, says the LORD.

The days are surely coming, says the LORD, when I will fulfill the promise I made to the house of Israel and the house of Judah. In those days and at that time I will cause a righteous Branch to spring up for David; and he shall execute justice and righteousness in the land. In those days Judah will be saved and Jerusalem will live in safety. And this is the name by which it will be called: "The LORD is our righteousness." (Jer. 33:12-16)

Psalm
Psalm 118:1-2, 19-29
Blessed is the one who comes

Additional Reading
Mark 10:32-34, 46-52
Jesus approaches Jerusalem

Hymn: Bless Now, O God, the Journey, ELW 326

You are the Lord who heals us. All that is broken and torn apart is restored through the saving grace of your Son, Jesus Christ. You spared nothing to make a path back to you, and for that we rejoice.

Holy Week

On the Sunday of the Passion, Christians enter into Holy Week. This day opens before the Christian community the final period of preparation before the celebration of the Three Days of the Lord's passion, death, and resurrection.

In many churches, palm branches will be given to worshipers for the procession into the worship space. Following an ancient custom, many Christians bring their palms home and place them in the household prayer center, behind a cross or sacred image, or above the indoor lintel of the entryway.

At sunset on Maundy Thursday, Lent comes to an end as the church begins the celebration of the events through which Christ has become the life and the resurrection for all who believe.

Prayer for Placing Palms in the Home

Use this blessing when placing palms in the home after the Palm Sunday liturgy.

Blessed is the one who comes in the name of the Lord!
May we who place these palms receive Christ into our midst
with the joy that marked the entrance to Jerusalem.
May we hold no betrayal in our hearts,
but peacefully welcome Christ
who lives and reigns with you and the Holy Spirit,
one God, now and forever. Amen.

Sunday, March 25, 2018
Sunday of the Passion
Palm Sunday

Annunciation of Our Lord (transferred to April 2)

Mark 14:1—15:47
The passion and death of Jesus

When it was noon, darkness came over the whole land until three in the afternoon. At three o'clock Jesus cried out with a loud voice, "Eloi, Eloi, lema sabachthani?" which means, "My God, my God, why have you forsaken me?" When some of the bystanders heard it, they said, "Listen, he is calling for Elijah." And someone ran, filled a sponge with sour wine, put it on a stick, and gave it to him to drink, saying, "Wait, let us see whether Elijah will come to take him down." Then Jesus gave a loud cry and breathed his last. And the curtain of the temple was torn in two, from top to bottom. Now when the centurion, who stood facing him, saw that in this way he breathed his last, he said, "Truly this man was God's Son!" (Mark 15:33-39)

Psalm
Psalm 31:9-16
I commend my spirit

Additional Readings
Isaiah 50:4-9a
The servant submits to suffering

Philippians 2:5-11
Death on a cross

Hymn: My Song Is Love Unknown, ELW 343

O God of mercy and might, in the mystery of the passion of your Son you offer your infinite life to the world. Gather us around the cross of Christ, and preserve us until the resurrection, through Jesus Christ, our Savior and Lord, who lives and reigns with you and the Holy Spirit, one God, now and forever.

Monday, March 26, 2018
Monday in Holy Week

Psalm 36:5-11

Refuge under the shadow of your wings

How precious is your steadfast love, O God!
>   All people may take refuge in the shadow of your wings.
They feast on the abundance of your house,
>   and you give them drink from the river of your delights.
For with you is the fountain of life;
>   in your light we see light. (Ps. 36:7-9)

Additional Readings

Isaiah 42:1-9
The servant brings forth justice

Hebrews 9:11-15
The blood of Christ redeems for eternal life

John 12:1-11
Mary of Bethany anoints Jesus

Hymn: Alas! And Did My Savior Bleed, ELW 337

O God, your Son chose the path that led to pain before joy and to the cross before glory. Plant his cross in our hearts, so that in its power and love we may come at last to joy and glory, through Jesus Christ, our Savior and Lord, who lives and reigns with you and the Holy Spirit, one God, now and forever.

Tuesday, March 27, 2018
Tuesday in Holy Week

1 Corinthians 1:18-31

The cross of Christ reveals God's power and wisdom

For since, in the wisdom of God, the world did not know God through wisdom, God decided, through the foolishness of our proclamation, to save those who believe. For Jews demand signs and Greeks desire wisdom, but we proclaim Christ crucified, a stumbling block to Jews and foolishness to Gentiles, but to those who are the called, both Jews and Greeks, Christ the power of God and the wisdom of God. For God's foolishness is wiser than human wisdom, and God's weakness is stronger than human strength. (1 Cor. 1:21-25)

Psalm

Psalm 71:1-14
From my mother's womb you have been my strength

Additional Readings

Isaiah 49:1-7
The servant brings salvation to earth's ends

John 12:20-36
Jesus speaks of his death

Hymn: Seed That in Earth Is Dying, ELW 330

Lord Jesus, you have called us to follow you. Grant that our love may not grow cold in your service, and that we may not fail or deny you in the time of trial, for you live and reign with the Father and the Holy Spirit, one God, now and forever.

Wednesday, March 28, 2018
Wednesday in Holy Week

Isaiah 50:4-9a
The servant is vindicated by God

The Lord GOD helps me;
> therefore I have not been disgraced;
therefore I have set my face like flint,
> and I know that I shall not be put to shame;
> he who vindicates me is near.
Who will contend with me?
> Let us stand up together.
Who are my adversaries?
> Let them confront me.
It is the Lord GOD who helps me;
> who will declare me guilty? (Isa. 50:7-9a)

Psalm

Psalm 70
Be pleased, O God, to deliver me

Additional Readings

Hebrews 12:1-3
Look to Jesus, who endured the cross

John 13:21-32
Jesus foretells his betrayal

Hymn: Ah, Holy Jesus, ELW 349

Almighty God, your Son our Savior suffered at human hands and endured the shame of the cross. Grant that we may walk in the way of his cross and find it the way of life and peace, through Jesus Christ, our Savior and Lord, who lives and reigns with you and the Holy Spirit, one God, now and forever.

The Three Days

As the sun sets on Maundy Thursday, so Lent ends and the Three Days begin, ending with sunset on Easter Day. During these central days, Christians prepare to celebrate God's gift of new life given in baptism. Indeed, the readings of the Three Days move toward the baptismal font where new brothers and sisters are born of water and the Spirit, and where the baptized renew their baptismal promises.

In the home and in the church community, special attention is given to these days through prayer and keeping greater silence until the great Vigil of Easter is celebrated. Many Christians keep a fast from food, work, and entertainment on Good Friday and Holy Saturday. In the home, preparations can be made for the celebration of Easter: cleaning, coloring eggs, baking Easter breads, gathering greens or flowers to adorn crosses and sacred images. In those communities where baptisms will be celebrated, prayers may be offered for those to be received into the church.

Table Prayer for the Three Days

Blessed are you, O Lord our God.
With this food strengthen us on our journey from death to life.
We glory in the cross of Christ.
Raise us, with him, to the joy of the resurrection,
through Jesus Christ our Lord. Amen.

Thursday, March 29, 2018
Maundy Thursday

Hans Nielsen Hauge, renewer of the church, died 1824

1 Corinthians 11:23-26
Proclaim the Lord's death

For I received from the Lord what I also handed on to you, that the Lord Jesus on the night when he was betrayed took a loaf of bread, and when he had given thanks, he broke it and said, "This is my body that is for you. Do this in remembrance of me." In the same way he took the cup also, after supper, saying, "This cup is the new covenant in my blood. Do this, as often as you drink it, in remembrance of me." For as often as you eat this bread and drink the cup, you proclaim the Lord's death until he comes. (1 Cor. 11:23-26)

Psalm
Psalm 116:1-2, 12-19
The cup of salvation

Additional Readings
Exodus 12:1-4 [5-10]
11-14
The passover of the Lord

John 13:1-17, 31b-35
The service of Christ: footwashing and meal

Hymn: Where Charity and Love Prevail, ELW 359

Holy God, source of all love, on the night of his betrayal, Jesus gave us a new commandment, to love one another as he loves us. Write this commandment in our hearts, and give us the will to serve others as he was the servant of all, your Son, Jesus Christ, our Savior and Lord, who lives and reigns with you and the Holy Spirit, one God, now and forever.

Friday, March 30, 2018
Good Friday

John 18:1—19:42

The passion and death of Jesus

Then Pilate entered the headquarters again, summoned Jesus, and asked him, "Are you the King of the Jews?" Jesus answered, "Do you ask this on your own, or did others tell you about me?" Pilate replied, "I am not a Jew, am I? Your own nation and the chief priests have handed you over to me. What have you done?" Jesus answered, "My kingdom is not from this world. If my kingdom were from this world, my followers would be fighting to keep me from being handed over to the Jews. But as it is, my kingdom is not from here." Pilate asked him, "So you are a king?" Jesus answered, "You say that I am a king. For this I was born, and for this I came into the world, to testify to the truth. Everyone who belongs to the truth listens to my voice." (John 18:33-37)

Psalm

Psalm 22
Why have you forsaken me?

Additional Readings

Isaiah 52:13—53:12
The suffering servant

Hebrews 10:16-25
The way to God is opened

Hymn: O Sacred Head, Now Wounded, ELW 351/352

Almighty God, look with loving mercy on your family, for whom our Lord Jesus Christ was willing to be betrayed, to be given over to the hands of sinners, and to suffer death on the cross; who now lives and reigns with you and the Holy Spirit, one God, now and forever.

Saturday, March 31, 2018
Resurrection of Our Lord
Vigil of Easter

John Donne, poet, died 1631

Romans 6:3-11
Dying and rising with Christ

Do you not know that all of us who have been baptized into Christ Jesus were baptized into his death? Therefore we have been buried with him by baptism into death, so that, just as Christ was raised from the dead by the glory of the Father, so we too might walk in newness of life.

For if we have been united with him in a death like his, we will certainly be united with him in a resurrection like his. We know that our old self was crucified with him so that the body of sin might be destroyed, and we might no longer be enslaved to sin. For whoever has died is freed from sin. (Rom. 6:3-7)

Psalm
Psalm 136:1-9, 23-26
God's mercy endures forever

Additional Readings
Genesis 1:1—2:4a
Creation

John 20:1-18
Seeing the risen Christ

Hymn: Come, You Faithful, Raise the Strain, ELW 363

Eternal giver of life and light, this holy night shines with the radiance of the risen Christ. Renew your church with the Spirit given us in baptism, that we may worship you in sincerity and truth and may shine as a light in the world, through your Son, Jesus Christ our Lord, who lives and reigns with you and the Holy Spirit, one God, now and forever.

Prayer List for April

_____

_____

_____

_____

_____

_____

_____

_____

_____

_____

Sunday, April 1, 2018
Resurrection of Our Lord
Easter Day

Mark 16:1-8

The resurrection is announced

As [Mary Magdalene, and Mary the mother of James, and Salome] entered the tomb, they saw a young man, dressed in a white robe, sitting on the right side; and they were alarmed. But he said to them, "Do not be alarmed; you are looking for Jesus of Nazareth, who was crucified. He has been raised; he is not here. Look, there is the place they laid him. But go, tell his disciples and Peter that he is going ahead of you to Galilee; there you will see him, just as he told you." So they went out and fled from the tomb, for terror and amazement had seized them; and they said nothing to anyone, for they were afraid. (Mark 16:5-8)

Psalm

Psalm 118:1-2, 14-24
On this day God has acted

Additional Readings

Acts 10:34-43
God raised Jesus on the third day

1 Corinthians 15:1-11
Witnesses to the risen Christ

Hymn: At the Lamb's High Feast We Sing, ELW 362

O God, you gave your only Son to suffer death on the cross for our redemption, and by his glorious resurrection you delivered us from the power of death. Make us die every day to sin, that we may live with him forever in the joy of the resurrection, through your Son, Jesus Christ our Lord, who lives and reigns with you and the Holy Spirit, one God, now and forever.

Easter

The Three Days flow into the rejoicing of the fifty days of Easter. During this "week of weeks," Christians explore the meaning of the central actions of baptism for daily life: the renouncing of evil and the professing of faith, washing in water, being marked with the cross, clothing in the white robe, receiving the light of the paschal/Easter candle, and eating and drinking the bread of life and the cup of salvation.

The fifty days were once called Pentecost, Greek for "fifty." On the fiftieth day of Easter, Christians celebrate the pentecostal mystery of the risen Christ breathing on the church the breath, the wind, and the fire of the Holy Spirit.

Table Prayer for the Season of Easter

O God of our risen Lord, we praise you, we bless you,
we worship you for the gifts of life you give us.
Always you offer us life, and for this we bless your holy name.
And we ask you,
give your life also to all who know only hunger and the pangs of death.
So may the whole world be raised to life,
through Jesus Christ, our Savior and Lord. Amen.

Monday, April 2, 2018
Annunciation of Our Lord (transferred)

Luke 1:26-38
The angel greets Mary

In the sixth month the angel Gabriel was sent by God to a town in Galilee called Nazareth, to a virgin engaged to a man whose name was Joseph, of the house of David. The virgin's name was Mary. And he came to her and said, "Greetings, favored one! The Lord is with you." But she was much perplexed by his words and pondered what sort of greeting this might be. The angel said to her, "Do not be afraid, Mary, for you have found favor with God. And now, you will conceive in your womb and bear a son, and you will name him Jesus." (Luke 1:26-31)

Psalm

Psalm 45
Your name will be remembered

Additional Readings

Isaiah 7:10-14
A young woman will bear a son

Hebrews 10:4-10
The offering of Jesus' body sanctifies us

Hymn: Signs and Wonders, ELW 672

Pour your grace into our hearts, O God, that we who have known the incarnation of your Son, Jesus Christ, announced by an angel, may by his cross and passion be brought to the glory of his resurrection; for he lives and reigns with you, in the unity of the Holy Spirit, one God, now and forever.

Tuesday, April 3, 2018
Week of Easter 1

Psalm 118:1-2, 14-24
On this day God has acted

I thank you that you have answered me
> and have become my salvation.
The stone that the builders rejected
> has become the chief cornerstone.
This is the LORD's doing;
> it is marvelous in our eyes.
This is the day that the LORD has made;
> let us rejoice and be glad in it. (Ps. 118:21-24)

Additional Reading
1 Corinthians 15:50-58
The dead will be raised

Genesis 1:20—2:4a
God creates

Hymn: This Joyful Eastertide, ELW 391

*Father of the Risen One, not only at Easter, but every day may we rejoice
and be glad in the resurrection promise. Help us carry in our hearts the
newness of creation and sing hymns of praise.*

Wednesday, April 4, 2018
Week of Easter 1

Benedict the African, confessor, died 1589

Mark 16:1-8
Mark's resurrection account

When the sabbath was over, Mary Magdalene, and Mary the mother of James, and Salome bought spices, so that they might go and anoint Jesus. And very early on the first day of the week, when the sun had risen, they went to the tomb. They had been saying to one another, "Who will roll away the stone for us from the entrance to the tomb?" When they looked up, they saw that the stone, which was very large, had already been rolled back. As they entered the tomb, they saw a young man, dressed in a white robe, sitting on the right side; and they were alarmed. But he said to them, "Do not be alarmed; you are looking for Jesus of Nazareth, who was crucified. He has been raised; he is not here. Look, there is the place they laid him. But go, tell his disciples and Peter that he is going ahead of you to Galilee; there you will see him, just as he told you." (Mark 16:1-7)

Psalm
Psalm 118:1-2, 14-24
On this day God has acted

Additional Reading
Song of Solomon 3:1-11
The song of the lover

Hymn: Christ Has Arisen, Alleluia, ELW 364

O God, as you led the women to the tomb, may you grant us similar courage to shout that Jesus is not here, but he is risen! Help us to believe and share the hope of the resurrection.

Thursday, April 5, 2018
Week of Easter 1

Psalm 133
How good it is to live in unity

How very good and pleasant it is
    when kindred live together in unity!
It is like the precious oil on the head,
    running down upon the beard,
on the beard of Aaron,
    running down over the collar of his robes.
It is like the dew of Hermon,
    which falls on the mountains of Zion.
For there the LORD ordained his blessing,
    life forevermore. (Ps. 133:1-3)

Additional Readings
Daniel 1:1-21
Daniel in the court of Nebuchadnezzar

Acts 2:42-47
The believers' common life

Hymn: The Risen Christ, ELW 390

God of the risen Christ, you call us to live in harmony and to worship and praise you. Teach us to speak out for the oppressed and to serve others with love and grace.

Friday, April 6, 2018
Week of Easter 1

Albrecht Dürer, died 1528; Matthias Grünewald, died 1529; Lucas Cranach, died 1553; artists

Daniel 2:1-23
The king searches for wisdom

Daniel said:

"Blessed be the name of God from age to age,
    for wisdom and power are his.
He changes times and seasons,
    deposes kings and sets up kings;
he gives wisdom to the wise
    and knowledge to those who have understanding.
He reveals deep and hidden things;
    he knows what is in the darkness,
    and light dwells with him.
To you, O God of my ancestors,
    I give thanks and praise,
for you have given me wisdom and power,
    and have now revealed to me what we asked of you,
    for you have revealed to us what the king ordered." (Dan. 2:20-23)

Psalm
Psalm 133
How good it is to live in unity

Additional Reading
Acts 4:23-31
Prayer after Peter and John's release

Hymn: Christ Is Alive! Let Christians Sing, ELW 389

O God, how good to sing your praises as the prophet Daniel, who gave thanks for your wisdom and power. May your light dwell within us as we praise the risen Christ who brings good news, hope, and truth.

Saturday, April 7, 2018
Week of Easter 1

John 12:44-50
Believe in the one who sent me

Then Jesus cried aloud: "Whoever believes in me believes not in me but in him who sent me. And whoever sees me sees him who sent me. I have come as light into the world, so that everyone who believes in me should not remain in the darkness. I do not judge anyone who hears my words and does not keep them, for I came not to judge the world, but to save the world. The one who rejects me and does not receive my word has a judge; on the last day the word that I have spoken will serve as judge, for I have not spoken on my own, but the Father who sent me has himself given me a commandment about what to say and what to speak. And I know that his commandment is eternal life. What I speak, therefore, I speak just as the Father has told me." (John 12:44-50)

Psalm
Psalm 133
How good it is to live in unity

Additional Reading
Daniel 2:24-49
Daniel's rise to power

Hymn: Now All the Vault of Heaven Resounds, ELW 367

Heavenly Father, thank you for sending your Son as light into the world to give us life. In our times of doubt or trial, help us to sing that Christ has triumphed!

Sunday, April 8, 2018
Second Sunday of Easter

John 20:19-31

Beholding the wounds of the risen Christ

A week later [Jesus'] disciples were again in the house, and Thomas was with them. Although the doors were shut, Jesus came and stood among them and said, "Peace be with you." Then he said to Thomas, "Put your finger here and see my hands. Reach out your hand and put it in my side. Do not doubt but believe." Thomas answered him, "My Lord and my God!" Jesus said to him, "Have you believed because you have seen me? Blessed are those who have not seen and yet have come to believe." (John 20:26-29)

Psalm

Psalm 133
How good it is to live in unity

Additional Readings

Acts 4:32-35
The believers' common life

1 John 1:1—2:2
Walking in the light

Hymn: We Walk by Faith, ELW 635

Almighty God, with joy we celebrate the day of our Lord's resurrection. By the grace of Christ among us, enable us to show the power of the resurrection in all that we say and do, through Jesus Christ, our Savior and Lord, who lives and reigns with you and the Holy Spirit, one God, now and forever.

Monday, April 9, 2018
Week of Easter 2

Dietrich Bonhoeffer, theologian, died 1945

Psalm 135
Praise to God

Praise the LORD!
>Praise the name of the LORD;
>give praise, O servants of the LORD,
you that stand in the house of the LORD,
>in the courts of the house of our God.
Praise the LORD, for the LORD is good;
>sing to his name, for he is gracious.
For the LORD has chosen Jacob for himself,
>Israel as his own possession. (Ps. 135:1-4)

Additional Readings
Daniel 3:1-30
God saves the three men from the fire

1 John 2:3-11
A new commandment

Hymn: You Servants of God, ELW 825

O God of Israel, when you liberated your chosen people from slavery in Egypt and brought them to the promised land, they sang hymns of thanks and praise. Remain so present to us today that may we praise you without ceasing.

Tuesday, April 10, 2018
Week of Easter 2

Mikael Agricola, Bishop of Turku, died 1557

Daniel 6:1-28
God saves Daniel from the lions

Then King Darius wrote to all peoples and nations of every language throughout the whole world: "May you have abundant prosperity! I make a decree, that in all my royal dominion people should tremble and fear before the God of Daniel:

> For he is the living God,
>> enduring forever.
> His kingdom shall never be destroyed,
>> and his dominion has no end.
> He delivers and rescues,
>> he works signs and wonders in heaven and on earth;
> for he has saved Daniel
>> from the power of the lions." (Dan. 6:25-27)

Psalm
Psalm 135
Praise to God

Additional Reading
1 John 2:12-17
The world is passing away

Hymn: Thine the Amen, ELW 826

O God of justice, as you delivered your servant Daniel from lions, rescue us from whatever threatens to devour us. Give us courage and hope as we live in the light of your resurrection love.

Wednesday, April 11, 2018
Week of Easter 2

Isaiah 26:1-15

Song of victory

O Lᴏʀᴅ, you will ordain peace for us,
    for indeed, all that we have done, you have done for us.
O Lᴏʀᴅ our God,
    other lords besides you have ruled over us,
    but we acknowledge your name alone.
The dead do not live;
    shades do not rise—
because you have punished and destroyed them,
    and wiped out all memory of them.
But you have increased the nation, O Lᴏʀᴅ,
    you have increased the nation; you are glorified;
    you have enlarged all the borders of the land. (Isa. 26:12-15)

Psalm

Psalm 135
Praise to God

Additional Reading

Mark 12:18-27
Jesus teaches about the resurrection

Hymn: Bring Peace to Earth Again, ELW 700

O God of compassion, when our homes, cities, or countries are torn apart, you bear our pain. Deliver us from enemies that wound us. Bring peace to our brokenness and give us gentle, loving hearts.

Thursday, April 12, 2018
Week of Easter 2

Psalm 4

God does wonders for the faithful

There are many who say, "O that we might see some good!
    Let the light of your face shine on us, O LORD!"
You have put gladness in my heart
    more than when their grain and wine abound.

I will both lie down and sleep in peace;
    for you alone, O LORD, make me lie down in safety. (Ps. 4:6-8)

Additional Readings

Daniel 9:1-19
Daniel pleads for the people in prayer

1 John 2:18-25
Remain in union with God

Hymn: Awake, My Heart, with Gladness, ELW 378

O God of hope, hear our prayer when we do not sleep in peace. Help us in times of trouble to trust that you will never leave us and that we are safe in you.

Friday, April 13, 2018
Week of Easter 2

1 John 2:26-28
Have confidence in the coming one

I write these things to you concerning those who would deceive you. As for you, the anointing that you received from him abides in you, and so you do not need anyone to teach you. But as his anointing teaches you about all things, and is true and is not a lie, and just as it has taught you, abide in him.

And now, little children, abide in him, so that when he is revealed we may have confidence and not be put to shame before him at his coming. (1 John 2:26-28)

Psalm
Psalm 4
God does wonders for the faithful

Additional Reading
Daniel 10:2-19
Daniel's vision strengthens him

Hymn: O God in Heaven, ELW 748

Holy God, grounded in your love we can face the future with courage. You will not abandon us in our times of weakness. Help us to live with the confidence of your abiding and eternal love.

Saturday, April 14, 2018
Week of Easter 2

Luke 22:24-30
Eating and drinking at Christ's table

A dispute also arose among the apostles as to which one of them was to be regarded as the greatest. But [Jesus] said to them, "The kings of the Gentiles lord it over them; and those in authority over them are called benefactors. But not so with you; rather the greatest among you must become like the youngest, and the leader like one who serves. For who is greater, the one who is at the table or the one who serves? Is it not the one at the table? But I am among you as one who serves.

"You are those who have stood by me in my trials; and I confer on you, just as my Father has conferred on me, a kingdom, so that you may eat and drink at my table in my kingdom, and you will sit on thrones judging the twelve tribes of Israel." (Luke 22:24-30)

Psalm
Psalm 4
God does wonders for the faithful

Additional Reading
Acts 3:1-10
A man lame from birth is healed

Hymn: I Come with Joy, ELW 482

O God of the risen Christ, what a privilege to be served at the table of your Son. He reminds us that all divisions cease when we share in his communion meal. Give us grace to become a community of love.

Sunday, April 15, 2018
Third Sunday of Easter

Luke 24:36b-48
Eating with the risen Christ

Then [Jesus] said to [the disciples,] "These are my words that I spoke to you while I was still with you—that everything written about me in the law of Moses, the prophets, and the psalms must be fulfilled." Then he opened their minds to understand the scriptures, and he said to them, "Thus it is written, that the Messiah is to suffer and to rise from the dead on the third day, and that repentance and forgiveness of sins is to be proclaimed in his name to all nations, beginning from Jerusalem. You are witnesses of these things." (Luke 24:44-48)

Psalm

Psalm 4
God does wonders for the faithful

Additional Readings

Acts 3:12-19
Health and forgiveness through Jesus

1 John 3:1-7
The revealing of the children of God

Hymn: With High Delight Let Us Unite, ELW 368

Holy and righteous God, you are the author of life, and you adopt us to be your children. Fill us with your words of life, that we may live as witnesses to the resurrection of your Son, Jesus Christ, our Savior and Lord, who lives and reigns with you and the Holy Spirit, one God, now and forever.

Monday, April 16, 2018
Week of Easter 3

Psalm 150
Praise to God

Praise the LORD!
Praise God in his sanctuary;
    praise him in his mighty firmament!
Praise him for his mighty deeds;
    praise him according to his surpassing greatness!

Praise him with trumpet sound;
    praise him with lute and harp!
Praise him with tambourine and dance;
    praise him with strings and pipe!
Praise him with clanging cymbals;
    praise him with loud clashing cymbals!
Let everything that breathes praise the LORD!
Praise the LORD! (Ps. 150:1-6)

Additional Readings
Jeremiah 30:1-11a
God will save the people

1 John 3:10-16
Lay down life for one another

Hymn: When in Our Music God Is Glorified, ELW 850/851

Redeemer God, as we savor Easter's fifty-day celebration, remind us to keep your music going in our lives. Let every voice and instrument praise you. Give us faith to sing and glorify your greatness today and always.

Tuesday, April 17, 2018
Week of Easter 3

2 John 1-6
Love one another

The elder to the elect lady and her children, whom I love in the truth, and not only I but also all who know the truth, because of the truth that abides in us and will be with us forever:

Grace, mercy, and peace will be with us from God the Father and from Jesus Christ, the Father's Son, in truth and love.

I was overjoyed to find some of your children walking in the truth, just as we have been commanded by the Father. But now, dear lady, I ask you, not as though I were writing you a new commandment, but one we have had from the beginning, let us love one another. And this is love, that we walk according to his commandments; this is the commandment just as you have heard it from the beginning—you must walk in it. (2 John 1-6)

Psalm
Psalm 150
Praise to God

Additional Reading
Hosea 5:15—6:6
Salvation on the third day

Hymn: We Are Called, ELW 720

O God of truth, you call us to love one another as you have loved us. Teach us to open our hearts and shine with joy and love. Help us whenever we stumble, and remind us that we are not alone.

Wednesday, April 18, 2018
Week of Easter 3

Proverbs 9:1-6

Wisdom invites to her feast

Wisdom has built her house,
>   she has hewn her seven pillars.
She has slaughtered her animals, she has mixed her wine,
>   she has also set her table.
She has sent out her servant girls, she calls
>   from the highest places in the town,
"You that are simple, turn in here!"
>   To those without sense she says,
"Come, eat of my bread
>   and drink of the wine I have mixed.
Lay aside immaturity, and live,
and walk in the way of insight." (Prov. 9:1-6)

Psalm
Psalm 150
Praise to God

Additional Reading
Mark 16:9-18
Jesus appears to the disciples

Hymn: We Eat the Bread of Teaching, ELW 518

Almighty God, you call even those having the least among us to your glorious celebration. May the promise of your eternal banquet remind us to welcome all who hunger to the table of salvation where we are one in you.

Thursday, April 19, 2018
Week of Easter 3

Olavus Petri, priest, died 1552; Laurentius Petri, Bishop of Uppsala, died 1573;
renewers of the church

Psalm 23
God our shepherd

The LORD is my shepherd, I shall not want.
    He makes me lie down in green pastures;
he leads me beside still waters;
    he restores my soul.
He leads me in right paths
    for his name's sake.

Even though I walk through the darkest valley,
    I fear no evil;
for you are with me;
    your rod and your staff—
    they comfort me. (Ps. 23:1-4)

Additional Readings
Genesis 30:25-43
Jacob the shepherd

Acts 3:17-26
Peter preaches in Solomon's Portico

Hymn: My Shepherd, You Supply My Need, ELW 782

O divine Shepherd, you reassure those who cry out in distress. When we wander, bring us back to you and lead us in the path of truth and grace. Grant that we not be afraid but comforted in your love.

Friday, April 20, 2018
Week of Easter 3

Acts 4:1-4

Peter and John arrested

While Peter and John were speaking to the people, the priests, the captain of the temple, and the Sadducees came to them, much annoyed because they were teaching the people and proclaiming that in Jesus there is the resurrection of the dead. So they arrested them and put them in custody until the next day, for it was already evening. But many of those who heard the word believed; and they numbered about five thousand. (Acts 4:1-4)

Psalm

Psalm 23
God our shepherd

Additional Reading

Genesis 46:28—47:6
The shepherds of Israel sojourn in Egypt

Hymn: The Day of Resurrection! ELW 361

O God of truth, help us to hear your word. Bathe us in the light of the resurrection so that we will know and believe in it. Help our unbelief so that we can share the good news with others.

Saturday, April 21, 2018
Week of Easter 3

Anselm, Bishop of Canterbury, died 1109

Mark 6:30-34
Like sheep without a shepherd

The apostles gathered around Jesus, and told him all that they had done and taught. He said to them, "Come away to a deserted place all by yourselves and rest a while." For many were coming and going, and they had no leisure even to eat. And they went away in the boat to a deserted place by themselves. Now many saw them going and recognized them, and they hurried there on foot from all the towns and arrived ahead of them. As he went ashore, he saw a great crowd; and he had compassion for them, because they were like sheep without a shepherd; and he began to teach them many things. (Mark 6:30-34)

Psalm
Psalm 23
God our shepherd

Additional Reading
Genesis 48:8-19
God has been my shepherd

Hymn: Savior, like a Shepherd Lead Us, ELW 789

God, our shepherd, when we are lost like sheep, find us and remind us that we are yours. You know when we are discouraged and need rest. Help us to show compassion to others who seek your goodness and mercy.

Sunday, April 22, 2018
Fourth Sunday of Easter

John 10:11-18

Christ the shepherd

[Jesus said,] "I am the good shepherd. The good shepherd lays down his life for the sheep. The hired hand, who is not the shepherd and does not own the sheep, sees the wolf coming and leaves the sheep and runs away—and the wolf snatches them and scatters them. The hired hand runs away because a hired hand does not care for the sheep. I am the good shepherd. I know my own and my own know me, just as the Father knows me and I know the Father. And I lay down my life for the sheep." (John 10:11-15)

Psalm

Psalm 23
God our shepherd

Additional Readings

Acts 4:5-12
Salvation in the name of Jesus

1 John 3:16-24
Love in truth and action

Hymn: Have No Fear, Little Flock, ELW 764

O Lord Christ, good shepherd of the sheep, you seek the lost and guide us into your fold. Feed us, and we shall be satisfied; heal us, and we shall be whole. Make us one with you, for you live and reign with the Father and the Holy Spirit, one God, now and forever.

Monday, April 23, 2018
Week of Easter 4

Toyohiko Kagawa, renewer of society, died 1960

Psalm 95
We are the sheep of God's hand

O come, let us worship and bow down,
>   let us kneel before the LORD, our Maker!
For he is our God,
>   and we are the people of his pasture,
>   and the sheep of his hand.

O that today you would listen to his voice! (Ps. 95:6-7)

Additional Readings
1 Samuel 16:1-13
The shepherd David is anointed

1 Peter 5:1-5
Christ the great shepherd

Hymn: All People That on Earth Do Dwell, ELW 883

Caring God, you command us to listen to your voice and yours alone. When we are lost, you call us back to you. Help us sing your praises with a cheerful voice today and always.

Tuesday, April 24, 2018
Week of Easter 4

Revelation 7:13-17
The Lamb will be the shepherd

Then one of the elders addressed me, saying, "Who are these, robed in white, and where have they come from?" I said to him, "Sir, you are the one that knows." Then he said to me, "These are they who have come out of the great ordeal; they have washed their robes and made them white in the blood of the Lamb.

> For this reason they are before the throne of God,
>> and worship him day and night within his temple,
>> and the one who is seated on the throne will shelter them.
> They will hunger no more, and thirst no more;
>> the sun will not strike them,
>> nor any scorching heat;
> for the Lamb at the center of the throne will be their shepherd,
>> and he will guide them to springs of the water of life,
> and God will wipe away every tear from their eyes." (Rev. 7:13-17)

Psalm
Psalm 95
We are the sheep of God's hand

Additional Reading
1 Chronicles 11:1-9
The shepherd David made king

Hymn: Sing with All the Saints in Glory, ELW 426

O God, we await the day when every tear will be wiped away and every sin washed clean. Give us courage to endure hardship and follow Jesus the lamb until we stand before your throne and all of heaven rejoices.

Wednesday, April 25, 2018
Mark, Evangelist

Mark 1:1-15

The beginning of the gospel of Jesus Christ

The beginning of the good news of Jesus Christ, the Son of God.

As it is written in the prophet Isaiah,

"See, I am sending my messenger ahead of you,
who will prepare your way;
the voice of one crying out in the wilderness:
'Prepare the way of the Lord,
make his paths straight,'"

John the baptizer appeared in the wilderness, proclaiming a baptism of repentance for the forgiveness of sins. And people from the whole Judean countryside and all the people of Jerusalem were going out to him, and were baptized by him in the river Jordan, confessing their sins. (Mark 1:1-5)

Psalm

Psalm 57
Be merciful to me, O God

Additional Readings

Isaiah 52:7-10
The messenger announces salvation

2 Timothy 4:6-11, 18
The good fight of faith

Hymn: By All Your Saints, st. 10, ELW 420

Almighty God, you have enriched your church with Mark's proclamation of the gospel. Give us grace to believe firmly in the good news of salvation and to walk daily in accord with it, through Jesus Christ, our Savior and Lord, who lives and reigns with you and the Holy Spirit, one God, now and forever.

Thursday, April 26, 2018
Week of Easter 4

Psalm 22:25-31
All shall turn to the Lord

From you comes my praise in the great congregation;
    my vows I will pay before those who fear him.
The poor shall eat and be satisfied;
    those who seek him shall praise the LORD.
    May your hearts live forever!

All the ends of the earth shall remember
    and turn to the LORD;
and all the families of the nations
    shall worship before him.
For dominion belongs to the LORD,
    and he rules over the nations. (Ps. 22:25-28)

Additional Readings
Amos 8:1-7
Amos' vision of the basket of fruit

Acts 8:1b-8
Philip's ministry in Samaria

Hymn: Sing Praise to God, the Highest Good, ELW 871

O ruler of every nation, all creation is called to praise and serve you. Open our arms to embrace those who are hungry, poor, afraid, and hopeless so that by our example they might know your love and peace.

Friday, April 27, 2018
Week of Easter 4

Amos 8:11-13

A famine of hearing the word of God

The time is surely coming, says the Lord GOD,
    when I will send a famine on the land;
not a famine of bread, or a thirst for water,
    but of hearing the words of the LORD.
They shall wander from sea to sea,
    and from north to east;
they shall run to and fro, seeking the word of the LORD,
    but they shall not find it.

In that day the beautiful young women and the young men
    shall faint for thirst. (Amos 8:11-13)

Psalm
Psalm 22:25-31
All shall turn to the Lord

Additional Reading
Acts 8:9-25
Philip and Simon the magician

Hymn: Word of God, Come Down on Earth, ELW 510

O God, we cannot imagine a world where anyone would be prevented from hearing your living word. Help us share your teachings with others so that all may find faith and hope in your steadfast love that endures forever.

Saturday, April 28, 2018
Week of Easter 4

Mark 4:30-32

The kingdom like a mustard seed

[Jesus] also said, "With what can we compare the kingdom of God, or what parable will we use for it? It is like a mustard seed, which, when sown upon the ground, is the smallest of all the seeds on earth; yet when it is sown it grows up and becomes the greatest of all shrubs, and puts forth large branches, so that the birds of the air can make nests in its shade." (Mark 4:30-32)

Psalm
Psalm 22:25-31
All shall turn to the Lord

Additional Reading
Amos 9:7-15
The mountains shall drip sweet wine

Hymn: On What Has Now Been Sown, ELW 550

Almighty God, you protect us when we feel small and vulnerable. Lead us to good soil so that we may grow in faith and be examples for others of your great love. To you be praise and glory!

Sunday, April 29, 2018
Fifth Sunday of Easter

Catherine of Siena, theologian, died 1380

John 15:1-8

Christ the vine

[Jesus said,] "I am the true vine, and my Father is the vinegrower. He removes every branch in me that bears no fruit. Every branch that bears fruit he prunes to make it bear more fruit. You have already been cleansed by the word that I have spoken to you. Abide in me as I abide in you. Just as the branch cannot bear fruit by itself unless it abides in the vine, neither can you unless you abide in me. I am the vine, you are the branches. Those who abide in me and I in them bear much fruit, because apart from me you can do nothing." (John 15:1-5)

Psalm

Psalm 22:25-31
All shall turn to the Lord

Additional Readings

Acts 8:26-40
Philip teaches and baptizes an Ethiopian

1 John 4:7-21
Loving one another

Hymn: O Blessed Spring, ELW 447

O God, you give us your Son as the vine apart from whom we cannot live. Nourish our life in his resurrection, that we may bear the fruit of love and know the fullness of your joy, through Jesus Christ, our Savior and Lord, who lives and reigns with you and the Holy Spirit, one God, now and forever.

Monday, April 30, 2018
Week of Easter 5

Psalm 80
Israel, the vine

Turn again, O God of hosts;
  look down from heaven, and see;
have regard for this vine,
  the stock that your right hand planted.
They have burned it with fire, they have cut it down;
  may they perish at the rebuke of your countenance.
But let your hand be upon the one at your right hand,
  the one whom you made strong for yourself.
Then we will never turn back from you;
  give us life, and we will call on your name. (Ps. 80:14-18)

Additional Readings
Isaiah 5:1-7
The unfaithful vineyard

Galatians 5:16-26
The fruits of the Spirit

Hymn: Alleluia! Jesus Is Risen! ELW 377

O God of compassion, you give us life, you give us strength. Respond to our cries for the troubles that are on our hearts. Restore us so that we may become healthy, strong vines once again.

Prayer List for May

_____

_____

_____

_____

_____

_____

_____

_____

_____

Tuesday, May 1, 2018
Philip and James, Apostles

John 14:8-14
Jesus and the Father are one

Philip said to [Jesus,]"Lord, show us the Father, and we will be satisfied." Jesus said to him, "Have I been with you all this time, Philip, and you still do not know me? Whoever has seen me has seen the Father. How can you say, 'Show us the Father'? Do you not believe that I am in the Father and the Father is in me? The words that I say to you I do not speak on my own; but the Father who dwells in me does his works." (John 14:8-10)

Psalm
Psalm 44:1-3, 20-26
Save us for the sake of your love

Additional Readings
Isaiah 30:18-21
God's mercy and justice

2 Corinthians 4:1-6
Proclaiming Jesus Christ as Lord

Hymn: You Are the Way, ELW 758

Almighty God, you gave to your apostles Philip and James grace and strength to bear witness to your Son. Grant that we, remembering their victory of faith, may glorify in life and death the name of our Lord Jesus Christ, who lives and reigns with you and the Holy Spirit, one God, now and forever.

Wednesday, May 2, 2018
Week of Easter 5

Athanasius, Bishop of Alexandria, died 373

John 14:18-31
Keeping God's word

[Jesus said,] "I will not leave you orphaned; I am coming to you. In a little while the world will no longer see me, but you will see me; because I live, you also will live. On that day you will know that I am in my Father, and you in me, and I in you. They who have my commandments and keep them are those who love me; and those who love me will be loved by my Father, and I will love them and reveal myself to them." (John 14:18-21)

Psalm
Psalm 80
Israel, the vine

Additional Reading
Isaiah 65:17-25
God's people like a tree

Hymn: Here, O Lord, Your Servants Gather, ELW 530

God of the resurrection, you live in us and we in you. Reveal yourself to us through the risen Christ, that grounded in the assurance of your presence we may boldly embody your command to love our neighbors as ourselves.

Thursday, May 3, 2018
Week of Easter 5

Psalm 98

Shout with joy to God

Make a joyful noise to the LORD, all the earth;
　　break forth into joyous song and sing praises.
Sing praises to the LORD with the lyre,
　　with the lyre and the sound of melody.
With trumpets and the sound of the horn
　　make a joyful noise before the King, the LORD. (Ps. 98:4-6)

Additional Readings

Isaiah 49:5-6
A light to the nations

Acts 10:1-34
Peter and Cornelius

Hymn: Oh, Sing to the Lord, ELW 822

God of the whole world, your love reaches beyond human borders, and the earth itself sings your praise. Fill us with the music of your grace in Jesus Christ that we may join your song of hope for all nations.

Friday, May 4, 2018
Week of Easter 5

Monica, mother of Augustine, died 387

Acts 10:34-43

God shows no partiality

Then Peter began to speak to [the people with Cornelius:] "I truly understand that God shows no partiality, but in every nation anyone who fears him and does what is right is acceptable to him. You know the message he sent to the people of Israel, preaching peace by Jesus Christ—he is Lord of all. That message spread throughout Judea, beginning in Galilee after the baptism that John announced: how God anointed Jesus of Nazareth with the Holy Spirit and with power; how he went about doing good and healing all who were oppressed by the devil, for God was with him." (Acts 10:34-38)

Psalm

Psalm 98
Shout with joy to God

Additional Reading

Isaiah 42:5-9
God declares new things

Hymn: Earth and All Stars! ELW 731

Lord of all, in Jesus of Nazareth you came among us with the Holy Spirit and with power, declaring peace, healing, and forgiveness. Grant these gifts to us today, that our words and deeds may proclaim your living presence.

Saturday, May 5, 2018
Week of Easter 5

Deuteronomy 32:44-47
Take to heart the command of God

Moses came and recited all the words of this song in the hearing of the people, he and Joshua son of Nun. When Moses had finished reciting all these words to all Israel, he said to them: "Take to heart all the words that I am giving in witness against you today; give them as a command to your children, so that they may diligently observe all the words of this law. This is no trifling matter for you, but rather your very life; through it you may live long in the land that you are crossing over the Jordan to possess." (Deut. 32:44-47)

Psalm
Psalm 98
Shout with joy to God

Additional Reading
Mark 10:42-45
Jesus came to serve

Hymn: We Sing to You, O God, ELW 791

God of all generations, you entrust your promise to us that we may have life. Place your word in our hearts, that elders and children alike may know the one who came as servant of all, Jesus Christ our Lord.

Sunday, May 6, 2018
Sixth Sunday of Easter

John 15:9-17

Christ, the friend and lover

[Jesus said,] "As the Father has loved me, so I have loved you; abide in my love. If you keep my commandments, you will abide in my love, just as I have kept my Father's commandments and abide in his love. I have said these things to you so that my joy may be in you, and that your joy may be complete." (John 15:9-11)

Psalm
Psalm 98
Shout with joy to God

Additional Readings
Acts 10:44-48
The Spirit poured out on the Gentiles

1 John 5:1-6
The victory of faith

Hymn: Great God, Your Love Has Called Us, ELW 358

O God, you have prepared for those who love you joys beyond understanding. Pour into our hearts such love for you that, loving you above all things, we may obtain your promises, which exceed all we can desire; through Jesus Christ, your Son and our Lord, who lives and reigns with you and the Holy Spirit, one God, now and forever.

Monday, May 7, 2018
Week of Easter 6

Psalm 93
God reigns above the floods

The LORD is king, he is robed in majesty;
> the LORD is robed, he is girded with strength.
He has established the world; it shall never be moved;
> your throne is established from of old;
> you are from everlasting.

The floods have lifted up, O LORD,
> the floods have lifted up their voice;
> the floods lift up their roaring.
More majestic than the thunders of mighty waters,
> more majestic than the waves of the sea,
> majestic on high is the LORD!

Your decrees are very sure;
> holiness befits your house,
> O LORD, forevermore. (Ps. 93:1-5)

Additional Readings
Deuteronomy 7:1-11
Keeping God's commandments

1 Timothy 6:11-12
Pursue righteousness

Hymn: Come, Thou Almighty King, ELW 408

Almighty God, your majestic power surpasses flood and crashing sea, and in Christ you defeated sin and death. Help us to trust in the eternal life that is ours through the waters of baptism that we may withstand all floods.

Tuesday, May 8, 2018
Week of Easter 6

Julian of Norwich, renewer of the church, died around 1416

1 Timothy 6:13-16
Keep the commandments until Christ comes

In the presence of God, who gives life to all things, and of Christ Jesus, who in his testimony before Pontius Pilate made the good confession, I charge you to keep the commandment without spot or blame until the manifestation of our Lord Jesus Christ, which he will bring about at the right time—he who is the blessed and only Sovereign, the King of kings and Lord of lords. It is he alone who has immortality and dwells in unapproachable light, whom no one has ever seen or can see; to him be honor and eternal dominion. Amen. (1 Tim. 6:13-16)

Psalm
Psalm 93
God reigns above the floods

Additional Reading
Deuteronomy 11:1-17
The rewards of obedience

Hymn: Come, Let Us Join Our Cheerful Songs, ELW 847

God of immortal light, your glory shines too bright for us to see, yet in Christ we know the fullness of your grace without end. Free us from fear that we may confess our faith in you with gladness.

Wednesday, May 9, 2018
Week of Easter 6

Nicolaus Ludwig von Zinzendorf, renewer of the church, hymnwriter, died 1760

Deuteronomy 11:18-21
Teach God's words to your children

You shall put these words of mine in your heart and soul, and you shall bind them as a sign on your hand, and fix them as an emblem on your forehead. Teach them to your children, talking about them when you are at home and when you are away, when you lie down and when you rise. Write them on the doorposts of your house and on your gates, so that your days and the days of your children may be multiplied in the land that the LORD swore to your ancestors to give them, as long as the heavens are above the earth. (Deut. 11:18-21)

Psalm
Psalm 93
God reigns above the floods

Additional Reading
Mark 16:19-20
An account of Jesus' ascension

Hymn: O God of Mercy, God of Light, ELW 714

God of grace, you dwell with us not in words alone but also in our hearts and minds through Jesus Christ. Awaken us to your presence, that we may seek and find you in our lives and in the world.

Thursday, May 10, 2018
Ascension of Our Lord

Luke 24:44-53

Christ present in all times and places

Then [Jesus] led them out as far as Bethany, and, lifting up his hands, he blessed them. While he was blessing them, he withdrew from them and was carried up into heaven. And they worshiped him, and returned to Jerusalem with great joy; and they were continually in the temple blessing God. (Luke 24:50-53)

Psalm

Psalm 47
God has gone up with a shout

Additional Readings

Acts 1:1-11
Jesus sends the apostles

Ephesians 1:15-23
Seeing the risen and ascended Christ

Hymn: Alleluia! Sing to Jesus, ELW 392

Almighty God, your only Son was taken into the heavens and in your presence intercedes for us. Receive us and our prayers for all the world, and in the end bring everything into your glory, through Jesus Christ, our Sovereign and Lord, who lives and reigns with you and the Holy Spirit, one God, now and forever.

Friday, May 11, 2018
Week of Easter 6

Psalm 47

God has gone up with a shout

God has gone up with a shout,
    the LORD with the sound of a trumpet.
Sing praises to God, sing praises;
    sing praises to our King, sing praises.
For God is the king of all the earth;
    sing praises with a psalm.

God is king over the nations;
    God sits on his holy throne.
The princes of the peoples gather
    as the people of the God of Abraham.
For the shields of the earth belong to God;
    he is highly exalted. (Ps. 47:5-9)

Additional Readings

Exodus 24:15-18
Moses on Mount Sinai for forty days

Revelation 1:9-18
A vision of the risen Christ

Hymn: A Hymn of Glory Let Us Sing! ELW 393

God of fire and trumpet sound, our words fail to express all that you are. As we live in faithful service and love for others, may our very lives be songs of praise to you.

Saturday, May 12, 2018
Week of Easter 6

John 16:4-11

Jesus will send the Advocate

[Jesus said,] "I did not say these things to you from the beginning, because I was with you. But now I am going to him who sent me; yet none of you asks me, 'Where are you going?' But because I have said these things to you, sorrow has filled your hearts. Nevertheless I tell you the truth: it is to your advantage that I go away, for if I do not go away, the Advocate will not come to you; but if I go, I will send him to you." (John 16:4b-7)

Psalm
Psalm 47
God has gone up with a shout

Additional Reading
Deuteronomy 34:1-7
Moses goes up to see the promised land

Hymn: Love Divine, All Loves Excelling, ELW 631

God of the horizon, you beckon us to follow you into places unknown. Remind us that wherever you send us, you also go ahead of us, giving us courage to answer your call.

Sunday, May 13, 2018
Seventh Sunday of Easter

John 17:6-19
Christ's prayer for his disciples

"But now I am coming to you, and I speak these things in the world so that they may have my joy made complete in themselves. I have given them your word, and the world has hated them because they do not belong to the world, just as I do not belong to the world. I am not asking you to take them out of the world, but I ask you to protect them from the evil one. They do not belong to the world, just as I do not belong to the world." (John 17:13-16)

Psalm

Psalm 1
The way of the righteous

Additional Readings

Acts 1:15-17, 21-26
Matthias added to the apostles

1 John 5:9-13
Life in the Son of God

Hymn: Lord, Who the Night You Were Betrayed, ELW 463

Gracious and glorious God, you have chosen us as your own, and by the powerful name of Christ you protect us from evil. By your Spirit transform us and your beloved world, that we may find our joy in your Son, Jesus Christ, our Savior and Lord, who lives and reigns with you and the Holy Spirit, one God, now and forever.

Monday, May 14, 2018
Matthias, Apostle

Luke 6:12-16
Jesus calls the Twelve

Now during those days [Jesus] went out to the mountain to pray; and he spent the night in prayer to God. And when day came, he called his disciples and chose twelve of them, whom he also named apostles: Simon, whom he named Peter, and his brother Andrew, and James, and John, and Philip, and Bartholomew, and Matthew, and Thomas, and James son of Alphaeus, and Simon, who was called the Zealot, and Judas son of James, and Judas Iscariot, who became a traitor. (Luke 6:12-16)

Psalm
Psalm 56
I am bound by the vow I made to you

Additional Readings
Isaiah 66:1-2
Heaven is God's throne, earth is God's footstool

Acts 1:15-26
The apostles cast lots for Matthias

Hymn: Give Thanks for Saints, ELW 428

Almighty God, you chose your faithful servant Matthias to be numbered among the Twelve. Grant that your church may always be taught and guided by faithful and true pastors, through Jesus Christ our shepherd, who lives and reigns with you and the Holy Spirit, one God, now and forever.

Tuesday, May 15, 2018
Week of Easter 7

Psalm 115
God's blessings on the chosen ones

The LORD has been mindful of us; he will bless us;
    he will bless the house of Israel;
    he will bless the house of Aaron;
he will bless those who fear the LORD,
    both small and great.

May the LORD give you increase,
    both you and your children.
May you be blessed by the LORD,
    who made heaven and earth. (Ps. 115:12-15)

Additional Readings
Numbers 8:5-22
The Levites consecrated for service

Titus 1:1-9
The ministry entrusted to Titus by Paul

Hymn: O Christ, Your Heart, Compassionate, ELW 722

God of our vocations, you call all your people, both small and great, into holy service. Grant that through your Spirit we may discern our purpose and joyfully undertake the work you would have us do, through Christ our Lord.

Wednesday, May 16, 2018
Week of Easter 7

John 16:16-24
Sorrow turned to joy

[Jesus said,] "Very truly, I tell you, you will weep and mourn, but the world will rejoice; you will have pain, but your pain will turn into joy. When a woman is in labor, she has pain, because her hour has come. But when her child is born, she no longer remembers the anguish because of the joy of having brought a human being into the world. So you have pain now; but I will see you again, and your hearts will rejoice, and no one will take your joy from you. On that day you will ask nothing of me. Very truly, I tell you, if you ask anything of the Father in my name, he will give it to you. Until now you have not asked for anything in my name. Ask and you will receive, so that your joy may be complete." (John 16:20-24)

Psalm
Psalm 115
God's blessings on the chosen ones

Additional Reading
Ezra 9:5-15
Ezra prays for the people

Hymn: Jerusalem, My Happy Home, ELW 628

God of hope, as the pain of childbirth becomes the joy of new life, you promise that our pain will not endure forever. Make us bold to ask for your Spirit, that our joy—and the world's—may be complete.

Thursday, May 17, 2018
Week of Easter 7

Psalm 33:12-22
Our help and our shield

Our soul waits for the LORD;
>   he is our help and shield.
Our heart is glad in him,
>   because we trust in his holy name.
Let your steadfast love, O LORD, be upon us,
>   even as we hope in you. (Ps. 33:20-22)

Additional Readings
Genesis 2:4b-7
God breathes life into humankind

1 Corinthians 15:42b-49
We bear Christ's image

Hymn: O God, Our Help in Ages Past, ELW 632

God, breath of life, we are made in your image; your holy name is our refuge.
May your love grant us wisdom, trust, and patience that we may persevere
in all circumstances and bear your good news to the world.

Friday, May 18, 2018
Week of Easter 7

Erik, King of Sweden, martyr, died 1160

1 Corinthians 15:50-57

The dead will be raised

When this perishable body puts on imperishability, and this mortal body puts on immortality, then the saying that is written will be fulfilled:

"Death has been swallowed up in victory."

"Where, O death, is your victory?

Where, O death, is your sting?"

The sting of death is sin, and the power of sin is the law. But thanks be to God, who gives us the victory through our Lord Jesus Christ. (1 Cor. 15:54-57)

Psalm
Psalm 33:12-22
Our help and our shield

Additional Reading
Job 37:1-13
The powerful breath of God

Hymn: Praise and Thanks and Adoration, ELW 783

Eternal God, through Christ's resurrection death is swallowed up by life and we are raised in victory. Grant us strength in the present and hope for the future, that through your Spirit we might live a new life in Christ.

Saturday, May 19, 2018
Vigil of Pentecost

Romans 8:14-17, 22-27

Praying with the Spirit

We know that the whole creation has been groaning in labor pains until now; and not only the creation, but we ourselves, who have the first fruits of the Spirit, groan inwardly while we wait for adoption, the redemption of our bodies. For in hope we were saved. Now hope that is seen is not hope. For who hopes for what is seen? But if we hope for what we do not see, we wait for it with patience. (Rom. 8:22-25)

Psalm

Psalm 33:12-22
Our help and our shield

Additional Readings

Exodus 19:1-9
The covenant at Sinai

John 7:37-39
The living water of the Spirit

Hymn: Like the Murmur of the Dove's Song, ELW 403

Almighty and ever-living God, you fulfilled the promise of Easter by sending the gift of your Holy Spirit. Look upon your people gathered in prayer, open to receive the Spirit's flame. May it come to rest in our hearts and heal the divisions of word and tongue, that with one voice and one song we may praise your name in joy and thanksgiving; through Jesus Christ, our Savior and Lord, who lives and reigns with you and the Holy Spirit, one God, now and forever.

Pentecost

Christians pray to God "in the power of the Spirit." The gifts of the Spirit are faith, hope, and love. Whenever two or more gather in Jesus' name, the Spirit is present. At every baptism and communion, we pray for the Spirit's presence to forgive and strengthen, inspire and refresh. In the household, we pray for the Spirit's guidance, for the deepening of faith, hope, and love, for the patience and wisdom to live in peace with each other and our neighbors.

Table Prayer for Pentecost

Blessed are you, O Lord our God,
who gathers the whole world into the Spirit of your Son.
You have given us food for another day:
blessed be God forever!
We beg you to pour out food for the needy,
that all peoples and languages may praise your name,
through Jesus Christ our Lord. Amen.

Thanksgiving for the Holy Spirit

Use this prayer during the week following Pentecost Sunday.

O Spirit of God, seek us;
Good Spirit, pray with us;
Spirit of counsel, inform us;
Spirit of might, free us;
Spirit of truth, enlighten us;
Spirit of Christ, raise us;
O Holy Spirit, dwell in us. Amen.

Sunday, May 20, 2018
Day of Pentecost

John 15:26-27; 16:4b-15
Christ sends the Spirit of truth

[Jesus said,] "I still have many things to say to you, but you cannot bear them now. When the Spirit of truth comes, he will guide you into all the truth; for he will not speak on his own, but will speak whatever he hears, and he will declare to you the things that are to come. He will glorify me, because he will take what is mine and declare it to you. All that the Father has is mine. For this reason I said that he will take what is mine and declare it to you." (John 16:12-15)

Psalm
Psalm 104:24-34, 35b
Renewing the face of the earth

Additional Readings
Acts 2:1-21
Filled with the Spirit

Romans 8:22-27
Praying with the Spirit

Hymn: Come, Holy Ghost, God and Lord, ELW 395

Mighty God, you breathe life into our bones, and your Spirit brings truth to the world. Send us this Spirit, transform us by your truth, and give us language to proclaim your gospel; through Jesus Christ, our Savior and Lord, who lives and reigns with you and the Holy Spirit, one God, now and forever.

Monday, May 21, 2018
Time after Pentecost

Helena, mother of Constantine, died around 330

Psalm 104:24-34, 35b
Renewing the face of the earth

May the glory of the LORD endure forever;
> may the LORD rejoice in his works—
who looks on the earth and it trembles,
> who touches the mountains and they smoke.
I will sing to the LORD as long as I live;
> I will sing praise to my God while I have being. (Ps. 104:31-33)

Additional Readings
Joel 2:18-29
God's spirit poured out

1 Corinthians 12:4-11
Various gifts, the same Spirit

Hymn: Oh, Worship the King, ELW 842

Holy God, when the earth trembles, the mountains smoke, and we know the fragility of our being, still your love for us endures. Pour out your Spirit that young and old may sing praise to you for all our days.

Tuesday, May 22, 2018
Time after Pentecost

1 Corinthians 12:12-27
Many members, one body of Christ

For just as the body is one and has many members, and all the members of the body, though many, are one body, so it is with Christ. For in the one Spirit we were all baptized into one body—Jews or Greeks, slaves or free—and we were all made to drink of one Spirit. . . .

Now you are the body of Christ and individually members of it.
(1 Cor. 12:12-13, 27)

Psalm
Psalm 104:24-34, 35b
Renewing the face of the earth

Additional Reading
Genesis 11:1-9
The fragmenting of human tongues

Hymn: All Creatures, Worship God Most High! ELW 835

God of all people, in baptism we drink of your Spirit, and in our human diversity we become members of Christ's body. Through your Spirit may we rejoice in holy difference and move beyond unholy division, finding unity in you.

Wednesday, May 23, 2018
Time after Pentecost

Ezekiel 37:1-14
Life to dry bones

So I prophesied as I had been commanded; and as I prophesied, suddenly there was a noise, a rattling, and the bones came together, bone to its bone. I looked, and there were sinews on them, and flesh had come upon them, and skin had covered them; but there was no breath in them. Then he said to me, "Prophesy to the breath, prophesy, mortal, and say to the breath: Thus says the Lord GOD: Come from the four winds, O breath, and breathe upon these slain, that they may live." I prophesied as he commanded me, and the breath came into them, and they lived, and stood on their feet, a vast multitude. (Ezek. 37:7-10)

Psalm
Psalm 104:24-34, 35b
Renewing the face of the earth

Additional Reading
John 20:19-23
Jesus breathes the Spirit

Hymn: The Word of God Is Source and Seed, ELW 506

God of the wilderness, in the places where all hope has dried up, your Spirit breathes life and possibility. Restore our faith, that we also may work to restore life in our communities and the world in Jesus' name.

Thursday, May 24, 2018
Time after Pentecost

Nicolaus Copernicus, died 1543; Leonhard Euler, died 1783; scientists

Psalm 29
Worship God in holiness

Ascribe to the LORD, O heavenly beings,
    ascribe to the LORD glory and strength.
Ascribe to the LORD the glory of his name;
    worship the LORD in holy splendor.

The voice of the LORD is over the waters;
    the God of glory thunders,
    the LORD, over mighty waters.
The voice of the LORD is powerful;
    the voice of the LORD is full of majesty. (Ps. 29:1-4)

Additional Readings
Isaiah 1:1-4, 16-20
A vision concerning God's people

Romans 8:1-8
The Spirit is life and peace

Hymn: All Glory Be to God on High, ELW 410

Mighty God, your voice thunders over the waters and drowns out every shout of sin, evil, and death. Speak the living word of Christ's grace into our hearts, that we may hear your voice and follow you alone.

Friday, May 25, 2018
Time after Pentecost

Romans 8:9-11
The Spirit dwells in you

But you are not in the flesh; you are in the Spirit, since the Spirit of God dwells in you. Anyone who does not have the Spirit of Christ does not belong to him. But if Christ is in you, though the body is dead because of sin, the Spirit is life because of righteousness. If the Spirit of him who raised Jesus from the dead dwells in you, he who raised Christ from the dead will give life to your mortal bodies also through his Spirit that dwells in you. (Rom. 8:9-11)

Psalm
Psalm 29
Worship God in holiness

Additional Reading
Isaiah 2:1-5
A vision concerning God's people

Hymn: Awake, O Sleeper, Rise from Death, ELW 452

God of freedom, in Christ you liberate us from sin and death that our bodies might live anew in your Spirit. Put to death all human strife and dwell in us, that we may help bring peace to the world.

Saturday, May 26, 2018
Time after Pentecost

John 15:18-20, 26-27

Testify in the face of persecution

[Jesus said,] "When the Advocate comes, whom I will send to you from the Father, the Spirit of truth who comes from the Father, he will testify on my behalf. You also are to testify because you have been with me from the beginning." (John 15:26-27)

Psalm

Psalm 29
Worship God in holiness

Additional Reading

Isaiah 5:15-24
A vision concerning God's people

Hymn: Gracious Spirit, Heed Our Pleading, ELW 401

God, voice of the voiceless, your Spirit testifies to your people, and we hear and receive the good news of your unfailing care for all in need. May our words and deeds testify to your grace for a hurting world.

Time after Pentecost
Summer

The weeks and months following the Day of Pentecost coincide with the natural seasons of summer, autumn, and late autumn/November. Christian communities refer to this time in different ways. Whatever time is used to describe the many weeks between Pentecost and Christ the King (the last Sunday of the year), the seasons and calendars of North America offer some distinctive periods through which we may shape prayer in the household.

The Day of Pentecost is celebrated close to the end of the school year. A connection exists between graduations/new beginnings and our prayer for the Spirit's guidance in new endeavors. For many people, the months of June, July, and August signal a slightly altered schedule attuned to the weather, harvests, and vacations. Summer months offer their unique grace to those who spend time in discerning the many images which link the scriptures and the patient growth of the seed in the soil.

Table Prayer for Summer

The earth is the Lord's and all that is in it,
the world, and those who live in it. (Ps. 24:1)

All here gathered, food from the land,
all is gift from your gracious hand.
Feed us today; feed all those who hunger;
teach us to feed one another.
We ask this in the name of the one who is our bread, Jesus Christ.
Amen.

Sunday, May 27, 2018
The Holy Trinity

John Calvin, renewer of the church, died 1564

John 3:1-17
Entering the reign of God

Nicodemus said to [Jesus,] "How can anyone be born after having grown old? Can one enter a second time into the mother's womb and be born?" Jesus answered, "Very truly, I tell you, no one can enter the kingdom of God without being born of water and Spirit. What is born of the flesh is flesh, and what is born of the Spirit is spirit. Do not be astonished that I said to you, 'You must be born from above.' The wind blows where it chooses, and you hear the sound of it, but you do not know where it comes from or where it goes. So it is with everyone who is born of the Spirit." (John 3:4-8)

Psalm
Psalm 29
Worship God in holiness

Additional Readings
Isaiah 6:1-8
Isaiah's vision and call

Romans 8:12-17
Living by the Spirit

Hymn: Holy, Holy, Holy, Lord God Almighty! ELW 413

Almighty Creator and ever-living God: we worship your glory, eternal Three-in-One, and we praise your power, majestic One-in-Three. Keep us steadfast in this faith, defend us in all adversity, and bring us at last into your presence, where you live in endless joy and love, Father, Son, and Holy Spirit, one God, now and forever.

Monday, May 28, 2018
Time after Pentecost

Psalm 20
The name of God

The Lord answer you in the day of trouble!
>   The name of the God of Jacob protect you!
May he send you help from the sanctuary,
>   and give you support from Zion.
May he remember all your offerings,
>   and regard with favor your burnt sacrifices. (Ps. 20:1-3)

Additional Readings
Numbers 9:15-23
God in the cloud and the fire

Revelation 4:1-8
Heaven's holy, holy, holy

Hymn: Jesus, Still Lead On, ELW 624

God of mystery, you are near us even when we cannot see you, and you never leave us to face our struggles alone. Finding your help close at hand, may we trust in you and live generously for others.

Tuesday, May 29, 2018
Time after Pentecost

Jiří Tranovský, hymnwriter, died 1637

1 Corinthians 2:1-10
God's wisdom revealed through the Spirit

When I came to you, brothers and sisters, I did not come proclaiming the mystery of God to you in lofty words or wisdom. For I decided to know nothing among you except Jesus Christ, and him crucified. And I came to you in weakness and in fear and in much trembling. My speech and my proclamation were not with plausible words of wisdom, but with a demonstration of the Spirit and of power, so that your faith might rest not on human wisdom but on the power of God. (1 Cor. 2:1-5)

Psalm
Psalm 20
The name of God

Additional Reading
Exodus 25:1-22
God in the ark and its mercy seat

Hymn: Holy Spirit, Ever Dwelling, ELW 582

God of all wisdom, through your Holy Spirit you teach us that true power is found in weakness, true strength in service, and true life in the cross. Open the eyes of our hearts to find Christ in our neighbors.

Wednesday, May 30, 2018
Time after Pentecost

Numbers 6:22-27
Aaronic blessing

The LORD spoke to Moses, saying: Speak to Aaron and his sons, saying, Thus you shall bless the Israelites: You shall say to them,

The LORD bless you and keep you;
the LORD make his face to shine upon you, and be gracious to you;
the LORD lift up his countenance upon you, and give you peace.

So they shall put my name on the Israelites, and I will bless them.
(Num. 6:22-27)

Psalm
Psalm 20
The name of God

Additional Reading
Mark 4:21-25
Secrets come to light

Hymn: Lord, Dismiss Us with Your Blessing, ELW 545

God of blessing, even our words of prayer and praise are gifts from your Spirit. Lead us in your way, that as we are blessed by the grace of Christ our lives may in turn bless the world with love.

Thursday, May 31, 2018
Visit of Mary to Elizabeth

Luke 1:39-57
Mary greets Elizabeth

In those days Mary set out and went with haste to a Judean town in the hill country, where she entered the house of Zechariah and greeted Elizabeth. When Elizabeth heard Mary's greeting, the child leaped in her womb. And Elizabeth was filled with the Holy Spirit and exclaimed with a loud cry, "Blessed are you among women, and blessed is the fruit of your womb." (Luke 1:39-42)

Psalm
Psalm 113
God, the helper of the needy

Additional Readings
1 Samuel 2:1-10
Hannah's thanksgiving

Romans 12:9-16b
Rejoice with those who rejoice

Hymn: Unexpected and Mysterious, ELW 258

Mighty God, by whose grace Elizabeth rejoiced with Mary and greeted her as the mother of the Lord: look with favor on your lowly servants that, with Mary, we may magnify your holy name and rejoice to acclaim her Son as our Savior, who lives and reigns with you and the Holy Spirit, one God, now and forever.

Prayer List for June

_____

_____

_____

_____

_____

_____

_____

_____

_____

Friday, June 1, 2018
Time after Pentecost

Justin, martyr at Rome, died around 165

Psalm 81:1-10
Raise a loud shout to the God of Jacob

Sing aloud to God our strength;
>   shout for joy to the God of Jacob.
Raise a song, sound the tambourine,
>   the sweet lyre with the harp.
Blow the trumpet at the new moon,
>   at the full moon, on our festal day.
For it is a statute for Israel,
>   an ordinance of the God of Jacob.
He made it a decree in Joseph,
>   when he went out over the land of Egypt. (Ps. 81:1-5)

Additional Readings
Leviticus 23:1-8
Sabbath, Passover, unleavened bread

Romans 8:31-39
Death cannot separate us from the love of God

Hymn: Give to Our God Immortal Praise! ELW 848

God our strength, our days and seasons are sustained by your generous goodness. With voice and instrument we raise our songs and shouts in praise of you. Help us live festal lives radiating your grace.

Saturday, June 2, 2018
Time after Pentecost

Leviticus 24:5-9

The bread for the tabernacle

You shall take choice flour, and bake twelve loaves of it; two-tenths of an ephah shall be in each loaf. You shall place them in two rows, six in a row, on the table of pure gold. You shall put pure frankincense with each row, to be a token offering for the bread, as an offering by fire to the LORD. Every sabbath day Aaron shall set them in order before the LORD regularly as a commitment of the people of Israel, as a covenant forever. They shall be for Aaron and his descendants, who shall eat them in a holy place, for they are most holy portions for him from the offerings by fire to the LORD, a perpetual due. (Lev. 24:5-9)

Psalm
Psalm 81:1-10
Raise a loud shout to the God of Jacob

Additional Reading
John 7:19-24
Circumcision and healing on the sabbath

Hymn: Glorious Things of You Are Spoken, ELW 647

Covenanting God, with choice gifts you feed your people. Our mouths water at the delights of your holy table. Set our lives in accordance with your gifts. Help us regularly offer sacrifices of praise and thanksgiving.

Sunday, June 3, 2018
Time after Pentecost

The Martyrs of Uganda, died 1886
John XXIII, Bishop of Rome, died 1963

Mark 2:23—3:6
Doing the work of God on the sabbath

One sabbath Jesus was going through the grainfields; and as they made their way his disciples began to pluck heads of grain. The Pharisees said to him, "Look, why are they doing what is not lawful on the sabbath?" And he said to them, "Have you never read what David did when he and his companions were hungry and in need of food? He entered the house of God, when Abiathar was high priest, and ate the bread of the Presence, which it is not lawful for any but the priests to eat, and he gave some to his companions." Then he said to them, "The sabbath was made for humankind, and not humankind for the sabbath." (Mark 2:23-27)

Psalm

Psalm 81:1-10
Raise a loud shout to the God of Jacob

Additional Readings

Deuteronomy 5:12-15
Sabbath commandments

2 Corinthians 4:5-12
Treasure in clay jars

Hymn: O Day of Rest and Gladness, ELW 521

Almighty and ever-living God, throughout time you free the oppressed, heal the sick, and make whole all that you have made. Look with compassion on the world wounded by sin, and by your power restore us to wholeness of life, through Jesus Christ, our Savior and Lord.

Monday, June 4, 2018
Time after Pentecost

Psalm 78:1-4, 52-72
God's care for the chosen people

Give ear, O my people, to my teaching;
    incline your ears to the words of my mouth.
I will open my mouth in a parable;
    I will utter dark sayings from of old,
things that we have heard and known,
    that our ancestors have told us.
We will not hide them from their children;
    we will tell to the coming generation
the glorious deeds of the LORD, and his might,
    and the wonders that he has done. (Ps. 78:1-4)

Additional Readings

Exodus 16:13-26
Concernng food on the sabbath

Romans 9:19-29
God's wrath and mercy

Hymn: Open Your Ears, O Faithful People, ELW 519

Mighty Lord, your glorious deeds are from the beginning through all of time. As we learn your wisdom from forebears in faith, help us hear you anew and share the wonders of your love with each generation.

Tuesday, June 5, 2018
Time after Pentecost

Boniface, Bishop of Mainz, missionary to Germany, martyr, died 754

Acts 15:1-5, 22-35

The church considers Jewish practices

Then certain individuals came down from Judea and were teaching the brothers, "Unless you are circumcised according to the custom of Moses, you cannot be saved." And after Paul and Barnabas had no small dissension and debate with them, Paul and Barnabas and some of the others were appointed to go up to Jerusalem to discuss this question with the apostles and the elders. So they were sent on their way by the church, and as they passed through both Phoenicia and Samaria, they reported the conversion of the Gentiles, and brought great joy to all the believers. When they came to Jerusalem, they were welcomed by the church and the apostles and the elders, and they reported all that God had done with them. But some believers who belonged to the sect of the Pharisees stood up and said, "It is necessary for them to be circumcised and ordered to keep the law of Moses." (Acts 15:1-5)

Psalm
Psalm 78:1-4, 52-72
God's care for the chosen people

Additional Reading
Exodus 16:27-36
Manna and the sabbath

Hymn: Salvation unto Us Has Come, ELW 590

Saving God, with surprising freedom you give newness of life. You call forth a church that questions and discusses, yet above all welcomes and shares joy. Enable us to gladly report all that you are doing.

Wednesday, June 6, 2018
Time after Pentecost

John 5:1-18
Jesus heals on the sabbath

Now the man who had been healed did not know who had told him to take up his mat and walk, for Jesus had disappeared in the crowd that was there. Later Jesus found him in the temple and said to him, "See, you have been made well! Do not sin any more, so that nothing worse happens to you." The man went away and told the Jews that it was Jesus who had made him well. Therefore the Jews started persecuting Jesus, because he was doing such things on the sabbath. But Jesus answered them, "My Father is still working, and I also am working." For this reason the Jews were seeking all the more to kill him, because he was not only breaking the sabbath, but was also calling God his own Father, thereby making himself equal to God. (John 5:13-18)

Psalm
Psalm 78:1-4, 52-72
God's care for the chosen people

Additional Reading
1 Samuel 21:1-6
David eats the bread of the Presence

Hymn: O Christ, the Healer, We Have Come, ELW 610

O Lord, your love breaks even the boundaries we think come from you. In Jesus your healing love knows no bounds and you draw ever near us. Work your way into our lives, that we too may be made well.

Thursday, June 7, 2018
Time after Pentecost

Seattle, chief of the Duwamish Confederacy, died 1866

Psalm 130
With you there is forgiveness

Out of the depths I cry to you, O LORD.
>   Lord, hear my voice!
Let your ears be attentive
>   to the voice of my supplications!

If you, O LORD, should mark iniquities,
>   Lord, who could stand?
But there is forgiveness with you,
>   so that you may be revered. (Ps. 130:1-4)

Additional Readings
Isaiah 28:9-13
The people of God refuse to hear

1 Peter 4:7-19
Entrusting ourselves to a faithful Creator

Hymn: Listen, God Is Calling, ELW 513

*There's not a one of us, O Lord, who hasn't sunk to the depths and cried out
to you. Hear us, bear with us, and forgive us for the sake of your faithfulness
and love for your people.*

Friday, June 8, 2018
Time after Pentecost

2 Corinthians 5:1-5

What is mortal is swallowed up in life

For we know that if the earthly tent we live in is destroyed, we have a building from God, a house not made with hands, eternal in the heavens. For in this tent we groan, longing to be clothed with our heavenly dwelling—if indeed, when we have taken it off we will not be found naked. For while we are still in this tent, we groan under our burden, because we wish not to be unclothed but to be further clothed, so that what is mortal may be swallowed up by life. He who has prepared us for this very thing is God, who has given us the Spirit as a guarantee. (2 Cor. 5:1-5)

Psalm
Psalm 130
With you there is forgiveness

Additional Reading
Deuteronomy 1:34-40
The innocent enter the good land

Hymn: Built on a Rock, ELW 652

Ever-giving God, you prepare us for an eternal and imperishable home, healed from the burdens and agonies of this life. In the longing of this hope, may the sure gift of your Spirit fill us with confidence and strength.

Saturday, June 9, 2018
Time after Pentecost

Columba, died 597; Aidan, died 651; Bede, died 735; renewers of the church

Genesis 2:4b-14

The tree of knowledge

In the day that the LORD God made the earth and the heavens, when no plant of the field was yet in the earth and no herb of the field had yet sprung up—for the LORD God had not caused it to rain upon the earth, and there was no one to till the ground; but a stream would rise from the earth, and water the whole face of the ground— then the LORD God formed man from the dust of the ground, and breathed into his nostrils the breath of life; and the man became a living being. And the LORD God planted a garden in Eden, in the east; and there he put the man whom he had formed. Out of the ground the LORD God made to grow every tree that is pleasant to the sight and good for food, the tree of life also in the midst of the garden, and the tree of the knowledge of good and evil. (Gen. 2:4b-9)

Psalm
Psalm 130
With you there is forgiveness

Additional Reading
Luke 8:4-15
Hearing and living the word of God

Hymn: Lord, Let My Heart Be Good Soil, ELW 512

You who formed humanity from the dust of the earth and breathed into us your very breath, giving us life out of the same ground from which you made all things: sustain us with the breath of your Holy Spirit.

Sunday, June 10, 2018
Time after Pentecost

Mark 3:20-35

Doing the work of God

Then [Jesus'] mother and his brothers came; and standing outside, they sent to him and called him. A crowd was sitting around him; and they said to him, "Your mother and your brothers and sisters are outside, asking for you." And he replied, "Who are my mother and my brothers?" And looking at those who sat around him, he said, "Here are my mother and my brothers! Whoever does the will of God is my brother and sister and mother." (Mark 3:31-34)

Psalm

Psalm 130
With you there is forgiveness

Additional Readings

Genesis 3:8-15
God confronts Adam and Eve

2 Corinthians 4:13—5:1
Renewed in the inner nature

Hymn: Joyful, Joyful We Adore Thee, ELW 836

All-powerful God, in Jesus Christ you turned death into life and defeat into victory. Increase our faith and trust in him, that we may triumph over all evil in the strength of the same Jesus Christ, our Savior and Lord.

Monday, June 11, 2018
Barnabas, Apostle

Acts 11:19-30; 13:1-3
Barnabas and Saul are set apart

Now in the church at Antioch there were prophets and teachers: Barnabas, Simeon who was called Niger, Lucius of Cyrene, Manaen a member of the court of Herod the ruler, and Saul. While they were worshiping the Lord and fasting, the Holy Spirit said, "Set apart for me Barnabas and Saul for the work to which I have called them." Then after fasting and praying they laid their hands on them and sent them off. (Acts 13:1-3)

Psalm

Psalm 112
Happy are the God-fearing

Additional Readings

Isaiah 42:5-12
The Lord calls us in righteousness

Matthew 10:7-16
Jesus sends out the Twelve

Hymn: O Zion, Haste, ELW 668

We praise you, O God, for the life of your faithful servant Barnabas, who, seeking not his own renown but the well-being of your church, gave generously of his life and possessions for the relief of the poor and the spread of the gospel. Grant that we may follow his example and by our actions give glory to you, Father, Son, and Holy Spirit, now and forever.

Tuesday, June 12, 2018
Time after Pentecost

Psalm 74
God will save us from the enemy

O God, why do you cast us off forever?
>   Why does your anger smoke against the sheep of your pasture?
Remember your congregation, which you acquired long ago,
>   which you redeemed to be the tribe of your heritage.
>   Remember Mount Zion, where you came to dwell.
Direct your steps to the perpetual ruins;
>   the enemy has destroyed everything in the sanctuary. (Ps. 74:1-3)

Additional Readings
1 Kings 18:17-40
Elijah destroys the evil prophets

Revelation 20:7-15
Satan's doom

Hymn: If You But Trust in God to Guide You, ELW 769

When all seems lost, holy God, when our lives have fallen into ruin, seek and find us, and remember us according to your grace and love for your people, for your presence is our comfort, strength, and hope.

Wednesday, June 13, 2018
Time after Pentecost

Luke 11:14-28
Jesus and Beelzebul

Now Jesus was casting out a demon that was mute; when the demon had gone out, the one who had been mute spoke, and the crowds were amazed. But some of them said, "He casts out demons by Beelzebul, the ruler of the demons." Others, to test him, kept demanding from him a sign from heaven. But he knew what they were thinking and said to them, "Every kingdom divided against itself becomes a desert, and house falls on house. If Satan also is divided against himself, how will his kingdom stand? —for you say that I cast out the demons by Beelzebul. Now if I cast out the demons by Beelzebul, by whom do your exorcists cast them out? Therefore they will be your judges." (Luke 11:14-19)

Psalm
Psalm 74
God will save us from the enemy

Additional Reading
Isaiah 26:16—27:1
God destroys Leviathan

Hymn: Abide, O Dearest Jesus, ELW 539

Your love, O Lord, frees us from powers that coerce and constrain us. Grant us health and wholeness of mind, body, and soul. We ask this in the strong name of Jesus.

Thursday, June 14, 2018
Time after Pentecost

Basil the Great, Bishop of Caesarea, died 379; Gregory, Bishop of Nyssa,
died around 385; Gregory of Nazianzus, Bishop of Constantinople, died around 389;
Macrina, teacher, died around 379

Psalm 92:1-4, 12-15
The righteous are like a cedar of Lebanon

The righteous flourish like the palm tree,
 and grow like a cedar in Lebanon.
They are planted in the house of the LORD;
 they flourish in the courts of our God.
In old age they still produce fruit;
 they are always green and full of sap,
showing that the LORD is upright;
 he is my rock, and there is no unrighteousness in him.
(Ps. 92:12-15)

Additional Readings
Genesis 3:14-24
Deprived of the tree of life

Hebrews 2:5-9
Christ tastes death for everyone

Hymn: Be Thou My Vision, ELW 793

*Your goodness flows through us, O Lord, like sap through a healthy tree.
Green with your life and vitality, we bend and do not break in the winds of
life; for in you our roots are deep.*

Friday, June 15, 2018
Time after Pentecost

Hebrews 11:4-7
Without faith no one can please God

By faith Abel offered to God a more acceptable sacrifice than Cain's. Through this he received approval as righteous, God himself giving approval to his gifts; he died, but through his faith he still speaks. By faith Enoch was taken so that he did not experience death; and "he was not found, because God had taken him." For it was attested before he was taken away that "he had pleased God." And without faith it is impossible to please God, for whoever would approach him must believe that he exists and that he rewards those who seek him. By faith Noah, warned by God about events as yet unseen, respected the warning and built an ark to save his household; by this he condemned the world and became an heir to the righteousness that is in accordance with faith. (Heb.11:4-7)

Psalm
Psalm 92:1-4, 12-15
The righteous are like a cedar of Lebanon

Additional Reading
1 Kings 10:26—11:8
Cedars more numerous than sycamores

Hymn: How Marvelous God's Greatness, ELW 830

As trusting children lean into loving parents with pleasing delight, we pray for the grace to trust and lean into you, O Lord. As did the saints of old, help us to live by God-pleasing faith.

Saturday, June 16, 2018
Time after Pentecost

Mark 4:1-20
The parable of the sower

[Jesus said,] "Listen! A sower went out to sow. And as he sowed, some seed fell on the path, and the birds came and ate it up. Other seed fell on rocky ground, where it did not have much soil, and it sprang up quickly, since it had no depth of soil. And when the sun rose, it was scorched; and since it had no root, it withered away. Other seed fell among thorns, and the thorns grew up and choked it, and it yielded no grain. Other seed fell into good soil and brought forth grain, growing up and increasing and yielding thirty and sixty and a hundredfold." And he said, "Let anyone with ears to hear listen!" (Mark 4:3-9)

Psalm
Psalm 92:1-4, 12-15
The righteous are like a cedar of Lebanon

Additional Reading
2 Kings 14:1-14
A thornbush confronts a cedar of Lebanon

Hymn: Almighty God, Your Word Is Cast, ELW 516

Prepare and enhance the soil of our hearts, eternal farmer. Sow the seed of your wild, loving grace in us, so that our words and deeds and all our lives may be a rich and bountiful harvest.

Sunday, June 17, 2018
Time after Pentecost

Mark 4:26-34

The parable of the mustard seed

[Jesus] also said, "With what can we compare the kingdom of God, or what parable will we use for it? It is like a mustard seed, which, when sown upon the ground, is the smallest of all the seeds on earth; yet when it is sown it grows up and becomes the greatest of all shrubs, and puts forth large branches, so that the birds of the air can make nests in its shade." (Mark 4:30-32)

Psalm

Psalm 92:1-4, 12-15
The righteous are like a cedar of Lebanon

Additional Readings

Ezekiel 17:22-24
The sign of the cedar

2 Corinthians 5:6-10 [11-13] 14-17
In Christ, a new creation

Hymn: Lord, Your Hands Have Formed, ELW 554

O God, you are the tree of life, offering shelter to all the world. Graft us into yourself and nurture our growth, that we may bear your truth and love to those in need, through Jesus Christ, our Savior and Lord.

Monday, June 18, 2018
Time after Pentecost

Psalm 52
Like an olive tree in God's house

Why do you boast, O mighty one,
    of mischief done against the godly?
    All day long you are plotting destruction.
Your tongue is like a sharp razor,
    you worker of treachery.
You love evil more than good,
    and lying more than speaking the truth.
You love all words that devour,
    O deceitful tongue.

But God will break you down forever;
    he will snatch and tear you from your tent;
    he will uproot you from the land of the living. (Ps. 52:1-5)

Additional Readings
Ezekiel 31:1-12
Evil can be a towering cedar

Galatians 6:11-18
A new creation is everything

Hymn: When I Survey the Wondrous Cross, ELW 803

O God of steadfast love, because of what you have done for us we have life. We trust in you and proclaim your name. Keep us from the deceitful boasting of self-sufficiency, which leads to nothing good.

Tuesday, June 19, 2018
Time after Pentecost

Revelation 21:22—22:5
The tree of life

Then the angel showed me the river of the water of life, bright as crystal, flowing from the throne of God and of the Lamb through the middle of the street of the city. On either side of the river is the tree of life with its twelve kinds of fruit, producing its fruit each month; and the leaves of the tree are for the healing of the nations. Nothing accursed will be found there any more. But the throne of God and of the Lamb will be in it, and his servants will worship him; they will see his face, and his name will be on their foreheads. And there will be no more night; they need no light of lamp or sun, for the Lord God will be their light, and they will reign forever and ever. (Rev. 22:1-5)

Psalm
Psalm 52
Like an olive tree in God's house

Additional Reading
Jeremiah 21:11-14
A fire in Judah's forest

Hymn: O Day Full of Grace, ELW 627

God, your wondrous love inspires millions to join in singing praise to you and to Christ the lamb. We thank you, gracious Lord, for your healing of the nations.

Wednesday, June 20, 2018
Time after Pentecost

Luke 6:43-45
A tree and its fruit

[Jesus said,] "No good tree bears bad fruit, nor again does a bad tree bear good fruit; for each tree is known by its own fruit. Figs are not gathered from thorns, nor are grapes picked from a bramble bush. The good person out of the good treasure of the heart produces good, and the evil person out of evil treasure produces evil; for it is out of the abundance of the heart that the mouth speaks." (Luke 6:43-45)

Psalm
Psalm 52
Like an olive tree in God's house

Additional Reading
Jeremiah 22:1-9
The evil will be cut down

Hymn: Lord of Glory, You Have Bought Us, ELW 707

Though we are all too often little more than thorns and bramble, we pray that you, O Lord, would make us into good and living trees. Produce in us good works—the fruit of your Holy Spirit in our lives—flowing with your abundant life.

Thursday, June 21, 2018
Time after Pentecost

Onesimos Nesib, translator, evangelist, died 1931

Psalm 107:1-3, 23-32
God stilled the storm

Then they cried to the LORD in their trouble,
>   and he brought them out from their distress;
he made the storm be still,
>   and the waves of the sea were hushed.
Then they were glad because they had quiet,
>   and he brought them to their desired haven.
Let them thank the LORD for his steadfast love,
>   for his wonderful works to humankind.
Let them extol him in the congregation of the people,
>   and praise him in the assembly of the elders. (Ps. 107:28-32)

Additional Readings
Job 29:1-20
Job makes his defense

Acts 20:1-16
Paul's travels

Hymn: Jesus, Savior, Pilot Me, ELW 755

We find ourselves tossed about in the many storms of life, O Lord, and we need you to be our safe haven. Come to us, O desire of our hearts, and give us the peace we need.

Friday, June 22, 2018
Time after Pentecost

Acts 21:1-16

Paul is warned about future persecution

While we were staying [in Caesarea] for several days, a prophet named Agabus came down from Judea. He came to us and took Paul's belt, bound his own feet and hands with it, and said, "Thus says the Holy Spirit, 'This is the way the Jews in Jerusalem will bind the man who owns this belt and will hand him over to the Gentiles.'" When we heard this, we and the people there urged him not to go up to Jerusalem. Then Paul answered, "What are you doing, weeping and breaking my heart? For I am ready not only to be bound but even to die in Jerusalem for the name of the Lord Jesus." Since he would not be persuaded, we remained silent except to say, "The Lord's will be done." (Acts 21:10-14)

Psalm
Psalm 107:1-3, 23-32
God stilled the storm

Additional Reading
Job 29:21—30:15
Job laments his losses

Hymn: Our Father, God in Heaven Above, ELW 746/747

You call us, O Lord, to follow the way of the cross that leads to the light of the resurrection. Grant us courage to be ready to follow you wherever you lead us, from death into life.

Saturday, June 23, 2018
Time after Pentecost

Luke 21:25-28
The roaring of the sea and the waves

[Jesus said,] "There will be signs in the sun, the moon, and the stars, and on the earth distress among nations confused by the roaring of the sea and the waves. People will faint from fear and foreboding of what is coming upon the world, for the powers of the heavens will be shaken. Then they will see 'the Son of Man coming in a cloud' with power and great glory. Now when these things begin to take place, stand up and raise your heads, because your redemption is drawing near." (Luke 21:25-28)

Psalm
Psalm 107:1-3, 23-32
God stilled the storm

Additional Reading
Job 37:1-13
Elihu extols God's power

Hymn: Lo! He Comes with Clouds Descending, ELW 435

Like those of old, Lord, we see signs of the times and are filled with fear and foreboding. Come to us in the midst all these things. Remove our fears and help us take hold of your redemption.

Sunday, June 24, 2018
Time after Pentecost

John the Baptist (transferred to June 25)

Mark 4:35-41
Christ calming the sea

On that day, when evening had come, [Jesus] said to them, "Let us go across to the other side." And leaving the crowd behind, they took him with them in the boat, just as he was. Other boats were with him. A great windstorm arose, and the waves beat into the boat, so that the boat was already being swamped. But he was in the stern, asleep on the cushion; and they woke him up and said to him, "Teacher, do you not care that we are perishing?" He woke up and rebuked the wind, and said to the sea, "Peace! Be still!" Then the wind ceased, and there was a dead calm. He said to them, "Why are you afraid? Have you still no faith?" And they were filled with great awe and said to one another, "Who then is this, that even the wind and the sea obey him?" (Mark 4:35-41)

Psalm

Psalm 107:1-3, 23-32
God stilled the storm

Additional Readings

Job 38:1-11
The Creator of earth and sea

2 Corinthians 6:1-13
Paul's defense of his ministry

Hymn: Eternal Father, Strong to Save, ELW 756

O God of creation, eternal majesty, you preside over land and sea, sunshine and storm. By your strength pilot us, by your power preserve us, by your wisdom instruct us, and by your hand protect us, through Jesus Christ, our Savior and Lord.

197

Monday, June 25, 2018
John the Baptist (transferred)

Presentation of the Augsburg Confession, 1530
Philipp Melanchthon, renewer of the church, died 1560

Luke 1:57-67 [68-80]
The birth and naming of John

On the eighth day [Elizabeth and her neighbors and relatives] came
to circumcise the child, and they were going to name him Zechariah
after his father. But his mother said, "No; he is to be called John." They
said to her, "None of your relatives has this name." Then they began
motioning to his father to find out what name he wanted to give him.
He asked for a writing tablet and wrote, "His name is John." And all of
them were amazed. Immediately his mouth was opened and his tongue
freed, and he began to speak, praising God. (Luke 1:59-64)

Psalm

Psalm 141
My eyes are turned to God

Additional Readings

Malachi 3:1-4
*My messenger, a refiner and
purifier*

Acts 13:13-26
*The gospel for the
descendents of Abraham*

Hymn: Blessed Be the God of Israel, ELW 552

*Almighty God, by your gracious providence your servant John the Baptist
was born to Elizabeth and Zechariah. Grant to your people the wisdom to
see your purpose and the openness to hear your will, that the light of Christ
may increase in us, through Jesus Christ, our Savior and Lord, who lives
and reigns with you and the Holy Spirit, one God, now and forever.*

Tuesday, June 26, 2018
Time after Pentecost

Psalm 65
God silences the seas

By awesome deeds you answer us with deliverance,
     O God of our salvation;
you are the hope of all the ends of the earth
     and of the farthest seas.
By your strength you established the mountains;
     you are girded with might.
You silence the roaring of the seas,
     the roaring of their waves,
     the tumult of the peoples.
Those who live at earth's farthest bounds are awed by your signs;
you make the gateways of the morning and the evening shout for joy.
(Ps. 65:5-8)

Additional Readings
Exodus 9:13-35
God sends hail

Acts 27:39-44
Safe arrival on land

Hymn: On Our Way Rejoicing, ELW 537

As deep as oceans, as high as mountains, as wide as grassy plains, O Lord, are the peoples of the earth. You hold us together and deliver us from affliction. Make us one in our songs of joy and praise.

Wednesday, June 27, 2018
Time after Pentecost

Cyril, Bishop of Alexandria, died 444

Mark 6:45-52

Jesus walks on the water

When evening came, the boat was out on the sea, and [Jesus] was alone on the land. When he saw that [the disciples] were straining at the oars against an adverse wind, he came towards them early in the morning, walking on the sea. He intended to pass them by. But when they saw him walking on the sea, they thought it was a ghost and cried out; for they all saw him and were terrified. But immediately he spoke to them and said, "Take heart, it is I; do not be afraid." Then he got into the boat with them and the wind ceased. And they were utterly astounded, for they did not understand about the loaves, but their hearts were hardened. (Mark 6:47-52)

Psalm

Psalm 65
God silences the seas

Additional Reading

Joshua 10:1-14
God makes the sun stand still

Hymn: God of the Sparrow, ELW 740

Lord of adverse winds, we cry out to you and you do not pass us by. Thank you for climbing into the boat with us—into the hardships of our lives—so we can let go of our fears.

Thursday, June 28, 2018
Time after Pentecost

Irenaeus, Bishop of Lyons, died around 202

Psalm 30
You have lifted me up

I will extol you, O LORD, for you have drawn me up,
    and did not let my foes rejoice over me.
O LORD my God, I cried to you for help,
    and you have healed me.
O LORD, you brought up my soul from Sheol,
    restored me to life from among those gone down to the Pit.
(Ps. 30:1-3)

Additional Readings
Lamentations 1:16-22
The Lord is in the right

2 Corinthians 7:2-16
Grief leads to repentance

Hymn: Come, Thou Fount of Every Blessing, ELW 807

O Lord, so much in life brings us down, down, down. But you draw us up, get us back on our feet again, arms and voices raised in praise of your healing, restoring, and life-giving help. We thank you.

Friday, June 29, 2018
Peter and Paul, Apostles

John 21:15-19

Jesus says to Peter: Tend my sheep

When they had finished breakfast, Jesus said to Simon Peter, "Simon son of John, do you love me more than these?" He said to him, "Yes, Lord; you know that I love you." Jesus said to him, "Feed my lambs." A second time he said to him, "Simon son of John, do you love me?" He said to him, "Yes, Lord; you know that I love you." Jesus said to him, "Tend my sheep." He said to him the third time, "Simon son of John, do you love me?" Peter felt hurt because he said to him the third time, "Do you love me?" And he said to him, "Lord, you know everything; you know that I love you." Jesus said to him, "Feed my sheep. Very truly, I tell you, when you were younger, you used to fasten your own belt and to go wherever you wished. But when you grow old, you will stretch out your hands, and someone else will fasten a belt around you and take you where you do not wish to go." (John 21:15-18)

Psalm

Psalm 87:1-3, 5-7
Glorious things are spoken of you

Additional Readings

Acts 12:1-11
Peter released from prison

2 Timothy 4:6-8, 17-18
The good fight of faith

Hymn: Faith of Our Fathers, ELW 812

Almighty God, we praise you that your blessed apostles Peter and Paul glorified you by their martyrdoms. Grant that your church throughout the world may always be instructed by their teaching and example, be knit together in unity by your Spirit, and ever stand firm upon the one foundation who is Jesus Christ our Lord, for he lives and reigns with you and the Holy Spirit, one God, now and forever.

Saturday, June 30, 2018
Time after Pentecost

Lamentations 2:18-22
Pour out your heart before God

Cry aloud to the Lord!
>O wall of daughter Zion!
Let tears stream down like a torrent
>day and night!
Give yourself no rest,
>your eyes no respite!

Arise, cry out in the night,
>at the beginning of the watches!
Pour out your heart like water
>before the presence of the Lord!
Lift your hands to him
>for the lives of your children,
who faint for hunger
>at the head of every street. (Lam. 2:18-19)

Psalm
Psalm 30
You have lifted me up

Additional Reading
Luke 4:31-37
The man with an unclean spirit

Hymn: Lost in the Night, ELW 243

To you, O Lord, we pour out our hearts. For your many children who live with injustice, we cry out in anguish. For those who experience no mercy, we plead. We lift our hands to you. Come quickly!

Prayer List for July

_____

_____

_____

_____

_____

_____

_____

_____

_____

_____

Sunday, July 1, 2018
Time after Pentecost

Catherine Winkworth, died 1878; John Mason Neale, died 1866; hymn translators

Mark 5:21-43

Christ heals a woman and Jairus' daughter

While [Jesus] was still speaking, some people came from the leader's house to say, "Your daughter is dead. Why trouble the teacher any further?" But overhearing what they said, Jesus said to the leader of the synagogue, "Do not fear, only believe." He allowed no one to follow him except Peter, James, and John, the brother of James. When they came to the house of the leader of the synagogue, he saw a commotion, people weeping and wailing loudly. When he had entered, he said to them, "Why do you make a commotion and weep? The child is not dead but sleeping." (Mark 5:35-39)

Psalm

Psalm 30
You have lifted me up

Additional Readings

Lamentations 3:22-33
Great is God's faithfulness

2 Corinthians 8:7-15
Excel in generosity, following Jesus

Hymn: We Come to You for Healing, Lord, ELW 617

Almighty and merciful God, we implore you to hear the prayers of your people. Be our strong defense against all harm and danger, that we may live and grow in faith and hope, through Jesus Christ, our Savior and Lord.

Monday, July 2, 2018
Time after Pentecost

Psalm 88
Prayer for restoration

O LORD, why do you cast me off?
> Why do you hide your face from me?
Wretched and close to death from my youth up,
> I suffer your terrors; I am desperate.
Your wrath has swept over me;
> your dread assaults destroy me.
They surround me like a flood all day long;
> from all sides they close in on me.
You have caused friend and neighbor to shun me;
> my companions are in darkness. (Ps. 88:14-18)

Additional Readings
Leviticus 21:1-15
Dead bodies are unclean

2 Corinthians 8:16-24
The administration of generous gifts

Hymn: My Faith Looks Up to Thee, ELW 759

Holy God, have mercy upon us. Open our hearts to recognize your gracious presence even when we feel abandoned and discouraged. Protect us from harm and danger. Forgive our sins and hold us close in your love.

Tuesday, July 3, 2018
Thomas, Apostle

John 14:1-7
Jesus, the way, the truth, the life

Thomas said to [Jesus,] "Lord, we do not know where you are going. How can we know the way?" Jesus said to him, "I am the way, and the truth, and the life. No one comes to the Father except through me. If you know me, you will know my Father also. From now on you do know him and have seen him." (John 14:5-7)

Psalm
Psalm 136:1-4, 23-26
God's mercy endures forever

Additional Readings
Judges 6:36-40
God affirms Gideon's calling

Ephesians 4:11-16
The body of Christ has various gifts

Hymn: O Sons and Daughters, Let Us Sing, ELW 386

Ever-living God, you strengthened your apostle Thomas with firm and certain faith in the resurrection of your Son. Grant that we too may confess our faith in Jesus Christ, our Lord and our God, who lives and reigns with you and the Holy Spirit, one God, now and forever.

Wednesday, July 4, 2018
Time after Pentecost

2 Kings 20:1-11

God heals Hezekiah

Hezekiah said to Isaiah, "What shall be the sign that the LORD will heal me, and that I shall go up to the house of the LORD on the third day?" Isaiah said, "This is the sign to you from the LORD, that the LORD will do the thing that he has promised: the shadow has now advanced ten intervals; shall it retreat ten intervals?" Hezekiah answered, "It is normal for the shadow to lengthen ten intervals; rather let the shadow retreat ten intervals." The prophet Isaiah cried to the LORD; and he brought the shadow back the ten intervals, by which the sun had declined on the dial of Ahaz. (2 Kings 20:8-11)

Psalm
Psalm 88
Prayer for restoration

Additional Reading
Mark 9:14-29
Jesus heals a child

Hymn: Where Cross the Crowded Ways of Life, ELW 719

Merciful God, your grace surrounds us every hour of the day. Give us faith to trust your promises. Bring healing and strength to all who suffer. Help us to see the signs of your unfailing presence in our lives.

Thursday, July 5, 2018
Time after Pentecost

Psalm 123
Our eyes look to you, O God

To you I lift up my eyes,
    O you who are enthroned in the heavens!
As the eyes of servants
    look to the hand of their master,
as the eyes of a maid
    to the hand of her mistress,
so our eyes look to the LORD our God,
    until he has mercy upon us.

Have mercy upon us, O LORD, have mercy upon us,
    for we have had more than enough of contempt.
Our soul has had more than its fill
    of the scorn of those who are at ease,
    of the contempt of the proud. (Ps. 123:1-4)

Additional Readings
Jeremiah 7:1-15
Do not trust deceptive words

1 Corinthians 4:8-13
We are weak, but you are strong

Hymn: Rise, O Sun of Righteousness, ELW 657

Compassionate God, we look to you in faith and trust. Look upon us with mercy. Uplift us when we are worn down. Hold us steady amid the difficulties we face and fill us with hope and peace.

Friday, July 6, 2018
Time after Pentecost

Jan Hus, martyr, died 1415

2 Corinthians 10:7-11
Paul's bodily presence is weak

Look at what is before your eyes. If you are confident that you belong to Christ, remind yourself of this, that just as you belong to Christ, so also do we. Now, even if I boast a little too much of our authority, which the Lord gave for building you up and not for tearing you down, I will not be ashamed of it. I do not want to seem as though I am trying to frighten you with my letters. For they say, "His letters are weighty and strong, but his bodily presence is weak, and his speech contemptible." Let such people understand that what we say by letter when absent, we will also do when present. (2 Cor. 10:7-11)

Psalm
Psalm 123
Our eyes look to you, O God

Additional Reading
Jeremiah 7:16-26
Walk in the way God commands

Hymn: Just a Closer Walk with Thee, ELW 697

Loving God, build us up in faith. Form your church into a vibrant community eager to grow in wisdom, compassion, and service. Strengthen us where we are weak. Make us bold to share the good news of Christ.

Saturday, July 7, 2018
Time after Pentecost

Matthew 8:18-22
The cost of discipleship

Now when Jesus saw great crowds around him, he gave orders to go over to the other side. A scribe then approached and said, "Teacher, I will follow you wherever you go." And Jesus said to him, "Foxes have holes, and birds of the air have nests; but the Son of Man has nowhere to lay his head." Another of his disciples said to him, "Lord, first let me go and bury my father." But Jesus said to him, "Follow me, and let the dead bury their own dead." (Matt. 8:18-22)

Psalm
Psalm 123
Our eyes look to you, O God

Additional Reading
Jeremiah 7:27-34
Disobeying the voice of the LORD

Hymn: I Want to Walk as a Child of the Light, ELW 815

Gracious God, overcome our reluctance to respond to your call to discipleship. Raise up faithful leaders for your church. Empower us to let go of all that hinders us. Give us courage to follow where you lead.

Sunday, July 8, 2018
Time after Pentecost

Mark 6:1-13

The Twelve sent to preach and heal

[Jesus] called the twelve and began to send them out two by two, and gave them authority over the unclean spirits. He ordered them to take nothing for their journey except a staff; no bread, no bag, no money in their belts; but to wear sandals and not to put on two tunics. He said to them, "Wherever you enter a house, stay there until you leave the place. If any place will not welcome you and they refuse to hear you, as you leave, shake off the dust that is on your feet as a testimony against them." So they went out and proclaimed that all should repent. They cast out many demons, and anointed with oil many who were sick and cured them. (Mark 6:7-13)

Psalm

Psalm 123
Our eyes look to you, O God

Additional Readings

Ezekiel 2:1-5
The call of Ezekiel

2 Corinthians 12:2-10
God's power made perfect in weakness

Hymn: Healer of Our Every Ill, ELW 612

God of the covenant, in our baptism you call us to proclaim the coming of your kingdom. Give us the courage you gave the apostles, that we may faithfully witness to your love and peace in every circumstance of life, in the name of Jesus Christ, our Savior and Lord.

Monday, July 9, 2018
Time after Pentecost

Psalm 119:81-88
The faithful persecuted

How long must your servant endure?
> When will you judge those who persecute me?
The arrogant have dug pitfalls for me;
> they flout your law.
All your commandments are enduring;
> I am persecuted without cause; help me!
They have almost made an end of me on earth;
> but I have not forsaken your precepts.
In your steadfast love spare my life,
> so that I may keep the decrees of your mouth. (Ps. 119:84-88)

Additional Readings
Ezekiel 2:8—3:11
Ezekiel to eat the scroll

2 Corinthians 11:16-33
Paul's sufferings

Hymn: How Long, O God, ELW 698

O God, in your mercy, protect us from every danger and shield us from those who would harm us. Uphold all who suffer persecution, giving them comfort and hope. Guide us in your ways of justice and truth.

Tuesday, July 10, 2018
Time after Pentecost

James 5:7-12
Suffering and patience

Be patient, therefore, beloved, until the coming of the Lord. The farmer waits for the precious crop from the earth, being patient with it until it receives the early and the late rains. You also must be patient. Strengthen your hearts, for the coming of the Lord is near. Beloved, do not grumble against one another, so that you may not be judged. See, the Judge is standing at the doors! As an example of suffering and patience, beloved, take the prophets who spoke in the name of the Lord. Indeed we call blessed those who showed endurance. You have heard of the endurance of Job, and you have seen the purpose of the Lord, how the Lord is compassionate and merciful. (James 5:7-11)

Psalm
Psalm 119:81-88
The faithful persecuted

Additional Reading
Jeremiah 16:1-13
Jeremiah's celibacy and message

Hymn: When Memory Fades, ELW 792

Loving God, teach us to exercise patience and practice compassion. In your mercy, come among us to bring an end to suffering. Strengthen us with the persistence to work for justice and peace throughout the world.

Wednesday, July 11, 2018
Time after Pentecost

Benedict of Nursia, Abbot of Monte Cassino, died around 540

John 7:1-9
Unbelief of Jesus' brothers

After this Jesus went about in Galilee. He did not wish to go about in Judea because the Jews were looking for an opportunity to kill him. Now the Jewish festival of Booths was near. So his brothers said to him, "Leave here and go to Judea so that your disciples also may see the works you are doing; for no one who wants to be widely known acts in secret. If you do these things, show yourself to the world." (For not even his brothers believed in him.) Jesus said to them, "My time has not yet come, but your time is always here. The world cannot hate you, but it hates me because I testify against it that its works are evil. Go to the festival yourselves. I am not going to this festival, for my time has not yet fully come." After saying this, he remained in Galilee. (John 7:1-9)

Psalm
Psalm 119:81-88
The faithful persecuted

Additional Reading
Jeremiah 16:14-21
God will forgive Israel

Hymn: God of Tempest, God of Whirlwind, ELW 400

Merciful God, grant us wisdom in the face of uncertainty and courage in times of fear. Help us to trust in you even when we harbor doubts. Keep us steadfast in your word and shelter us in your love.

Thursday, July 12, 2018
Time after Pentecost

Nathan Söderblom, Bishop of Uppsala, died 1931

Psalm 85:8-13

Listen to what God is saying

Steadfast love and faithfulness will meet;
>   righteousness and peace will kiss each other.
Faithfulness will spring up from the ground,
>   and righteousness will look down from the sky.
The LORD will give what is good,
>   and our land will yield its increase.
Righteousness will go before him,
>   and will make a path for his steps. (Ps. 85:10-13)

Additional Readings
Amos 2:6-16
God's condemnation of Israel

Colossians 2:1-5
Christ, the mystery of God

Hymn: Christ, Whose Glory Fills the Skies, ELW 553

Gracious God, you watch over your whole creation and provide for the needs of all. Shower us with your mercy. Plant your peace in our hearts so our lives may show forth the fruit of your love.

Friday, July 13, 2018
Time after Pentecost

Colossians 4:2-18
Declaring the mystery of Christ

Devote yourselves to prayer, keeping alert in it with thanksgiving. At the same time pray for us as well that God will open to us a door for the word, that we may declare the mystery of Christ, for which I am in prison, so that I may reveal it clearly, as I should.

Conduct yourselves wisely toward outsiders, making the most of the time. Let your speech always be gracious, seasoned with salt, so that you may know how you ought to answer everyone. (Col. 4:2-6)

Psalm
Psalm 85:8-13
Listen to what God is saying

Additional Reading
Amos 3:1-12
Who can but prophesy?

Hymn: Lord, Teach Us How to Pray Aright, ELW 745

Gracious God, open us to the mysteries of your grace. Grant us your wisdom. Inspire our speech to bear testimony to your love. Teach us to pray without ceasing, calling upon you in trust and faith.

Saturday, July 14, 2018
Time after Pentecost

Luke 1:57-80
The birth of John the Baptist

On the eighth day [Elizabeth and her neighbors and relatives] came
to circumcise the child, and they were going to name him Zechariah
after his father. But his mother said, "No; he is to be called John." They
said to her, "None of your relatives has this name." Then they began
motioning to his father to find out what name he wanted to give him.
He asked for a writing tablet and wrote, "His name is John." And all of
them were amazed. (Luke 1:59-63)

Psalm
Psalm 85:8-13
Listen to what God is saying

Additional Reading
Amos 4:6-13
Prepare to meet your God

Hymn: Blessed Be the God of Israel, ELW 250

*Creator God, in the waters of baptism you give us new birth and name us as
your own beloved children. Nurture us in faith and fill us with your wisdom.
Guide our lives in accordance with your will.*

Sunday, July 15, 2018
Time after Pentecost

Mark 6:14-29

The death of John the Baptist

King Herod heard of [the disciples' preaching,] for Jesus' name had become known. Some were saying, "John the baptizer has been raised from the dead; and for this reason these powers are at work in him." But others said, "It is Elijah." And others said, "It is a prophet, like one of the prophets of old." But when Herod heard of it, he said, "John, whom I beheaded, has been raised." (Mark 6:14-16)

Psalm
Psalm 85:8-13
Listen to what God is saying

Additional Readings
Amos 7:7-15
The sign of the plumb line

Ephesians 1:3-14
Chosen to live in praise of God

Hymn: Lead On, O King Eternal! ELW 805

O God, from you come all holy desires, all good counsels, and all just works. Give to us, your servants, that peace which the world cannot give, that our hearts may be set to obey your commandments; and also that we, being defended from the fear of our enemies, may live in peace and quietness, through Jesus Christ, our Savior and Lord.

Monday, July 16, 2018
Time after Pentecost

Psalm 142
Prayer for deliverance

I cry to you, O Lord;
>   I say, "You are my refuge,
>   my portion in the land of the living."
Give heed to my cry,
>   for I am brought very low.

Save me from my persecutors,
>   for they are too strong for me.
Bring me out of prison,
>   so that I may give thanks to your name.
The righteous will surround me,
>   for you will deal bountifully with me. (Ps. 142:5-7)

Additional Readings
Amos 5:1-9
Seek me and live

Acts 21:27-39
Paul arrested

Hymn: Out of the Depths I Cry to You, ELW 600

O God our redeemer, you are our refuge and strength. Unbind the chains of injustice. Help those who are in trouble. Bring freedom and peace to all who suffer. Sustain us with your mercy and love.

Tuesday, July 17, 2018
Time after Pentecost

Bartolomé de Las Casas, missionary to the Indies, died 1566

Amos 9:1-4

God searches out rebellious Israel

I saw the Lord standing beside the altar, and he said:
Strike the capitals until the thresholds shake,
and shatter them on the heads of all the people;
and those who are left I will kill with the sword;
not one of them shall flee away,
not one of them shall escape.

Though they dig into Sheol,
from there shall my hand take them;
though they climb up to heaven,
from there I will bring them down. (Amos 9:1-2)

Psalm
Psalm 142
Prayer for deliverance

Additional Reading
Acts 23:12-35
Plot to kill Paul

Hymn: O God of Every Nation, ELW 713

Almighty God, you desire that all would turn toward you in faith and hope. Overcome our rebellion against your will. Shatter the power of sin, deliver us from evil, and lead us into your everlasting mercy.

Wednesday, July 18, 2018
Time after Pentecost

Luke 7:31-35
Refusing the witness of John the Baptist and Jesus

[Jesus said,] "To what then will I compare the people of this generation, and what are they like?

They are like children sitting in the marketplace and calling to one another,

'We played the flute for you, and you did not dance;
we wailed, and you did not weep.'

For John the Baptist has come eating no bread and drinking no wine, and you say, 'He has a demon'; the Son of Man has come eating and drinking, and you say, 'Look, a glutton and a drunkard, a friend of tax collectors and sinners!' Nevertheless, wisdom is vindicated by all her children." (Luke 7:31-35)

Psalm
Psalm 142
Prayer for deliverance

Additional Reading
Amos 9:11-15
God will restore the fortunes of Israel

Hymn: O Christ the Same, ELW 760

Loving God, you befriend sinners and welcome outcasts. Melt away our resistance to your word of life. Extend your arms of mercy to those who have been rejected or ignored. Draw all people into your loving embrace.

Thursday, July 19, 2018
Time after Pentecost

Psalm 23
The Lord is my shepherd

The LORD is my shepherd, I shall not want.
>He makes me lie down in green pastures;
he leads me beside still waters;
>he restores my soul.
He leads me in right paths
>for his name's sake.

Even though I walk through the darkest valley,
>I fear no evil;
for you are with me;
>your rod and your staff—
>they comfort me. (Ps. 23:1-4)

Additional Readings
Jeremiah 10:1-16
Following scarecrows

Colossians 1:15-23
God reconciles all things through Christ

Hymn: Shepherd Me, O God, ELW 780

O God, your goodness and mercy surrounds us. Guide us in your paths of righteousness. Provide food for all who hunger. Shepherd us through places of danger and times of fear. Comfort us with your presence.

Friday, July 20, 2018
Time after Pentecost

Jeremiah 10:17-25
Stupid shepherds scatter the flock

Woe is me because of my hurt!
    My wound is severe.
But I said, "Truly this is my punishment,
    and I must bear it."
My tent is destroyed,
    and all my cords are broken;
my children have gone from me,
    and they are no more;
there is no one to spread my tent again,
    and to set up my curtains.
For the shepherds are stupid,
    and do not inquire of the LORD;
therefore they have not prospered,
    and all their flock is scattered. (Jer. 10:19-21)

Psalm
Psalm 23
The Lord is my shepherd

Additional Reading
Acts 17:16-31
Assurance for all through Christ

Hymn: Have No Fear, Little Flock, ELW 764

Gracious God, you bind up the wounds of the brokenhearted. Give hope to those who despair. Comfort those who feel abandoned and strengthen all who suffer disappointment and loss. Give us your wisdom and grant us your peace.

Saturday, July 21, 2018
Time after Pentecost

Luke 18:35-43
Jesus heals a blind beggar

As Jesus approached Jericho, a blind man was sitting by the roadside begging. When he heard a crowd going by, he asked what was happening. They told him, "Jesus of Nazareth is passing by." Then he shouted, "Jesus, Son of David, have mercy on me!" Those who were in front sternly ordered him to be quiet; but he shouted even more loudly, "Son of David, have mercy on me!" Jesus stood still and ordered the man to be brought to him; and when he came near, he asked him, "What do you want me to do for you?" He said, "Lord, let me see again." Jesus said to him, "Receive your sight; your faith has saved you." Immediately he regained his sight and followed him, glorifying God; and all the people, when they saw it, praised God. (Luke 18:35-43)

Psalm
Psalm 23
The Lord is my shepherd

Additional Reading
Jeremiah 12:1-13
Shepherds who destroy God's vineyard

Hymn: God, Whose Almighty Word, ELW 673

Merciful God, you hear the cries of the needy. In your compassion, heal the pain of all who suffer. Make us bold to ask for what we need and to receive your gifts with thanksgiving and praise.

Sunday, July 22, 2018
Time after Pentecost

Mary Magdalene, Apostle (transferred to July 23)

Mark 6:30-34, 53-56

Christ healing the multitudes

The apostles gathered around Jesus, and told him all that they had done and taught. He said to them, "Come away to a deserted place all by yourselves and rest a while." For many were coming and going, and they had no leisure even to eat. And they went away in the boat to a deserted place by themselves. Now many saw them going and recognized them, and they hurried there on foot from all the towns and arrived ahead of them. As he went ashore, he saw a great crowd; and he had compassion for them, because they were like sheep without a shepherd; and he began to teach them many things. (Mark 6:30-34)

Psalm

Psalm 23
The Lord is my shepherd

Additional Readings

Jeremiah 23:1-6
A righteous shepherd for Israel

Ephesians 2:11-22
Reconciled to God through Christ

Hymn: I Heard the Voice of Jesus Say, ELW 611

O God, powerful and compassionate, you shepherd your people, faithfully feeding and protecting us. Heal each of us, and make us a whole people, that we may embody the justice and peace of your Son, Jesus Christ, our Savior and Lord.

Monday, July 23, 2018
Mary Magdalene, Apostle (transferred)

Birgitta of Sweden, renewer of the church, died 1373

John 20:1-2, 11-18
Mary Magdalene meets Jesus in the garden

Jesus said to [Mary Magdalene,] "Woman, why are you weeping? Whom are you looking for?" Supposing him to be the gardener, she said to him, "Sir, if you have carried him away, tell me where you have laid him, and I will take him away." Jesus said to her, "Mary!" She turned and said to him in Hebrew, "Rabbouni!" (which means Teacher). Jesus said to her, "Do not hold on to me, because I have not yet ascended to the Father. But go to my brothers and say to them, 'I am ascending to my Father and your Father, to my God and your God.' " Mary Magdalene went and announced to the disciples, "I have seen the Lord"; and she told them that he had said these things to her. (John 20:15-18)

Psalm
Psalm 73:23-28
I will speak of all God's works

Additional Readings
Ruth 1:6-18
Ruth stays with Naomi

Acts 13:26-33a
The raising of Jesus fulfills God's promise

Hymn: For All the Faithful Women, st. 9, ELW 419

Almighty God, your Son first entrusted the apostle Mary Magdalene with the joyful news of his resurrection. Following the example of her witness, may we proclaim Christ as our living Lord and one day see him in glory, for he lives and reigns with you and the Holy Spirit, one God, now and forever.

Tuesday, July 24, 2018
Time after Pentecost

Psalm 100
We are God's sheep

Make a joyful noise to the LORD, all the earth.
>Worship the LORD with gladness;
>come into his presence with singing.

Know that the LORD is God.
>It is he that made us, and we are his;
>we are his people, and the sheep of his pasture.

Enter his gates with thanksgiving,
>and his courts with praise.
>Give thanks to him, bless his name.

For the LORD is good;
>his steadfast love endures forever,
>and his faithfulness to all generations. (Ps. 100:1-5)

Additional Readings
Zechariah 9:14—10:2
God will save the flock

Acts 20:17-38
The elders are shepherds

Hymn: Savior, like a Shepherd Lead Us, ELW 789

Creator God, your steadfast love endures forever. You take delight in your whole creation. We lift up our voices in praise, giving thanks for your gracious and tender care. Fill our hearts with gladness and our lives with joy.

Wednesday, July 25, 2018
James, Apostle

Mark 10:35-45

Whoever wishes to be great must serve

James and John, the sons of Zebedee, came forward to [Jesus] and said to him, "Teacher, we want you to do for us whatever we ask of you." And he said to them, "What is it you want me to do for you?" And they said to him, "Grant us to sit, one at your right hand and one at your left, in your glory." But Jesus said to them, "You do not know what you are asking. Are you able to drink the cup that I drink, or be baptized with the baptism that I am baptized with?" They replied, "We are able." Then Jesus said to them, "The cup that I drink you will drink; and with the baptism with which I am baptized, you will be baptized; but to sit at my right hand or at my left is not mine to grant, but it is for those for whom it has been prepared." (Mark 10:35-40)

Psalm
Psalm 7:1-10
God, my shield and defense

Additional Readings
1 Kings 19:9-18
Elijah hears God in the midst of silence

Acts 11:27—12:3a
James is killed by Herod

Hymn: In Our Day of Thanksgiving, ELW 429

Gracious God, we remember before you today your servant and apostle James, the first among the twelve to be martyred for the name of Jesus Christ. Pour out on the leaders of your church that spirit of self-denying service which is the true mark of authority among your people, through Jesus Christ our servant, who lives and reigns with you and the Holy Spirit, one God, now and forever.

Thursday, July 26, 2018
Time after Pentecost

Psalm 145:10-18
You open wide your hand

The eyes of all look to you,
 and you give them their food in due season.
You open your hand,
 satisfying the desire of every living thing.
The LORD is just in all his ways,
 and kind in all his doings.
The LORD is near to all who call on him,
 to all who call on him in truth. (Ps. 145:15-18)

Additional Readings
1 Kings 19:19-21
Elisha becomes Elijah's disciple

Colossians 1:9-14
Growing in the knowledge of God

Hymn: Sing to the Lord of Harvest, ELW 694

*Loving God, you fill the hungry with good things. Open your hand to satisfy
the needs of every living creature. Open our eyes to recognize the needs of
our neighbors. Open our lives to share your love.*

Friday, July 27, 2018
Time after Pentecost

Colossians 3:12-17

Let the peace of Christ rule in your hearts

As God's chosen ones, holy and beloved, clothe yourselves with compassion, kindness, humility, meekness, and patience. Bear with one another and, if anyone has a complaint against another, forgive each other; just as the Lord has forgiven you, so you also must forgive. Above all, clothe yourselves with love, which binds everything together in perfect harmony. And let the peace of Christ rule in your hearts, to which indeed you were called in the one body. And be thankful. Let the word of Christ dwell in you richly; teach and admonish one another in all wisdom; and with gratitude in your hearts sing psalms, hymns, and spiritual songs to God. And whatever you do, in word or deed, do everything in the name of the Lord Jesus, giving thanks to God the Father through him. (Col. 3:12-17)

Psalm
Psalm 145:10-18
You open wide your hand

Additional Reading
2 Kings 3:4-20
Elisha and the miracle of water

Hymn: Oh, for a Thousand Tongues to Sing, ELW 886

Holy God, you knit us together as one body in Christ. Clothe us with compassion and kindness. Inspire us to forgive others as you have forgiven us. Draw us together and teach us to live in harmony with one another.

Saturday, July 28, 2018
Time after Pentecost

Johann Sebastian Bach, died 1750; Heinrich Schütz, died 1672; George Frederick Handel, died 1759; musicians

2 Kings 4:38-41

Elisha purifies the pot of stew

When Elisha returned to Gilgal, there was a famine in the land. As the company of prophets was sitting before him, he said to his servant, "Put the large pot on, and make some stew for the company of prophets." One of them went out into the field to gather herbs; he found a wild vine and gathered from it a lapful of wild gourds, and came and cut them up into the pot of stew, not knowing what they were. They served some for the men to eat. But while they were eating the stew, they cried out, "O man of God, there is death in the pot!" They could not eat it. He said, "Then bring some flour." He threw it into the pot, and said, "Serve the people and let them eat." And there was nothing harmful in the pot. (2 Kings 4:38-41)

Psalm

Psalm 145:10-18
You open wide your hand

Additional Reading

John 4:31-38
Food that you do not know about

Hymn: Guide Me Ever, Great Redeemer, ELW 618

Gracious God, you nourish the land and fill creation with your goodness. Help us to recognize what is life-giving. Protect your people from harm and danger. Bring an end to famine and hunger. Provide safe and abundant food for all.

Sunday, July 29, 2018
Time after Pentecost

Mary, Martha, and Lazarus of Bethany
Olaf, King of Norway, martyr, died 1030

John 6:1-21
Jesus feeds 5000

One of Jesus' disciples, Andrew, Simon Peter's brother, said to him, "There is a boy here who has five barley loaves and two fish. But what are they among so many people?" Jesus said, "Make the people sit down." Now there was a great deal of grass in the place; so they sat down, about five thousand in all. Then Jesus took the loaves, and when he had given thanks, he distributed them to those who were seated; so also the fish, as much as they wanted. (John 6:8-11)

Psalm
Psalm 145:10-18
You open wide your hand

Additional Readings
2 Kings 4:42-44
Elisha feeds a hundred people

Ephesians 3:14-21
Prayer to Christ

Hymn: All Who Hunger, Gather Gladly, ELW 461

Gracious God, you have placed within the hearts of all your children a longing for your word and a hunger for your truth. Grant that we may know your Son to be the true bread of heaven and share this bread with all the world, through Jesus Christ, our Savior and Lord.

Monday, July 30, 2018
Time after Pentecost

Psalm 111
God gives food

Praise the LORD!
I will give thanks to the LORD with my whole heart,
    in the company of the upright, in the congregation.
Great are the works of the LORD,
    studied by all who delight in them.
Full of honor and majesty is his work,
    and his righteousness endures forever.
He has gained renown by his wonderful deeds;
    the LORD is gracious and merciful.
He provides food for those who fear him;
    he is ever mindful of his covenant. (Ps. 111:1-5)

Additional Readings
Genesis 18:1-15
God eats with Abraham and Sarah

Philippians 4:10-20
Christian generosity

Hymn: Praise to the Lord, the Almighty, ELW 858

Merciful God, your glory and majesty fills the whole earth. Work in us your deeds of mercy and kindle in us a delight for your word. Keep us mindful of your goodness and faithful to your covenant.

Tuesday, July 31, 2018
Time after Pentecost

Romans 15:22-33

Gentiles share their material blessings

This is the reason that I have so often been hindered from coming to you. But now, with no further place for me in these regions, I desire, as I have for many years, to come to you when I go to Spain. For I do hope to see you on my journey and to be sent on by you, once I have enjoyed your company for a little while. At present, however, I am going to Jerusalem in a ministry to the saints; for Macedonia and Achaia have been pleased to share their resources with the poor among the saints at Jerusalem. (Rom. 15:22-26)

Psalm
Psalm 111
God gives food

Additional Reading
Exodus 24:1-11
The elders eat with God

Hymn: O Bread of Life from Heaven, ELW 480

God of love, we give you thanks for all your blessings. Everything we have comes as a gift from you. Inspire us to live generously, sharing your abundance with others. Deepen our connections with one another.

Prayer List for August

Wednesday, August 1, 2018
Time after Pentecost

Isaiah 25:6-10a
A feast on the mountain

On this mountain the LORD of hosts will make for all peoples
    a feast of rich food, a feast of well-aged wines,
    of rich food filled with marrow, of well-aged wines strained clear.
And he will destroy on this mountain
    the shroud that is cast over all peoples,
    the sheet that is spread over all nations;
    he will swallow up death forever.
Then the Lord GOD will wipe away the tears from all faces,
    and the disgrace of his people he will take away from all the earth,
    for the LORD has spoken. (Isa. 25:6-8)

Psalm
Psalm 111
God gives food

Additional Reading
Mark 6:35-44
Jesus feeds 5000

Hymn: Arise, My Soul, Arise! ELW 827

Gracious God, one day in the future you shall wipe away all tears. Death shall be no more. Our waiting shall be turned into gladness as we rejoice in the fullness of your promises and savor the eternal feast.

Thursday, August 2, 2018
Time after Pentecost

Psalm 78:23-29
Manna rains down

Yet he commanded the skies above,
    and opened the doors of heaven;
he rained down on them manna to eat,
    and gave them the grain of heaven.
Mortals ate of the bread of angels;
    he sent them food in abundance. (Ps. 78:23-25)

Additional Readings
Exodus 12:33-42
Unleavened bread for the exodus

1 Corinthians 11:17-22
Abuses at the Lord's supper

Hymn: Praise, Praise! You Are My Rock, ELW 862

Holy One, long ago you opened the heavens and rained manna on the earth. On this day, open our hearts to trust you to provide for our needs. Help us to share our bounty so no one hungers.

Friday, August 3, 2018
Time after Pentecost

1 Corinthians 11:27-34
Discerning the body of Christ

Whoever, therefore, eats the bread or drinks the cup of the Lord in an unworthy manner will be answerable for the body and blood of the Lord. Examine yourselves, and only then eat of the bread and drink of the cup. For all who eat and drink without discerning the body, eat and drink judgment against themselves.

So then, my brothers and sisters, when you come together to eat, wait for one another. If you are hungry, eat at home, so that when you come together, it will not be for your condemnation. (1 Cor. 11:27-29; 33-34a)

Psalm
Psalm 78:23-29
Manna rains down

Additional Reading
Exodus 12:43—13:2
Directions for the Passover

Hymn: I Come with Joy, ELW 482

Mighty One, we humbly acknowledge our unworthiness to receive your gift of the body and blood of Christ at the eucharistic table, and yet we hear your invitation. Prepare our hearts to receive such a gift.

Saturday, August 4, 2018
Time after Pentecost

Exodus 13:3-10
The festival of unleavened bread

Moses said to the people, "Remember this day on which you came out of Egypt, out of the house of slavery, because the LORD brought you out from there by strength of hand; no leavened bread shall be eaten. Today, in the month of Abib, you are going out. When the LORD brings you into the land of the Canaanites, the Hittites, the Amorites, the Hivites, and the Jebusites, which he swore to your ancestors to give you, a land flowing with milk and honey, you shall keep this observance in this month. Seven days you shall eat unleavened bread, and on the seventh day there shall be a festival to the LORD." (Exod. 13:3-6)

Psalm
Psalm 78:23-29
Manna rains down

Additional Reading
Matthew 16:5-12
Bread as a sign of other things

Hymn: Bless Now, O God, the Journey, ELW 326

God of Moses, we remember how you freed the Hebrew slaves and guided them to a new life. Where there was and is no hope, you promise a future. Where there was and is no possibility, you give a new reality. Thank you.

Sunday, August 5, 2018
Time after Pentecost

John 6:24-35

Christ, the bread of life

So when the crowd saw that neither Jesus nor his disciples were there, they themselves got into the boats and went to Capernaum looking for Jesus.

When they found him on the other side of the sea, they said to him, "Rabbi, when did you come here?" Jesus answered them, "Very truly, I tell you, you are looking for me, not because you saw signs, but because you ate your fill of the loaves. Do not work for the food that perishes, but for the food that endures for eternal life, which the Son of Man will give you. For it is on him that God the Father has set his seal." (John 6:24-27)

Psalm

Psalm 78:23-29
Manna rains down

Additional Readings

Exodus 16:2-4, 9-15
Manna in the wilderness

Ephesians 4:1-16
Maintain the unity of the faith

Hymn: What Feast of Love, ELW 487

O God, eternal goodness, immeasurable love, you place your gifts before us; we eat and are satisfied. Fill us and this world in all its need with the life that comes only from you, through Jesus Christ, our Savior and Lord.

Monday, August 6, 2018
Time after Pentecost

Psalm 107:1-3, 33-43
God feeds the hungry

He turns rivers into a desert,
>   springs of water into thirsty ground,
a fruitful land into a salty waste,
>   because of the wickedness of its inhabitants.
He turns a desert into pools of water,
>   a parched land into springs of water.
And there he lets the hungry live,
>   and they establish a town to live in;
they sow fields, and plant vineyards,
>   and get a fruitful yield.
By his blessing they multiply greatly,
>   and he does not let their cattle decrease. (Ps. 107:33-38)

Additional Readings

Numbers 11:16-23, 31-32
God sends quail

Ephesians 4:17-24
The new life

Hymn: We Come to the Hungry Feast, ELW 479

Source of all blessings, you know our wounds and parched spirits. You bountifully shower us with healing water. It is you who transforms the desert of our lives into a garden. How can we begin to thank you?

Tuesday, August 7, 2018
Time after Pentecost

1 Corinthians 12:27-31
You are the body of Christ

Now you are the body of Christ and individually members of it. And God has appointed in the church first apostles, second prophets, third teachers; then deeds of power, then gifts of healing, forms of assistance, forms of leadership, various kinds of tongues. Are all apostles? Are all prophets? Are all teachers? Do all work miracles? Do all possess gifts of healing? Do all speak in tongues? Do all interpret? But strive for the greater gifts. And I will show you a still more excellent way. (1 Cor. 12:27-31)

Psalm
Psalm 107:1-3, 33-43
God feeds the hungry

Additional Reading
Deuteronomy 8:1-20
You will eat your fill

Hymn: Come to Us, Creative Spirit, ELW 687

Giver of all gifts, stir in us a passion for the more excellent way of love. Help us not only to identify our gifts but to use them fully to build up the body of Christ and to serve for the sake of the world.

Wednesday, August 8, 2018
Time after Pentecost

Dominic, founder of the Order of Preachers (Dominicans), died 1221

Mark 8:1-10
Jesus feeds 4000

In those days when there was again a great crowd without anything to eat, [Jesus] called his disciples and said to them, "I have compassion for the crowd, because they have been with me now for three days and have nothing to eat. If I send them away hungry to their homes, they will faint on the way—and some of them have come from a great distance." His disciples replied, "How can one feed these people with bread here in the desert?" He asked them, "How many loaves do you have?" They said, "Seven." Then he ordered the crowd to sit down on the ground; and he took the seven loaves, and after giving thanks he broke them and gave them to his disciples to distribute; and they distributed them to the crowd. (Mark 8:1-6)

Psalm
Psalm 107:1-3, 33-43
God feeds the hungry

Additional Reading
Isaiah 55:1-9
Come and eat

Hymn: Bread of Life from Heaven, ELW 474

Great Shepherd, we know of your compassion through Jesus who heard the cry of the hungry and responded with food. Stir our imaginations to use our resources to feed thousands, trusting in your blessing to multiply our efforts.

Thursday, August 9, 2018
Time after Pentecost

Psalm 34:1-8
Taste and see

I sought the LORD, and he answered me,
>and delivered me from all my fears.
Look to him, and be radiant;
>so your faces shall never be ashamed.
This poor soul cried, and was heard by the LORD,
>and was saved from every trouble.
The angel of the LORD encamps
>around those who fear him, and delivers them.
O taste and see that the LORD is good;
>happy are those who take refuge in him. (Ps. 34:4-8)

Additional Readings
1 Samuel 28:20-25
Food for Saul's journey

Romans 15:1-6
Living in harmony

Hymn: Taste and See, ELW 493

Deliver us from our fears and troubles, O God. In our time of need, call us to trust that you will provide a place of refuge. Send your Holy Spirit to strengthen us, giving us courage to live this day filled with the love of Christ.

Friday, August 10, 2018
Time after Pentecost

Lawrence, deacon, martyr, died 258

Galatians 6:1-10

Bear one another's burdens

My friends, if anyone is detected in a transgression, you who have received the Spirit should restore such a one in a spirit of gentleness. Take care that you yourselves are not tempted. Bear one another's burdens, and in this way you will fulfill the law of Christ. For if those who are nothing think they are something, they deceive themselves. All must test their own work; then that work, rather than their neighbor's work, will become a cause for pride. For all must carry their own loads. (Gal. 6:1-5)

Psalm

Psalm 34:1-8
Taste and see

Additional Reading

2 Samuel 17:15-29
Food in the wilderness

Hymn: Will You Let Me Be Your Servant, ELW 659

Gentle and loving God, embrace each of us with a spirit of gentleness so that we might speak the truth in love, encourage each other to follow Christ in daily life, act with kindness, and share each other's burdens.

Saturday, August 11, 2018
Time after Pentecost

Clare, Abbess of San Damiano, died 1253

Matthew 7:7-11

Bread and stones

[Jesus said,] "Ask, and it will be given you; search, and you will find; knock, and the door will be opened for you. For everyone who asks receives, and everyone who searches finds, and for everyone who knocks, the door will be opened. Is there anyone among you who, if your child asks for bread, will give a stone? Or if the child asks for a fish, will give a snake? If you then, who are evil, know how to give good gifts to your children, how much more will your Father in heaven give good things to those who ask him!" (Matt. 7:7-11)

Psalm
Psalm 34:1-8
Taste and see

Additional Reading
1 Kings 2:1-9
David's instructions to Solomon

Hymn: Eternal Spirit of the Living Christ, ELW 402

Gracious God, as a loving parent you open doors, seek the lost, and forgive. Strengthen our faith as we ask questions and seek answers. Help us to never take for granted the grace we have received through Jesus Christ.

Sunday, August 12, 2018
Time after Pentecost

John 6:35, 41-51
Christ, the bread of life

Jesus answered [the Jews,] "Very truly, I tell you, whoever believes has eternal life. I am the bread of life. Your ancestors ate the manna in the wilderness, and they died. This is the bread that comes down from heaven, so that one may eat of it and not die. I am the living bread that came down from heaven. Whoever eats of this bread will live forever; and the bread that I will give for the life of the world is my flesh." (John 6:43a, 47-51)

Psalm

Psalm 34:1-8
Taste and see

Additional Readings

1 Kings 19:4-8
Elijah given bread for his journey

Ephesians 4:25—5:2
Put away evil, live in love

Hymn: O Living Bread from Heaven, ELW 542

Gracious God, your blessed Son came down from heaven to be the true bread that gives life to the world. Give us this bread always, that he may live in us and we in him, and that, strengthened by this food, we may live as his body in the world, through Jesus Christ, our Savior and Lord.

Monday, August 13, 2018
Time after Pentecost

Florence Nightingale, died 1910; Clara Maass, died 1901; renewers of society

Psalm 81
God will feed us

"But my people did not listen to my voice;
    Israel would not submit to me.
So I gave them over to their stubborn hearts,
    to follow their own counsels.
O that my people would listen to me,
    that Israel would walk in my ways!
Then I would quickly subdue their enemies,
    and turn my hand against their foes.
Those who hate the LORD would cringe before him,
    and their doom would last forever.
I would feed you with the finest of the wheat,
    and with honey from the rock I would satisfy you." (Ps. 81:11-16)

Additional Readings
1 Kings 17:1-16
God feeds the widow of Zarephath

Ephesians 5:1-14
Fruits of the light

Hymn: You Satisfy the Hungry Heart, ELW 484

Creator of all, create in us each day a yearning spirit that longs to hear your word, seek your guidance, and receive your good gifts. May we never give you any concern about our stubborn hearts and meandering ways.

Tuesday, August 14, 2018
Time after Pentecost

Maximilian Kolbe, died 1941; Kaj Munk, died 1944; martyrs

2 Peter 3:14-18
Grow in grace and knowledge

Therefore, beloved, while you are waiting for these things, strive to be found by him at peace, without spot or blemish; and regard the patience of our Lord as salvation. So also our beloved brother Paul wrote to you according to the wisdom given him, speaking of this as he does in all his letters. There are some things in them hard to understand, which the ignorant and unstable twist to their own destruction, as they do the other scriptures. You therefore, beloved, since you are forewarned, beware that you are not carried away with the error of the lawless and lose your own stability. But grow in the grace and knowledge of our Lord and Savior Jesus Christ. To him be the glory both now and to the day of eternity. Amen. (2 Peter 3:14-18)

Psalm
Psalm 81
God will feed us

Additional Reading
Ruth 2:1-23
Ruth gleans in Boaz's field

Hymn: O Master, Let Me Walk with You, ELW 818

Source of all wisdom, help us to grow in grace and knowledge. Despite the troubles of this world and everything which we do not understand, turn our attention to your glory and love revealed in Jesus Christ.

Wednesday, August 15, 2018
Mary, Mother of Our Lord

Luke 1:46-55

Mary's thanksgiving

And Mary said,
"My soul magnifies the Lord,
    and my spirit rejoices in God my Savior,
for he has looked with favor on the lowliness of his servant.
    Surely, from now on all generations will call me blessed;
for the Mighty One has done great things for me,
    and holy is his name." (Luke 1:46-49)

Psalm

Psalm 34:1-9
O magnify the Lord with me

Additional Readings

Isaiah 61:7-11
God will cause righteousness to spring up

Galatians 4:4-7
We are no longer slaves, but children

Hymn: Canticle of the Turning, ELW 723

Almighty God, in choosing the virgin Mary to be the mother of your Son, you made known your gracious regard for the poor, the lowly, and the despised. Grant us grace to receive your word in humility, and so to be made one with your Son, Jesus Christ our Savior and Lord, who lives and reigns with you and the Holy Spirit, one God, now and forever.

Thursday, August 16, 2018
Time after Pentecost

Psalm 34:9-14

Seeking God

Come, O children, listen to me;
　　I will teach you the fear of the LORD.
Which of you desires life,
　　and covets many days to enjoy good?
Keep your tongue from evil,
　　and your lips from speaking deceit.
Depart from evil, and do good;
　　seek peace, and pursue it. (Ps. 34:11-14)

Additional Readings

Job 11:1-20
Zophar counsels Job about wisdom

Acts 6:8-15
Stephen's compelling wisdom

Hymn: There's a Wideness in God's Mercy, ELW 587/588

God of hope, do not lose hope in us. Teach us to do good, seek peace, and pursue it. Open our ears to listen to your teachings, shape our lives so we covet your guidance, and use our own voices to sing of your shalom.

Friday, August 17, 2018
Time after Pentecost

Romans 16:17-20
Being wise in what is good

I urge you, brothers and sisters, to keep an eye on those who cause dissensions and offenses, in opposition to the teaching that you have learned; avoid them. For such people do not serve our Lord Christ, but their own appetites, and by smooth talk and flattery they deceive the hearts of the simple-minded. For while your obedience is known to all, so that I rejoice over you, I want you to be wise in what is good and guileless in what is evil. The God of peace will shortly crush Satan under your feet. The grace of our Lord Jesus Christ be with you. (Rom. 16:17-20)

Psalm
Psalm 34:9-14
Seeking God

Additional Reading
Job 12:1-25
Job sees wisdom and strength in God

Hymn: O Day of Peace, ELW 711

Eternal One, keep us alert to people who draw us away from you and the love of Christ because of their flattery, seductive behavior, and evil ways. Awaken our desire to please you and empower us to serve with joy.

Saturday, August 18, 2018
Time after Pentecost

John 4:7-26

Christ, the living water

The woman said to [Jesus,] "Sir, you have no bucket, and the well is deep. Where do you get that living water? Are you greater than our ancestor Jacob, who gave us the well, and with his sons and his flocks drank from it?" Jesus said to her, "Everyone who drinks of this water will be thirsty again, but those who drink of the water that I will give them will never be thirsty. The water that I will give will become in them a spring of water gushing up to eternal life." The woman said to him, "Sir, give me this water, so that I may never be thirsty or have to keep coming here to draw water." (John 4:11-15)

Psalm
Psalm 34:9-14
Seeking God

Additional Reading
Job 13:1-19
When silence is wisdom

Hymn: Come to Me, All Pilgrims Thirsty, ELW 777

Great wellspring, each of us cries out for the water that only you can give. We too are thirsty, seeking to quench our parched spirits. We too want to drink from your eternal water.

Sunday, August 19, 2018
Time after Pentecost

John 6:51-58

Christ, the true food and drink

The Jews then disputed among themselves, saying, "How can this man give us his flesh to eat?" So Jesus said to them, "Very truly, I tell you, unless you eat the flesh of the Son of Man and drink his blood, you have no life in you. Those who eat my flesh and drink my blood have eternal life, and I will raise them up on the last day; for my flesh is true food and my blood is true drink." (John 6:52-55)

Psalm

Psalm 34:9-14
Seeking God

Additional Readings

Proverbs 9:1-6
Invited to dine at wisdom's feast

Ephesians 5:15-20
Filled with the Spirit

Hymn: We Eat the Bread of Teaching, ELW 518

Ever-loving God, your Son gives himself as living bread for the life of the world. Fill us with such a knowledge of his presence that we may be strengthened and sustained by his risen life to serve you continually, through Jesus Christ, our Savior and Lord.

Monday, August 20, 2018
Time after Pentecost

Bernard, Abbot of Clairvaux, died 1153

Psalm 36
God saves humans and animals

Your steadfast love, O LORD, extends to the heavens,
    your faithfulness to the clouds.
Your righteousness is like the mighty mountains,
    your judgments are like the great deep;
    you save humans and animals alike, O LORD.

How precious is your steadfast love, O God!
    All people may take refuge in the shadow of your wings.
They feast on the abundance of your house,
    and you give them drink from the river of your delights.
For with you is the fountain of life;
    in your light we see light. (Ps. 36:5-9)

Additional Readings

Genesis 43:1-15
Joseph's brothers need food

Acts 6:1-7
Deacons chosen to distribute food

Hymn: Thy Holy Wings, ELW 613

How precious is your steadfast love, O God! We offer praise to you for providing refuge for the weary, light to cast away all darkness, shade for those who need protection, and the promise of an abundant, eternal feast.

Tuesday, August 21, 2018
Time after Pentecost

Acts 7:9-16
Joseph's family is fed in Egypt

"The patriarchs, jealous of Joseph, sold him into Egypt; but God was with him, and rescued him from all his afflictions, and enabled him to win favor and to show wisdom when he stood before Pharaoh, king of Egypt, who appointed him ruler over Egypt and over all his household. Now there came a famine throughout Egypt and Canaan, and great suffering, and our ancestors could find no food. But when Jacob heard that there was grain in Egypt, he sent our ancestors there on their first visit. On the second visit Joseph made himself known to his brothers, and Joseph's family became known to Pharaoh. Then Joseph sent and invited his father Jacob and all his relatives to come to him, seventy-five in all; so Jacob went down to Egypt. He himself died there as well as our ancestors, and their bodies were brought back to Shechem and laid in the tomb that Abraham had bought for a sum of silver from the sons of Hamor in Shechem." (Acts 7:9-16)

Psalm
Psalm 36
God saves humans and animals

Additional Reading
Genesis 45:1-15
Joseph provides food

Hymn: As Rain from the Clouds, ELW 508

The brothers of Joseph meant him harm. But God, in your infinite wisdom, you brought good from evil. Joseph became an instrument of your blessing. Release us from anger caused by those who have harmed us and open us to your blessing.

Wednesday, August 22, 2018
Time after Pentecost

Genesis 47:13-26
Famine even in Egypt

So Joseph bought all the land of Egypt for Pharaoh. All the Egyptians sold their fields, because the famine was severe upon them; and the land became Pharaoh's. As for the people, he made slaves of them from one end of Egypt to the other. Only the land of the priests he did not buy; for the priests had a fixed allowance from Pharaoh, and lived on the allowance that Pharaoh gave them; therefore they did not sell their land. Then Joseph said to the people, "Now that I have this day bought you and your land for Pharaoh, here is seed for you; sow the land. And at the harvests you shall give one-fifth to Pharaoh, and four-fifths shall be your own, as seed for the field and as food for yourselves and your households, and as food for your little ones." They said, "You have saved our lives; may it please my lord, we will be slaves to Pharaoh." So Joseph made it a statute concerning the land of Egypt, and it stands to this day, that Pharaoh should have the fifth. The land of the priests alone did not become Pharaoh's. (Gen. 47:20-26)

Psalm
Psalm 36
God saves humans and animals

Additional Reading
Mark 8:14-21
Jesus teaches about bread

Hymn: We Plow the Fields and Scatter, ELW 680/681

God of life, it is so difficult to think straight when we are hungry, tired, and thirsty. We need people like Joseph who have vision, courage, and passion to act on behalf of those in need. Stir us to be like him.

Thursday, August 23, 2018
Time after Pentecost

Psalm 34:15-22
God's eyes are upon the righteous

The eyes of the LORD are on the righteous,
    and his ears are open to their cry.
The face of the LORD is against evildoers,
    to cut off the remembrance of them from the earth.
When the righteous cry for help, the LORD hears,
    and rescues them from all their troubles.
The LORD is near to the brokenhearted,
    and saves the crushed in spirit. (Ps. 34:15-18)

Additional Readings
Joshua 22:1-9
Joshua blesses eastern tribes

1 Thessalonians 5:1-11
The breastplate of faith and love

Hymn: O Jesus, Joy of Loving Hearts, ELW 658

Compassionate One, you are near to the brokenhearted. Open our ears to hear those crushed in spirit. Give us wisdom to discern the root of these cries. Fill us with determination to change unjust policies so justice reigns.

Friday, August 24, 2018
Bartholomew, Apostle

John 1:43-51

Jesus says: Follow me

When Jesus saw Nathanael coming toward him, he said of him, "Here is truly an Israelite in whom there is no deceit!" Nathanael asked him, "Where did you get to know me?" Jesus answered, "I saw you under the fig tree before Philip called you." Nathanael replied, "Rabbi, you are the Son of God! You are the King of Israel!" Jesus answered, "Do you believe because I told you that I saw you under the fig tree? You will see greater things than these." And he said to him, "Very truly, I tell you, you will see heaven opened and the angels of God ascending and descending upon the Son of Man." (John 1:47-51)

Psalm

Psalm 12
A plea for help in evil times

Additional Readings

Exodus 19:1-6
Israel is God's priestly kingdom

1 Corinthians 12:27-31a
The body of Christ

Hymn: We All Are One in Mission, ELW 576

Almighty and everlasting God, you gave to your apostle Bartholomew grace truly to believe and courageously to preach your word. Grant that your church may proclaim the good news to the ends of the earth, through Jesus Christ, our Savior and Lord, who lives and reigns with you and the Holy Spirit, one God, now and forever.

Saturday, August 25, 2018
Time after Pentecost

Luke 11:5-13

Ask, and it will be given

[Jesus said,] "So I say to you, Ask, and it will be given you; search, and you will find; knock, and the door will be opened for you. For everyone who asks receives, and everyone who searches finds, and for everyone who knocks, the door will be opened. Is there anyone among you who, if your child asks for a fish, will give a snake instead of a fish? Or if the child asks for an egg, will give a scorpion? If you then, who are evil, know how to give good gifts to your children, how much more will the heavenly Father give the Holy Spirit to those who ask him!" (Luke 11:9-13)

Psalm
Psalm 34:15-22
God's eyes are upon the righteous

Additional Reading
Joshua 22:21-34
An altar to the one LORD

Hymn: Our Father, God in Heaven Above, ELW 746/747

God, how can we hear the hungry beg for food and not respond? That raw cry for hunger is haunting. Send your Holy Spirit to give us courage to share our good gifts and to seek ways to end hunger.

Sunday, August 26, 2018
Time after Pentecost

John 6:56-69

The bread of eternal life

Jesus said, "Those who eat my flesh and drink my blood abide in me, and I in them. Just as the living Father sent me, and I live because of the Father, so whoever eats me will live because of me. This is the bread that came down from heaven, not like that which your ancestors ate, and they died. But the one who eats this bread will live forever." [Jesus] said these things while he was teaching in the synagogue at Capernaum. (John 6:56-59)

Psalm

Psalm 34:15-22
God's eyes are upon the righteous

Additional Readings

Joshua 24:1-2a, 14-18
Serve the LORD

Ephesians 6:10-20
Put on the armor of God

Hymn: Come, Gracious Spirit, Heavenly Dove, ELW 404

Holy God, your word feeds your people with life that is eternal. Direct our choices and preserve us in your truth, that, renouncing what is false and evil, we may live in you, through your Son, Jesus Christ, our Savior and Lord.

Monday, August 27, 2018
Time after Pentecost

Psalm 119:97-104
God's word is sweet

Oh, how I love your law!
> It is my meditation all day long.
Your commandment makes me wiser than my enemies,
> for it is always with me. . . .
How sweet are your words to my taste,
> sweeter than honey to my mouth!
Through your precepts I get understanding;
> therefore I hate every false way. (Ps. 119:97-98, 103-104)

Additional Readings
Nehemiah 9:1-15
God's care of the people

Ephesians 5:21—6:9
A household code

Hymn: Spirit of Gentleness, ELW 396

Faithful God, how we wander through life without thinking about who claimed us in baptism! Yet your Word made flesh in Christ is sweeter than honey. Focus our attention today, free us from distraction, and fill us with your grace.

Tuesday, August 28, 2018
Time after Pentecost

Augustine, Bishop of Hippo, died 430
Moses the Black, monk, martyr, died around 400

Nehemiah 9:16-31
Nehemiah confesses the people's sin

[Ezra said to the Lord,] "Forty years you sustained [our ancestors] in the wilderness so that they lacked nothing; their clothes did not wear out and their feet did not swell. And you gave them kingdoms and peoples, and allotted to them every corner, so they took possession of the land of King Sihon of Heshbon and the land of King Og of Bashan. You multiplied their descendants like the stars of heaven, and brought them into the land that you had told their ancestors to enter and possess. So the descendants went in and possessed the land, and you subdued before them the inhabitants of the land, the Canaanites, and gave them into their hands, with their kings and the peoples of the land, to do with them as they pleased. And they captured fortress cities and a rich land, and took possession of houses filled with all sorts of goods, hewn cisterns, vineyards, olive orchards, and fruit trees in abundance; so they ate, and were filled and became fat, and delighted themselves in your great goodness." (Neh. 9:21-25)

Psalm
Psalm 119:97-104
God's word is sweet

Additional Reading
Ephesians 6:21-24
Peace to the whole community

Hymn: I Love to Tell the Story, ELW 661

Awesome God, you sent Jesus into our world to free us from the power of sin and death. And yet, like our ancestors, we rebel against you, chasing after our own dreams and ambitions. Forgive us.

Wednesday, August 29, 2018
Time after Pentecost

Isaiah 33:10-16
The righteous will eat

Hear, you who are far away, what I have done;
> and you who are near, acknowledge my might.
The sinners in Zion are afraid;
> trembling has seized the godless:
"Who among us can live with the devouring fire?
> Who among us can live with everlasting flames?"
Those who walk righteously and speak uprightly,
> who despise the gain of oppression,
who wave away a bribe instead of accepting it,
> who stop their ears from hearing of bloodshed
> and shut their eyes from looking on evil,
they will live on the heights;
> their refuge will be the fortresses of rocks;
> their food will be supplied, their water assured. (Isa. 33:13-16)

Psalm
Psalm 119:97-104
God's word is sweet

Additional Reading
John 15:16-25
I chose you

Hymn: Around You, O Lord Jesus, ELW 468

Rock of ages, as we face the troubles of this world, be our fortress. When we cannot take another step, be our refuge. Throughout every circumstance, use us as living witnesses of what it means to lean solely on you.

Thursday, August 30, 2018
Time after Pentecost

Psalm 15
Dwelling in God's tabernacle

O LORD, who may abide in your tent?
>   Who may dwell on your holy hill?

Those who walk blamelessly, and do what is right,
>   and speak the truth from their heart;
who do not slander with their tongue,
>   and do no evil to their friends,
>   nor take up a reproach against their neighbors;
in whose eyes the wicked are despised,
>   but who honor those who fear the LORD;
who stand by their oath even to their hurt;
who do not lend money at interest,
>   and do not take a bribe against the innocent.

Those who do these things shall never be moved. (Ps. 15:1-5)

Additional Readings

Exodus 32:1-14
The Israelites make themselves a god

James 1:1-8
One who doubts is like a wave of the sea

Hymn: Oh, That the Lord Would Guide My Ways, ELW 772

Gracious God, include us in those who seek to walk blamelessly, do what is right, and speak the truth in love. Abide in us and allow our words and actions to echo the teachings of Jesus Christ.

Friday, August 31, 2018
Time after Pentecost

James 1:9-16

Blessed are those who endure temptation

Blessed is anyone who endures temptation. Such a one has stood the test and will receive the crown of life that the Lord has promised to those who love him. No one, when tempted, should say, "I am being tempted by God"; for God cannot be tempted by evil and he himself tempts no one. But one is tempted by one's own desire, being lured and enticed by it; then, when that desire has conceived, it gives birth to sin, and that sin, when it is fully grown, gives birth to death. Do not be deceived, my beloved. (James 1:12-16)

Psalm

Psalm 15
Dwelling in God's tabernacle

Additional Reading

Exodus 32:15-35
Moses punishes the Israelites' evil

Hymn: Holy Spirit, Truth Divine, ELW 398

Blessed is anyone who endures temptation, O God. We fervently appeal for you to strengthen us in facing and overcoming the many challenges of this life, especially those temptations that lead us away from your love revealed in Jesus Christ.

Prayer List for September

_____

_____

_____

_____

_____

_____

_____

_____

_____

_____

Time after Pentecost

Autumn

The days of early autumn (September and October) herald the resumption of a more regular schedule: school begins, church education programs commence, and the steady rhythms of work are accompanied by cooling breezes and the changing colors of the landscape. During these months, various crops are harvested and appear on roadside stands and in grocery stores. In many countries the harvest days of September and October are marked with prayer, feasting, and special care for the poor and hungry.

Table Prayer for Autumn

We praise you and bless you, O God,
for autumn days,
and for the gifts of this table.
Grant us grace to share your goodness,
until all people are fed by the harvest of the earth.
We ask this through Christ our Lord. Amen.

Saturday, September 1, 2018
Time after Pentecost

John 18:28-32
Ritual defilement and the Passover

Then [the police] took Jesus from Caiaphas to Pilate's headquarters. It was early in the morning. They themselves did not enter the headquarters, so as to avoid ritual defilement and to be able to eat the Passover. So Pilate went out to them and said, "What accusation do you bring against this man?" They answered, "If this man were not a criminal, we would not have handed him over to you." Pilate said to them, "Take him yourselves and judge him according to your law." The Jews replied, "We are not permitted to put anyone to death." (This was to fulfill what Jesus had said when he indicated the kind of death he was to die.) (John 18:28-32)

Psalm
Psalm 15
Dwelling in God's tabernacle

Additional Reading
Exodus 34:8-28
The covenant renewed

Hymn: My Lord of Light, ELW 832

Faithful God, who is worthy of all praise, guide our hearts in worship. Lead us in your way. Grant us wisdom that we may dwell with reverence in your presence and know what is your holy will.

Sunday, September 2, 2018
Time after Pentecost

Nikolai Frederik Severin Grundtvig, bishop, renewer of the church, died 1872

Mark 7:1-8, 14-15, 21-23
Authentic religion

So the Pharisees and the scribes asked [Jesus,] "Why do your disciples not live according to the tradition of the elders, but eat with defiled hands?" He said to them, "Isaiah prophesied rightly about you hypocrites, as it is written,

> 'This people honors me with their lips,
>> but their hearts are far from me;
> in vain do they worship me,
>> teaching human precepts as doctrines.'

You abandon the commandment of God and hold to human tradition."
(Mark 7:5-8)

Psalm
Psalm 15
Dwelling in God's tabernacle

Additional Readings
Deuteronomy 4:1-2, 6-9
God's law: sign of a great nation

James 1:17-27
Be doers of the word

Hymn: O God, My Faithful God, ELW 806

O God our strength, without you we are weak and wayward creatures. Protect us from all dangers that attack us from the outside, and cleanse us from all evil that arises from within ourselves, that we may be preserved through your Son, Jesus Christ, our Savior and Lord.

Monday, September 3, 2018
Time after Pentecost

Psalm 106:1-6, 13-23, 47-48
God will remember the people

Praise the LORD!
> O give thanks to the LORD, for he is good;
> > for his steadfast love endures forever.
> Who can utter the mighty doings of the LORD,
> > or declare all his praise?
> Happy are those who observe justice,
> > who do righteousness at all times.

> Remember me, O LORD, when you show favor to your people;
> > help me when you deliver them;
> that I may see the prosperity of your chosen ones,
> > that I may rejoice in the gladness of your nation,
> > that I may glory in your heritage. (Ps. 106:1-5)

Additional Readings

Deuteronomy 4:9-14
Teach your children

1 Timothy 4:6-16
Set the believers an example

Hymn: Voices Raised to You, ELW 845

Glory to you, O God. You show us great help and favor. We praise you for your enduring love and unending righteousness. We rejoice with gladness in your mighty words. Help us to walk always in your favor.

Tuesday, September 4, 2018
Time after Pentecost

Deuteronomy 4:15-20
Do not be led astray

Since you saw no form when the LORD spoke to you at Horeb out of the fire, take care and watch yourselves closely, so that you do not act corruptly by making an idol for yourselves, in the form of any figure—the likeness of male or female, the likeness of any animal that is on the earth, the likeness of any winged bird that flies in the air, the likeness of anything that creeps on the ground, the likeness of any fish that is in the water under the earth. And when you look up to the heavens and see the sun, the moon, and the stars, all the host of heaven, do not be led astray and bow down to them and serve them, things that the LORD your God has allotted to all the peoples everywhere under heaven. But the LORD has taken you and brought you out of the iron-smelter, out of Egypt, to become a people of his very own possession, as you are now. (Deut. 4:15-20)

Psalm
Psalm 106:1-6, 13-23, 47-48
God will remember the people

Additional Reading
1 Peter 2:19-25
Christ leaves an example

Hymn: Praise the Lord! O Heavens, ELW 823

God of our freedom, you have given us all things under the heavens. We worship you and you alone. Guide us that we may offer praise worthy of your majesty. Show us how to live uprightly.

Wednesday, September 5, 2018
Time after Pentecost

Mark 7:9-23
Jesus teaches about tradition

Then [Jesus] said to [the Pharisees and scribes,] "You have a fine way of rejecting the commandment of God in order to keep your tradition! For Moses said, 'Honor your father and your mother'; and, 'Whoever speaks evil of father or mother must surely die.' But you say that if anyone tells father or mother, 'Whatever support you might have had from me is Corban' (that is, an offering to GOD)—then you no longer permit doing anything for a father or mother, thus making void the word of God through your tradition that you have handed on. And you do many things like this." (Mark 7:9-13)

Psalm
Psalm 106:1-6, 13-23, 47-48
God will remember the people

Additional Reading
Deuteronomy 4:21-40
Moses urges faithfulness

Hymn: God's Word Is Our Great Heritage, ELW 509

God, our guidance through the trials of the world, help us keep our faith in you. Show us how to be obedient to your commandments, offering you praise and glory for your faithfulness in all things.

Thursday, September 6, 2018
Time after Pentecost

Psalm 146
Help and hope come from God

The LORD sets the prisoners free;
    the LORD opens the eyes of the blind.
The LORD lifts up those who are bowed down;
    the LORD loves the righteous.
The LORD watches over the strangers;
    he upholds the orphan and the widow,
    but the way of the wicked he brings to ruin.

The LORD will reign forever,
    your God, O Zion, for all generations.
Praise the LORD! (Ps. 146:7c-10)

Additional Readings
Isaiah 30:27-33
God sifts the nations

Romans 2:1-11
Divine judgment applies to all

Hymn: Praise the One Who Breaks the Darkness, ELW 843

Praise to you, O God, for you set us free from sin, heal us, and give us hope.
Implant your love in our hearts and grant us grace to show your love toward
our neighbors.

Friday, September 7, 2018
Time after Pentecost

Romans 2:12-16

Gentiles obey the law instinctively

All who have sinned apart from the law will also perish apart from the law, and all who have sinned under the law will be judged by the law. For it is not the hearers of the law who are righteous in God's sight, but the doers of the law who will be justified. When Gentiles, who do not possess the law, do instinctively what the law requires, these, though not having the law, are a law to themselves. They show that what the law requires is written on their hearts, to which their own conscience also bears witness; and their conflicting thoughts will accuse or perhaps excuse them on the day when, according to my gospel, God, through Jesus Christ, will judge the secret thoughts of all. (Rom. 2:12-16)

Psalm

Psalm 146
Help and hope come from God

Additional Reading

Isaiah 32:1-8
The noble stand by noble things

Hymn: Salvation unto Us Has Come, ELW 590

Gracious God, thank you for the gift of salvation through the death of your Son, whose promise of new life carries us through our daily struggles. Keep our hearts in your word and keep our thoughts free from sin.

Saturday, September 8, 2018
Time after Pentecost

Isaiah 33:1-9

The fear of God is Zion's treasure

O Lord, be gracious to us; we wait for you.
>   Be our arm every morning,
>   our salvation in the time of trouble.
At the sound of tumult, peoples fled;
>   before your majesty, nations scattered.
Spoil was gathered as the caterpillar gathers;
>   as locusts leap, they leaped upon it.
The Lord is exalted, he dwells on high;
>   he filled Zion with justice and righteousness;
he will be the stability of your times,
>   abundance of salvation, wisdom, and knowledge;
>   the fear of the Lord is Zion's treasure. (Isa. 33:2-6)

Psalm

Psalm 146
Help and hope come from God

Additional Reading

Matthew 15:21-31
Jesus heals

Hymn: O Savior, Precious Savior, ELW 820

Lord on high, praise be to you. You are our help in times of trouble and our security in uncertainty. Show us your wisdom and help us always to wait on you, for your justice and righteousness endure forever.

Sunday, September 9, 2018
Time after Pentecost

Peter Claver, priest, missionary to Colombia, died 1654

Mark 7:24-37

Christ heals a little girl and a deaf man

Then [Jesus] returned from the region of Tyre, and went by way of
Sidon towards the Sea of Galilee, in the region of the Decapolis. [The
disciples] brought to him a deaf man who had an impediment in his
speech; and they begged him to lay his hand on him. He took him aside
in private, away from the crowd, and put his fingers into his ears, and
he spat and touched his tongue. Then looking up to heaven, he sighed
and said to him, "Ephphatha," that is, "Be opened." And immediately
his ears were opened, his tongue was released, and he spoke plainly.
(Mark 7:31-35)

Psalm

Psalm 146
*Help and hope come from
God*

Additional Readings

Isaiah 35:4-7a
God comes with healing

James 2:1-10 [11-13]
14-17
Faith without works is dead

Hymn: Lord of All Nations, Grant Me Grace, ELW 716

*Gracious God, throughout the ages you transform sickness into health and
death into life. Open us to the power of your presence, and make us a people
ready to proclaim your promises to the whole world, through Jesus Christ,
our healer and Lord.*

Monday, September 10, 2018
Time after Pentecost

Isaiah 38:10-20
Prayer for health

O Lord, by these things people live,
>and in all these is the life of my spirit.
>Oh, restore me to health and make me live!
Surely it was for my welfare
>that I had great bitterness;
but you have held back my life
>from the pit of destruction,
for you have cast all my sins
>behind your back.
For Sheol cannot thank you,
>death cannot praise you;
those who go down to the Pit cannot hope
>for your faithfulness.
The living, the living, they thank you,
>as I do this day;
fathers make known to children
>your faithfulness. (Isa. 38:16-19)

Additional Readings

Joshua 6:1-21
The Israelites conquer Jericho

Hebrews 11:29—12:2
The heroes of faith

Hymn: Great Is Thy Faithfulness, ELW 733

*God of mercy, you grant us healing from pain and forgiveness from sin.
Help us to place our hope in your promises, for your faithfulness exceeds
our imagination. We thank and praise you always.*

Tuesday, September 11, 2018
Time after Pentecost

Hebrews 12:3-13
Trials for the sake of discipline

Endure trials for the sake of discipline. God is treating you as children;
for what child is there whom a parent does not discipline? If you do
not have that discipline in which all children share, then you are
illegitimate and not his children. Moreover, we had human parents
to discipline us, and we respected them. Should we not be even
more willing to be subject to the Father of spirits and live? For they
disciplined us for a short time as seemed best to them, but he disciplines
us for our good, in order that we may share his holiness. Now, discipline
always seems painful rather than pleasant at the time, but later it yields
the peaceful fruit of righteousness to those who have been trained by it.
(Heb. 12:7-11)

Psalm
Isaiah 38:10-20
Prayer for health

Additional Reading
Joshua 8:1-23
The Israelites conquer Ai

Hymn: How Clear Is Our Vocation, Lord, ELW 580

*God, you are the holiest of holies. Your light guides us through life. Lead us
to keep your commandments. Train us in your ways that we may be fruitful
and share in your holiness.*

Wednesday, September 12, 2018
Time after Pentecost

Matthew 17:14-21
Healing by faith

When [Jesus and the disciples] came to the crowd, a man came to [Jesus,] knelt before him, and said, "Lord, have mercy on my son, for he is an epileptic and he suffers terribly; he often falls into the fire and often into the water. And I brought him to your disciples, but they could not cure him." Jesus answered, "You faithless and perverse generation, how much longer must I be with you? How much longer must I put up with you? Bring him here to me." And Jesus rebuked the demon, and it came out of him, and the boy was cured instantly. Then the disciples came to Jesus privately and said, "Why could we not cast it out?" He said to them, "Because of your little faith. For truly I tell you, if you have faith the size of a mustard seed, you will say to this mountain, 'Move from here to there,' and it will move; and nothing will be impossible for you." (Matt. 17:14-20)

Psalm
Isaiah 38:10-20
Prayer for health

Additional Reading
Judges 15:9-20
Samson slays the Philistines

Hymn: Now to the Holy Spirit Let Us Pray, ELW 743

God of help, you are faithful in all things. You meet us in our suffering. You grant us your perfect comfort in our sorrows. Give us the faith we need to perform mighty works for you.

Thursday, September 13, 2018
Time after Pentecost

John Chrysostom, Bishop of Constantinople, died 407

Psalm 116:1-9

I will walk in God's presence

Gracious is the LORD, and righteous;
>   our God is merciful.
The LORD protects the simple;
>   when I was brought low, he saved me.
Return, O my soul, to your rest,
>   for the LORD has dealt bountifully with you.

For you have delivered my soul from death,
>   my eyes from tears,
>   my feet from stumbling.
I walk before the LORD
>   in the land of the living. (Ps. 116:5-9)

Additional Readings

Joshua 2:1-14
Rahab shelters Joshua's spies

Hebrews 11:17-22
Abraham, Isaac, and Jacob act on faith

Hymn: All Depends on Our Possessing, ELW 589

God of deliverance, you lift us up from sin. You save us from death. You raise us from valleys and let us walk always in your presence. Help us to walk in you without stumbling.

Friday, September 14, 2018
Holy Cross Day

John 3:13-17
The Son of Man will be lifted up

[Jesus said to Nicodemus,] "No one has ascended into heaven except the one who descended from heaven, the Son of Man. And just as Moses lifted up the serpent in the wilderness, so must the Son of Man be lifted up, that whoever believes in him may have eternal life.

"For God so loved the world that he gave his only Son, so that everyone who believes in him may not perish but may have eternal life.

"Indeed, God did not send the Son into the world to condemn the world, but in order that the world might be saved through him." (John 3:13-17)

Psalm
Psalm 98:1-4
God has done marvelous things

Additional Readings
Numbers 21:4b-9
A bronze serpent in the wilderness

1 Corinthians 1:18-24
The cross is the power of God

Hymn: Lift High the Cross, ELW 660

Almighty God, your Son, Jesus Christ, was lifted high upon the cross so that he might draw the whole world to himself. To those who look upon the cross, grant your wisdom, healing, and eternal life, through Jesus Christ, our Savior and Lord, who lives and reigns with you and the Holy Spirit, one God, now and forever.

Saturday, September 15, 2018
Time after Pentecost

Matthew 21:23-32
The faith of tax collectors and prostitutes

[Jesus said,] "What do you think? A man had two sons; he went to the first and said, 'Son, go and work in the vineyard today.' He answered, 'I will not'; but later he changed his mind and went. The father went to the second and said the same; and he answered, 'I go, sir'; but he did not go. Which of the two did the will of his father?" They said, "The first." Jesus said to them, "Truly I tell you, the tax collectors and the prostitutes are going into the kingdom of God ahead of you. For John came to you in the way of righteousness and you did not believe him, but the tax collectors and the prostitutes believed him; and even after you saw it, you did not change your minds and believe him." (Matt. 21:28-32)

Psalm
Psalm 116:1-9
I will walk in God's presence

Additional Reading
Joshua 6:22-27
Rahab and her family are spared

Hymn: Let Us Ever Walk with Jesus, ELW 802

God of mercy, thank you for your salvation which is given to us freely. Guide us to follow your example in showing love to all we encounter. Fill us with your grace that we may walk in the ways of righteousness.

Sunday, September 16, 2018
Time after Pentecost

Cyprian, Bishop of Carthage, martyr, died around 258

Mark 8:27-38

Peter's confession of faith

Jesus went on with his disciples to the villages of Caesarea Philippi; and on the way he asked his disciples, "Who do people say that I am?" And they answered him, "John the Baptist; and others, Elijah; and still others, one of the prophets." He asked them, "But who do you say that I am?" Peter answered him, "You are the Messiah." And he sternly ordered them not to tell anyone about him. (Mark 8:27-30)

Psalm

Psalm 116:1-9
I will walk in God's presence

Additional Readings

Isaiah 50:4-9a
The servant is vindicated by God

James 3:1-12
Dangers of the unbridled tongue

Hymn: O Jesus, I Have Promised, ELW 810

O God, through suffering and rejection you bring forth our salvation, and by the glory of the cross you transform our lives. Grant that for the sake of the gospel we may turn from the lure of evil, take up our cross, and follow your Son, Jesus Christ, our Savior and Lord.

Monday, September 17, 2018
Time after Pentecost

Hildegard, Abbess of Bingen, died 1179

Psalm 119:169-176
God's law my delight

Let your hand be ready to help me,
    for I have chosen your precepts.
I long for your salvation, O LORD,
    and your law is my delight.
Let me live that I may praise you,
    and let your ordinances help me.
I have gone astray like a lost sheep; seek out your servant,
    for I do not forget your commandments. (Ps. 119:173-176)

Additional Readings

1 Kings 13:1-10
Obeying the word of God

Romans 3:9-20
The unrighteous tongue deceives

Hymn: O Holy Spirit, Root of Life, ELW 399

As the shepherd sought to save the one lost sheep who wandered from the flock, so have you sought us, God. Lead us in your paths and keep us safe within your fold. May we delight in your commandments and praise your name forever.

Tuesday, September 18, 2018
Time after Pentecost

Dag Hammarskjöld, renewer of society, died 1961

Colossians 3:1-11
Rid your mouth of abusive language

Put to death, therefore, whatever in you is earthly: fornication, impurity, passion, evil desire, and greed (which is idolatry). On account of these the wrath of God is coming on those who are disobedient. These are the ways you also once followed, when you were living that life. But now you must get rid of all such things—anger, wrath, malice, slander, and abusive language from your mouth. Do not lie to one another, seeing that you have stripped off the old self with its practices and have clothed yourselves with the new self, which is being renewed in knowledge according to the image of its creator. (Col. 3:5-10)

Psalm
Psalm 119:169-176
God's law my delight

Additional Reading
1 Kings 13:11-25
Disobeying the word of God

Hymn: Let Us Ever Walk with Jesus, ELW 802

God of truth, show us your wisdom. You have saved us and crafted us into new creatures. Help us to set aside the ways of the world and take joy in your freedom so we may serve you always.

Wednesday, September 19, 2018
Time after Pentecost

John 7:25-36
Jesus the messiah

Now some of the people of Jerusalem were saying, "Is not this the man whom they are trying to kill? And here he is, speaking openly, but they say nothing to him! Can it be that the authorities really know that this is the Messiah? Yet we know where this man is from; but when the Messiah comes, no one will know where he is from." Then Jesus cried out as he was teaching in the temple, "You know me, and you know where I am from. I have not come on my own. But the one who sent me is true, and you do not know him. I know him, because I am from him, and he sent me." (John 7:25-29)

Psalm
Psalm 119:169-176
God's law my delight

Additional Reading
Isaiah 10:12-20
Evil will be destroyed

Hymn: He Comes to Us as One Unknown, ELW 737

God of our salvation, thank you for sending your son as a sacrifice for our sins. Help us always to see your work in our lives and follow the road of righteousness you have set before us.

Thursday, September 20, 2018
Time after Pentecost

Psalm 54
God is my helper

Save me, O God, by your name,
    and vindicate me by your might.
Hear my prayer, O God;
    give ear to the words of my mouth.

For the insolent have risen against me,
    the ruthless seek my life;
    they do not set God before them.

But surely, God is my helper;
    the Lord is the upholder of my life.
He will repay my enemies for their evil.
    In your faithfulness, put an end to them. (Ps. 54:1-5)

Additional Readings
Judges 6:1-10
Israel ignores a prophet of God

1 Corinthians 2:1-5
Beyond human wisdom

Hymn: Lord of Our Life, ELW 766

Lord, you are our help. You have promised never to leave us or forsake us. You hear our cries and answer our prayers. Hold us in your love. May we trust you with all our hearts.

Friday, September 21, 2018
Matthew, Apostle and Evangelist

Matthew 9:9-13

Jesus calls to Matthew: Follow me

As Jesus was walking along, he saw a man called Matthew sitting at the tax booth; and he said to him, "Follow me." And he got up and followed him.

And as he sat at dinner in the house, many tax collectors and sinners came and were sitting with him and his disciples. When the Pharisees saw this, they said to his disciples, "Why does your teacher eat with tax collectors and sinners?" But when he heard this, he said, "Those who are well have no need of a physician, but those who are sick. Go and learn what this means, 'I desire mercy, not sacrifice.' For I have come to call not the righteous but sinners." (Matt. 9:9-13)

Psalm

Psalm 119:33-40
Give me understanding

Additional Readings

Ezekiel 2:8—3:11
A prophet to the house of Israel

Ephesians 2:4-10
By grace you have been saved

Hymn: Gracious Spirit, Heed Our Pleading, ELW 401

Almighty God, your Son our Savior called a despised tax collector to become one of his apostles. Help us, like Matthew, to respond to the transforming call of Jesus Christ, who lives and reigns with you and the Holy Spirit, one God, now and forever.

Saturday, September 22, 2018
Time after Pentecost

2 Kings 17:5-18
Israel refuses to listen to the prophets

Yet the LORD warned Israel and Judah by every prophet and every seer, saying, "Turn from your evil ways and keep my commandments and my statutes, in accordance with all the law that I commanded your ancestors and that I sent to you by my servants the prophets." They would not listen but were stubborn, as their ancestors had been, who did not believe in the LORD their God. (2 Kings 17:13-14)

Psalm
Psalm 54
God is my helper

Additional Reading
Matthew 23:29-39
Woe to those who kill and crucify the prophets

Hymn: Open Your Ears, O Faithful People, ELW 519

God, as you saved Israel and Judah repeatedly, so you also save us no matter how many times we stumble. Open our hearts to your words. Guide us as we follow your commandments. Help us to cease our straying and walk in you.

Sunday, September 23, 2018
Time after Pentecost

Mark 9:30-37
Prediction of the passion

[Jesus and the disciples] went on from there and passed through Galilee. He did not want anyone to know it; for he was teaching his disciples, saying to them, "The Son of Man is to be betrayed into human hands, and they will kill him, and three days after being killed, he will rise again." But they did not understand what he was saying and were afraid to ask him. (Mark 9:30-32)

Psalm

Psalm 54
God is my helper

Additional Readings

Jeremiah 11:18-20
The prophet is like a lamb

James 3:13—4:3, 7-8a
The wisdom from above

Hymn: Children of the Heavenly Father, ELW 781

O God, our teacher and guide, you draw us to yourself and welcome us as beloved children. Help us to lay aside all envy and selfish ambition, that we may walk in your ways of wisdom and understanding as servants of your Son, Jesus Christ, our Savior and Lord.

Monday, September 24, 2018
Time after Pentecost

Psalm 139:1-18
Formed in my mother's womb

For it was you who formed my inward parts;
> you knit me together in my mother's womb.
I praise you, for I am fearfully and wonderfully made.
> Wonderful are your works;
that I know very well.
> My frame was not hidden from you,
when I was being made in secret,
> intricately woven in the depths of the earth. (Ps. 139:13-15)

Additional Readings
2 Kings 5:1-14
The girl servant saves her master

James 4:8-17
Draw near to God

Hymn: Borning Cry, ELW 732

God, our divine designer, praise be to you for you have gifted us with life and directed our lives with purpose. Show us how we may live fully for you. Guide us to carry out your will.

Tuesday, September 25, 2018
Time after Pentecost

James 5:1-6
A warning to those who trust in riches

Come now, you rich people, weep and wail for the miseries that are coming to you. Your riches have rotted, and your clothes are moth-eaten. Your gold and silver have rusted, and their rust will be evidence against you, and it will eat your flesh like fire. You have laid up treasure for the last days. Listen! The wages of the laborers who mowed your fields, which you kept back by fraud, cry out, and the cries of the harvesters have reached the ears of the Lord of hosts. You have lived on the earth in luxury and in pleasure; you have fattened your hearts in a day of slaughter. You have condemned and murdered the righteous one, who does not resist you. (James 5:1-6)

Psalm
Psalm 139:1-18
Formed in my mother's womb

Additional Reading
2 Kings 11:21—12:16
The boy king repairs the temple

Hymn: Jesus Calls Us; o'er the Tumult, ELW 696

Generous God, you have given us salvation from sin and have provided for our needs. As you care even for the sparrow, so much more do you care for us. Guide us to live for you, storing up heavenly riches and dedicating ourselves to your service.

Wednesday, September 26, 2018
Time after Pentecost

Jeremiah 1:4-10
God calls Jeremiah

Now the word of the LORD came to me saying,

> "Before I formed you in the womb I knew you,
> and before you were born I consecrated you;
> I appointed you a prophet to the nations."

Then I said, "Ah, Lord GOD! Truly I do not know how to speak, for I am only a boy." But the LORD said to me,

> "Do not say, 'I am only a boy';
> for you shall go to all to whom I send you,
> and you shall speak whatever I command you,
> Do not be afraid of them,
> for I am with you to deliver you,
> says the LORD." (Jer. 1:4-8)

Psalm
Psalm 139:1-18
Formed in my mother's womb

Additional Reading
John 8:21-38
Being disciples of Jesus

Hymn: Lord, Take My Hand and Lead Me, ELW 767

God, as you have called us to go into all the world, so send us to places where the needs are greatest. Direct us as we show your love and share the gospel with boldness.

Thursday, September 27, 2018
Time after Pentecost

Psalm 19:7-14
The law gives light

The law of the Lord is perfect,
    reviving the soul;
the decrees of the Lord are sure,
    making wise the simple;
the precepts of the Lord are right,
    rejoicing the heart;
the commandment of the Lord is clear,
    enlightening the eyes;
the fear of the Lord is pure,
    enduring forever;
the ordinances of the Lord are true
    and righteous altogether.
More to be desired are they than gold,
    even much fine gold;
sweeter also than honey,
    and drippings of the honeycomb. (Ps. 19:7-10)

Additional Readings
Exodus 18:13-27
Moses appoints judges to keep peace

Acts 4:13-31
The believers pray for boldness

Hymn: O Spirit of Life, ELW 405

Lord of purity and light everlasting, your love is without end and your glory without comparison. We rejoice in you. Make our hearts yearn for you, O God. Help us to keep our desires always in you.

Friday, September 28, 2018
Time after Pentecost

Acts 12:20-25
A leader fails to give glory to God

Now Herod was angry with the people of Tyre and Sidon. So they came to him in a body; and after winning over Blastus, the king's chamberlain, they asked for a reconciliation, because their country depended on the king's country for food. On an appointed day Herod put on his royal robes, took his seat on the platform, and delivered a public address to them. The people kept shouting, "The voice of a god, and not of a mortal!" And immediately, because he had not given the glory to God, an angel of the Lord struck him down, and he was eaten by worms and died.

But the word of God continued to advance and gain adherents. Then after completing their mission Barnabas and Saul returned to Jerusalem and brought with them John, whose other name was Mark. (Acts 12:20-25)

Psalm
Psalm 19:7-14
The law gives light

Additional Reading
Deuteronomy 1:1-18
Moses charges the judges

Hymn: O Word of God Incarnate, ELW 514

Enduring God, you are holy and always worthy of praise. Your word continues forever. Give us faith as we go forth, sharing the gospel with all the world. Use us to bring hope to people around us.

Saturday, September 29, 2018
Michael and All Angels

Luke 10:17-20
Jesus gives his followers authority

The seventy returned with joy, saying, "Lord, in your name even the demons submit to us!" Jesus said to them, "I watched Satan fall from heaven like a flash of lightning. See, I have given you authority to tread on snakes and scorpions, and over all the power of the enemy; and nothing will hurt you. Nevertheless, do not rejoice at this, that the spirits submit to you, but rejoice that your names are written in heaven." (Luke 10:17-20)

Psalm
Psalm 103:1-5, 20-22
Bless the Lord, you angels

Additional Readings
Daniel 10:10-14; 12:1-3
Michael shall arise

Revelation 12:7-12
Michael defeats Satan in a cosmic battle

Hymn: Ye Watchers and Ye Holy Ones, ELW 424

Everlasting God, you have wonderfully established the ministries of angels and mortals. Mercifully grant that as Michael and the angels contend against the cosmic forces of evil, so by your direction they may help and defend us here on earth, through your Son, Jesus Christ our Lord, who lives and reigns with you and the Holy Spirit, one God whom we worship and praise with angels and archangels and all the company of heaven, now and forever.

Sunday, September 30, 2018
Time after Pentecost

Jerome, translator, teacher, died 420

Mark 9:38-50
Warnings to those who obstruct faith

[Jesus said,] "If any of you put a stumbling block before one of these little ones who believe in me, it would be better for you if a great millstone were hung around your neck and you were thrown into the sea. If your hand causes you to stumble, cut it off; it is better for you to enter life maimed than to have two hands and to go to hell, to the unquenchable fire. And if your foot causes you to stumble, cut it off; it is better for you to enter life lame than to have two feet and to be thrown into hell. And if your eye causes you to stumble, tear it out; it is better for you to enter the kingdom of God with one eye than to have two eyes and to be thrown into hell, where their worm never dies, and the fire is never quenched." (Mark 9:42-48)

Psalm
Psalm 19:7-14
The law gives light

Additional Readings
Numbers 11:4-6, 10-16, 24-29
The spirit is upon seventy elders

James 5:13-20
Prayer and anointing in the community

Hymn: Where Cross the Crowded Ways of Life, ELW 719

Generous God, your Son gave his life that we might come to peace with you. Give us a share of your Spirit, and in all we do empower us to bear the name of Jesus Christ, our Savior and Lord.

Prayer List for October

_____

_____

_____

_____

_____

_____

_____

_____

_____

Monday, October 1, 2018
Time after Pentecost

Psalm 5
Lead me in righteousness

Lead me, O Lord, in your righteousness
>   because of my enemies;
>   make your way straight before me.

For there is no truth in their mouths;
>   their hearts are destruction;
their throats are open graves;
>   they flatter with their tongues.
Make them bear their guilt, O God;
>   let them fall by their own counsels;
because of their many transgressions cast them out,
>   for they have rebelled against you. (Ps. 5:8-10)

Additional Readings

Zechariah 6:9-15
Far and near led to build the temple

1 Peter 1:3-9
The outcome of faith is salvation

Hymn: Precious Lord, Take My Hand, ELW 773

Almighty God, you transcend our human divisions and invite all people to come to you with trust in your mercy. Grant us your wisdom and kindness to pray for the welfare of our enemies and learn to do good to those in our lives for whom it is hardest to show love and care.

Tuesday, October 2, 2018
Time after Pentecost

Zechariah 8:18-23

The nations seek God in Jerusalem

Thus says the LORD of hosts: Peoples shall yet come, the inhabitants of many cities; the inhabitants of one city shall go to another, saying, "Come, let us go to entreat the favor of the LORD, and to seek the LORD of hosts; I myself am going." Many peoples and strong nations shall come to seek the LORD of hosts in Jerusalem, and to entreat the favor of the LORD. Thus says the LORD of hosts: In those days ten men from nations of every language shall take hold of a Jew, grasping his garment and saying, "Let us go with you, for we have heard that God is with you." (Zech. 8:20-23)

Psalm
Psalm 5
Lead me in righteousness

Additional Reading
1 John 2:18-25
Anointed by the Holy One

Hymn: Come, We That Love the Lord, ELW 625

God of Israel, you went ahead of your people with a pillar of cloud showing a way through the wilderness. Give us the courage to follow where you are leading us, the strength to use the gifts you have given us, and the longing to share your grace with people in places we have yet to encounter.

Wednesday, October 3, 2018
Time after Pentecost

Matthew 18:6-9
Causing others to stumble

[Jesus said,] "If any of you put a stumbling block before one of these little ones who believe in me, it would be better for you if a great millstone were fastened around your neck and you were drowned in the depth of the sea. Woe to the world because of stumbling blocks! Occasions for stumbling are bound to come, but woe to the one by whom the stumbling block comes!

"If your hand or your foot causes you to stumble, cut it off and throw it away; it is better for you to enter life maimed or lame than to have two hands or two feet and to be thrown into the eternal fire. And if your eye causes you to stumble, tear it out and throw it away; it is better for you to enter life with one eye than to have two eyes and to be thrown into the hell of fire." (Matt. 18:6-9)

Psalm
Psalm 5
Lead me in righteousness

Additional Reading
Zechariah 10:1-12
God will gather the people

Hymn: Lord, Speak to Us, That We May Speak, ELW 676

Holy God, you have sent your life-giving Spirit into our hearts to remove every part of us that leads to death. Help us to let go of old addictions, ideas, and hatreds. Teach us instead to be soothed by the grace revealed in your Son, Jesus Christ.

Thursday, October 4, 2018
Time after Pentecost

Francis of Assisi, renewer of the church, died 1226
Theodor Fliedner, renewer of society, died 1864

Psalm 8
You adorn us with glory and honor

When I look at your heavens, the work of your fingers,
    the moon and the stars that you have established;
what are human beings that you are mindful of them,
    mortals that you care for them?

Yet you have made them a little lower than God,
    and crowned them with glory and honor.
You have given them dominion over the works of your hands;
    you have put all things under their feet,
all sheep and oxen,
    and also the beasts of the field,
the birds of the air, and the fish of the sea,
    whatever passes along the paths of the seas. (Ps. 8:3-8)

Additional Readings
Genesis 20:1-18
Abraham pretends Sarah is his sister

Galatians 3:23-29
Children of God in Christ

Hymn: Many and Great, O God, ELW 837

God of abundance, you have poured out blessings on our lives that are heaping up and running over. Fill us each moment with the awe and gratitude that is proper to your generosity. Lead us every day to praise you and to give thanks for your glorious love.

Friday, October 5, 2018
Time after Pentecost

Romans 8:1-11
Life in the Spirit

There is therefore now no condemnation for those who are in Christ Jesus. For the law of the Spirit of life in Christ Jesus has set you free from the law of sin and of death. For God has done what the law, weakened by the flesh, could not do: by sending his own Son in the likeness of sinful flesh, and to deal with sin, he condemned sin in the flesh, so that the just requirement of the law might be fulfilled in us, who walk not according to the flesh but according to the Spirit. For those who live according to the flesh set their minds on the things of the flesh, but those who live according to the Spirit set their minds on the things of the Spirit. (Rom. 8:1-5)

Psalm
Psalm 8
You adorn us with glory and honor

Additional Reading
Genesis 21:22-34
Abraham reconciles with Abimelech

Hymn: O Holy Spirit, Enter In, ELW 786

Redeeming God, you rescued us from the powers of evil holding us captive. Help us to live the freedom you have won for us and to give ourselves away in service to others.

Saturday, October 6, 2018
Time after Pentecost

William Tyndale, translator, martyr, died 1536

Luke 16:14-18
The law endures

The Pharisees, who were lovers of money, heard all this, and they ridiculed [Jesus.] So he said to them, "You are those who justify yourselves in the sight of others; but God knows your hearts; for what is prized by human beings is an abomination in the sight of God.

"The law and the prophets were in effect until John came; since then the good news of the kingdom of God is proclaimed, and everyone tries to enter it by force. But it is easier for heaven and earth to pass away, than for one stroke of a letter in the law to be dropped.

"Anyone who divorces his wife and marries another commits adultery, and whoever marries a woman divorced from her husband commits adultery." (Luke 16:14-18)

Psalm
Psalm 8
You adorn us with glory and honor

Additional Reading
Genesis 23:1-20
Abraham buries Sarah

Hymn: Spirit of Gentleness, ELW 396

Merciful Lord, through your law you confront us with our own failings and our need for you. Summon us to look squarely into the mirror that the law holds up to our lives, trusting that every deficiency will be healed through the grace of your Son, Jesus Christ.

Sunday, October 7, 2018
Time after Pentecost

Henry Melchior Muhlenberg, pastor in North America, died 1787

Mark 10:2-16
Teaching on marriage

Some Pharisees came, and to test Jesus they asked, "Is it lawful for a man to divorce his wife?" He answered them, "What did Moses command you?" They said, "Moses allowed a man to write a certificate of dismissal and to divorce her." But Jesus said to them, "Because of your hardness of heart he wrote this commandment for you. But from the beginning of creation, 'God made them male and female.'" (Mark 10:2-6)

Psalm
Psalm 8
You adorn us with glory and honor

Additional Readings
Genesis 2:18-24
Created for relationship

Hebrews 1:1-4; 2:5-12
God has spoken by a Son

Hymn: All Are Welcome, ELW 641

Sovereign God, you have created us to live in loving community with one another. Form us for life that is faithful and steadfast, and teach us to trust like little children, that we may reflect the image of your Son, Jesus Christ, our Savior and Lord.

Monday, October 8, 2018
Time after Pentecost

Day of Thanksgiving (Canada)

A Blessing of the Household for Thanksgiving Day is provided on page 356.

Psalm 112

Happy are those who fear God

Praise the LORD!
>Happy are those who fear the LORD,
>>who greatly delight in his commandments.
>Their descendants will be mighty in the land;
>>the generation of the upright will be blessed.
>Wealth and riches are in their houses,
>>and their righteousness endures forever.
>They rise in the darkness as a light for the upright;
>>they are gracious, merciful, and righteous. (Ps. 112:1-4)

Additional Readings

Deuteronomy 22:13-30
Laws about sexual relations

1 Corinthians 7:1-9
Guidance for the married

Hymn: Drawn to the Light, ELW 593

Righteous God, we give you thanks for women and men of faith before us who held out your mercy to the unmerciful and your righteousness among the unrighteous. Embolden us through their witness to shine where light is needed in this world.

Tuesday, October 9, 2018
Time after Pentecost

Deuteronomy 24:1-5
Laws about divorce

Suppose a man enters into marriage with a woman, but she does not please him because he finds something objectionable about her, and so he writes her a certificate of divorce, puts it in her hand, and sends her out of his house; she then leaves his house and goes off to become another man's wife. Then suppose the second man dislikes her, writes her a bill of divorce, puts it in her hand, and sends her out of his house (or the second man who married her dies); her first husband, who sent her away, is not permitted to take her again to be his wife after she has been defiled; for that would be abhorrent to the LORD, and you shall not bring guilt on the land that the LORD your God is giving you as a possession.

When a man is newly married, he shall not go out with the army or be charged with any related duty. He shall be free at home one year, to be happy with the wife whom he has married. (Deut. 24:1-5)

Psalm
Psalm 112
Happy are those who fear God

Additional Reading
1 Corinthians 7:10-16
Divorce discouraged

Hymn: Hear Us Now, Our God and Father, ELW 585

Holy Trinity, you formed us in your image to be in relationship with one another and with the world around us, yet we struggle to live into this grace. Make our homes and communities into spaces of healing where care and love are shared without discrimination.

Wednesday, October 10, 2018
Time after Pentecost

Matthew 5:27-36
Teachings about marriage and vow-making

[Jesus said,] "You have heard that it was said, 'You shall not commit adultery.' But I say to you that everyone who looks at a woman with lust has already committed adultery with her in his heart. If your right eye causes you to sin, tear it out and throw it away; it is better for you to lose one of your members than for your whole body to be thrown into hell. And if your right hand causes you to sin, cut it off and throw it away; it is better for you to lose one of your members than for your whole body to go into hell." (Matt. 5:27-30)

Psalm
Psalm 112
Happy are those who fear God

Additional Reading
Jeremiah 3:6-14
God will forgive the unfaithful

Hymn: Chief of Sinners Though I Be, ELW 609

Sanctifying God, you call on us to turn to you daily in repentance, dying to old ways and rising to new life. Renew our baptism as an ever-present gift that overflows with the promises of your mercy, forgiveness, and faithfulness.

Thursday, October 11, 2018
Time after Pentecost

Psalm 90:12-17
Teach us to number our days

So teach us to count our days
> that we may gain a wise heart.

Turn, O Lord! How long?
> Have compassion on your servants!
Satisfy us in the morning with your steadfast love,
> so that we may rejoice and be glad all our days.
Make us glad as many days as you have afflicted us,
> and as many years as we have seen evil.
Let your work be manifest to your servants,
> and your glorious power to their children.
Let the favor of the Lord our God be upon us,
> and prosper for us the work of our hands—
> O prosper the work of our hands! (Ps. 90:12-17)

Additional Readings

Deuteronomy 5:1-21
The ten commandments

Hebrews 3:7-19
Against disobedience

Hymn: How Small Our Span of Life, ELW 636

O God our creator, each moment of our lives is a gift from you. Teach us to treasure our days and the graces with which you fill them. Strengthen our faith in your goodness even when we experience misfortune, loss, and grief.

Friday, October 12, 2018
Time after Pentecost

Deuteronomy 5:22-33
Moses meditates on God's word

The LORD heard your words when you spoke to me, and the LORD said to me: "I have heard the words of this people, which they have spoken to you; they are right in all that they have spoken. If only they had such a mind as this, to fear me and to keep all my commandments always, so that it might go well with them and with their children forever! Go say to them, 'Return to your tents.' But you, stand here by me, and I will tell you all the commandments, the statutes and the ordinances, that you shall teach them, so that they may do them in the land that I am giving them to possess." (Deut. 5:28-31)

Psalm
Psalm 90:12-17
Teach us to number our days

Additional Reading
Hebrews 4:1-11
The rest that God promised

Hymn: Praise, My Soul, the God of Heaven, ELW 864

Gracious God, all the nations of the world are in your hands. Send your voice of peace into the ears of leaders from every nation. Grant them your wisdom that they may govern with justice, mercy, and compassion on behalf of the common good.

Saturday, October 13, 2018
Time after Pentecost

Matthew 15:1-9
Jesus teaches true commandments

Then Pharisees and scribes came to Jesus from Jerusalem and said, "Why do your disciples break the tradition of the elders? For they do not wash their hands before they eat." He answered them, "And why do you break the commandment of God for the sake of your tradition? For God said, 'Honor your father and your mother,' and, 'Whoever speaks evil of father or mother must surely die.' But you say that whoever tells father or mother, 'Whatever support you might have had from me is given to God,' then that person need not honor the father. So, for the sake of your tradition, you make void the word of God." (Matt. 15:1-6)

Psalm
Psalm 90:12-17
Teach us to number our days

Additional Reading
Amos 3:13—4:5
Judgment against oppressors

Hymn: Our Father, by Whose Name, ELW 640

Ever-reforming God, you have guided your church through all the ages with your living, confronting, and transforming word. Break in on us once again and lead us with your voice.

Sunday, October 14, 2018
Time after Pentecost

Mark 10:17-31
Teaching on wealth and reward

Then Jesus looked around and said to his disciples, "How hard it will be for those who have wealth to enter the kingdom of God!" And the disciples were perplexed at these words. But Jesus said to them again, "Children, how hard it is to enter the kingdom of God! It is easier for a camel to go through the eye of a needle than for someone who is rich to enter the kingdom of God." They were greatly astounded and said to one another, "Then who can be saved?" Jesus looked at them and said, "For mortals it is impossible, but not for God; for God all things are possible." (Mark 10:23-27)

Psalm

Psalm 90:12-17
Teach us to number our days

Additional Readings

Amos 5:6-7, 10-15
Turn from injustice to the poor

Hebrews 4:12-16
Approach the throne of grace

Hymn: Son of God, Eternal Savior, ELW 655

Almighty and ever-living God, increase in us your gift of faith, that, forsaking what lies behind and reaching out to what lies ahead, we may follow the way of your commandments and receive the crown of everlasting joy, through Jesus Christ, our Savior and Lord.

Monday, October 15, 2018
Time after Pentecost

Teresa of Avila, teacher, renewer of the church, died 1582

Psalm 26
Prayer for acceptance

O Lord, I love the house in which you dwell,
    and the place where your glory abides.
Do not sweep me away with sinners,
    nor my life with the bloodthirsty,
those in whose hands are evil devices,
    and whose right hands are full of bribes.

But as for me, I walk in my integrity;
    redeem me, and be gracious to me.
My foot stands on level ground;
    in the great congregation I will bless the Lord. (Ps. 26:8-12)

Additional Readings
Obadiah 1-9
Those who ate your bread set a trap

Revelation 7:9-17
The nations stand before God's throne

Hymn: We Praise You, O God, ELW 870

Ever-present God, through the mouths of our sisters and brothers in Christ you communicate your powerful word of grace. Help us to appreciate the gift of your church and to remember those who live in solitude, without support or companionship.

Tuesday, October 16, 2018
Time after Pentecost

Revelation 8:1-5
The saints' prayers before God

When the Lamb opened the seventh seal, there was silence in heaven for about half an hour. And I saw the seven angels who stand before God, and seven trumpets were given to them.

Another angel with a golden censer came and stood at the altar; he was given a great quantity of incense to offer with the prayers of all the saints on the golden altar that is before the throne. And the smoke of the incense, with the prayers of the saints, rose before God from the hand of the angel. Then the angel took the censer and filled it with fire from the altar and threw it on the earth; and there were peals of thunder, rumblings, flashes of lightning, and an earthquake. (Rev. 8:1-5)

Psalm
Psalm 26
Prayer for acceptance

Additional Reading
Obadiah 10-16
Do not gloat over another's misfortune

Hymn: Evening and Morning, ELW 761

Lord of the heavenly host, your power echoes through the universe and shakes the foundations of the earth, yet as a loving parent you tenderly invite us to lift our prayers before you. Stoke in us the desire to come to you with every need.

Wednesday, October 17, 2018
Time after Pentecost

Ignatius, Bishop of Antioch, martyr, died around 115

Obadiah 17-21
The dispossessed shall possess the land

But on Mount Zion there shall be those that escape,
>and it shall be holy;

and the house of Jacob shall take possession of those who dispossessed
>them.

The house of Jacob shall be a fire,
>the house of Joseph a flame,

>and the house of Esau stubble;

they shall burn them and consume them,
>and there shall be no survivor of the house of Esau;

>>for the LORD has spoken. (Obad. 17-18)

Psalm
Psalm 26
Prayer for acceptance

Additional Reading
Luke 16:19-31
Lazarus comforted by Abraham

Hymn: To Be Your Presence, ELW 546

God of the displaced, you call your people to remember that we were once slaves in Egypt. Rouse us to show compassion to immigrants and refugees, and to others without homes, that by our hospitality they would come to know the mercy of your embrace.

Thursday, October 18, 2018
Luke, Evangelist

Luke 1:1-4; 24:44-53
Luke witnesses to the ministry of Jesus

Since many have undertaken to set down an orderly account of the events that have been fulfilled among us, just as they were handed on to us by those who from the beginning were eyewitnesses and servants of the word, I too decided, after investigating everything carefully from the very first, to write an orderly account for you, most excellent Theophilus, so that you may know the truth concerning the things about which you have been instructed. (Luke 1:1-4)

Psalm

Psalm 124
Our help is in God

Additional Readings

Isaiah 43:8-13
You are my witness

2 Timothy 4:5-11
The good fight of faith

Hymn: O Christ, the Healer, We Have Come, ELW 610

Almighty God, you inspired your servant Luke to reveal in his gospel the love and healing power of your Son. Give your church the same love and power to heal, and to proclaim your salvation among the nations to the glory of your name, through Jesus Christ, your Son, our healer, who lives and reigns with you and the Holy Spirit, one God, now and forever.

Friday, October 19, 2018
Time after Pentecost

Psalm 91:9-16
The Most High, your refuge

Because you have made the LORD your refuge,
     the Most High your dwelling place,
no evil shall befall you,
     no scourge come near your tent.

For he will command his angels concerning you
     to guard you in all your ways.
On their hands they will bear you up,
     so that you will not dash your foot against a stone.
You will tread on the lion and the adder,
     the young lion and the serpent you will trample under foot.
(Ps. 91:9-13)

Additional Reading
Isaiah 47:1-9
Throneless nations

Revelation 17:1-18
Earth's kings conquered

Hymn: If God My Lord Be for Me, ELW 788

Life-giving God, from the moment of each birth to the moment of each death you are with us. In the coos of infants, the discoveries of youth, the labors of adulthood, and the focused movements of elders, grant us your vision throughout the journeys of our lives.

Saturday, October 20, 2018
Time after Pentecost

Luke 22:24-30
The greatness of one who serves

A dispute also arose among the apostles as to which one of them was to be regarded as the greatest. But [Jesus] said to them, "The kings of the Gentiles lord it over them; and those in authority over them are called benefactors. But not so with you; rather the greatest among you must become like the youngest, and the leader like one who serves. For who is greater, the one who is at the table or the one who serves? Is it not the one at the table? But I am among you as one who serves.

"You are those who have stood by me in my trials; and I confer on you, just as my Father has conferred on me, a kingdom, so that you may eat and drink at my table in my kingdom, and you will sit on thrones judging the twelve tribes of Israel." (Luke 22:24-30)

Psalm
Psalm 91:9-16
The Most High, your refuge

Additional Reading
Isaiah 47:10-15
Futile trust in those who cannot save

Hymn: Lord, Whose Love in Humble Service, ELW 712

God of grace, you have poured out wondrous gifts on all your people to set your grace at work through our many callings. Grant us joy and courage to use all that you have given us for the building up of your kingdom and a vision to see our purpose within your great design.

Sunday, October 21, 2018
Time after Pentecost

Mark 10:35-45

Warnings to ambitious disciples

James and John, the sons of Zebedee, came forward to [Jesus] and said to him, "Teacher, we want you to do for us whatever we ask of you." And he said to them, "What is it you want me to do for you?" And they said to him, "Grant us to sit, one at your right hand and one at your left, in your glory." But Jesus said to them, "You do not know what you are asking. Are you able to drink the cup that I drink, or be baptized with the baptism that I am baptized with?" They replied, "We are able." Then Jesus said to them, "The cup that I drink you will drink; and with the baptism with which I am baptized, you will be baptized; but to sit at my right hand or at my left is not mine to grant, but it is for those for whom it has been prepared." (Mark 10:35-40)

Psalm

Psalm 91:9-16
The Most High, your refuge

Additional Readings

Isaiah 53:4-12
The suffering servant

Hebrews 5:1-10
Through suffering Christ saves

Hymn: O Christ, What Can It Mean for Us, ELW 431

Sovereign God, you turn your greatness into goodness for all the peoples on earth. Shape us into willing servants of your kingdom, and make us desire always and only your will, through Jesus Christ, our Savior and Lord.

Monday, October 22, 2018
Time after Pentecost

Psalm 37:23-40

God will exalt the righteous

I have been young, and now am old,
>   yet I have not seen the righteous forsaken
>   or their children begging bread.
They are ever giving liberally and lending,
>   and their children become a blessing.

Depart from evil, and do good;
>   so you shall abide forever.
For the LORD loves justice;
>   he will not forsake his faithful ones.

The righteous shall be kept safe forever,
>   but the children of the wicked shall be cut off.
The righteous shall inherit the land,
>   and live in it forever. (Ps. 37:25-29)

Additional Readings
1 Samuel 8:1-18
Samuel warns against kings

Hebrews 6:1-12
The peril of falling away

Hymn: Let Streams of Living Justice, ELW 710

Gracious God, you cause rain to fall on the just and the unjust alike, providing all that we need out of the generosity of your heart. Make us your tools to provide food, clothing, and shelter to those who are most vulnerable in our communities.

Tuesday, October 23, 2018
Time after Pentecost

James of Jerusalem, martyr, died around 62

1 Samuel 10:17-25

Saul proclaimed king

Then Samuel brought all the tribes of Israel near, and the tribe of Benjamin was taken by lot. He brought the tribe of Benjamin near by its families, and the family of the Matrites was taken by lot. Finally he brought the family of the Matrites near man by man, and Saul the son of Kish was taken by lot. But when they sought him, he could not be found. So they inquired again of the LORD, "Did the man come here?" and the LORD said, "See, he has hidden himself among the baggage." Then they ran and brought him from there. When he took his stand among the people, he was head and shoulders taller than any of them. Samuel said to all the people, "Do you see the one whom the LORD has chosen? There is no one like him among all the people." And all the people shouted, "Long live the king!" (1 Sam. 10:20-24)

Psalm
Psalm 37:23-40
God will exalt the righteous

Additional Reading
Hebrews 6:13-20
The hope of God's promise

Hymn: Give to Our God Immortal Praise! ELW 848

Mothering God, through our civil authorities you seek to protect all people and care for the needs of those living on the edges of our society. Raise up leaders who will exercise your justice, mercy, and compassion on behalf of the common good.

Wednesday, October 24, 2018
Time after Pentecost

John 13:1-17
Jesus washes the disciples' feet

And during supper Jesus, knowing that the Father had given all things into his hands, and that he had come from God and was going to God, got up from the table, took off his outer robe, and tied a towel around himself. Then he poured water into a basin and began to wash the disciples' feet and to wipe them with the towel that was tied around him. He came to Simon Peter, who said to him, "Lord, are you going to wash my feet?" Jesus answered, "You do not know now what I am doing, but later you will understand." Peter said to him, "You will never wash my feet." Jesus answered, "Unless I wash you, you have no share with me." (John 13:2b-8)

Psalm
Psalm 37:23-40
God will exalt the righteous

Additional Reading
1 Samuel 12:1-25
Israel admonished to fear God

Hymn: Jesu, Jesu, Fill Us with Your Love, ELW 708

Lord God, you sent your Son among us as one who serves. Give us servant hearts that seek not to be served but to serve. Grant that we may follow the example of your Son, keeping his commandment to love one another.

Thursday, October 25, 2018
Time after Pentecost

Psalm 126
Sowing with tears, reaping with joy

Restore our fortunes, O Lord,
    like the watercourses in the Negeb.
May those who sow in tears
    reap with shouts of joy.
Those who go out weeping,
    bearing the seed for sowing,
shall come home with shouts of joy,
    carrying their sheaves. (Ps. 126:4-6)

Additional Readings
Jeremiah 23:9-15
False prophets of hope denounced

Hebrews 7:1-10
The priestly order of Melchizedek

Hymn: Sing to the Lord of Harvest, ELW 694

Lord of the harvest, from the abundance of the earth you bring forth all that we need to sustain our lives. Bless the work of all who steward these gifts from farm to table, and lead us to share our plenty with all who suffer from hunger.

Friday, October 26, 2018
Time after Pentecost

Philipp Nicolai, died 1608; Johann Heermann, died 1647; Paul Gerhardt, died 1676; hymnwriters

Hebrews 7:11-22
Jesus is like Melchizedek

Now if perfection had been attainable through the levitical priesthood—for the people received the law under this priesthood—what further need would there have been to speak of another priest arising according to the order of Melchizedek, rather than one according to the order of Aaron? For when there is a change in the priesthood, there is necessarily a change in the law as well. Now the one of whom these things are spoken belonged to another tribe, from which no one has ever served at the altar. For it is evident that our Lord was descended from Judah, and in connection with that tribe Moses said nothing about priests. (Heb. 7:11-14)

Psalm
Psalm 126
Sowing with tears, reaping with joy

Additional Reading
Jeremiah 26:12-24
Jeremiah threatened with death

Hymn: Soli Deo Gloria, ELW 878

Shepherding God, you have led the church through many generations by raising up leaders among us. Support our spiritual leaders today—bishops, pastors, deacons, and lay workers—giving them wisdom and vision to lead us in your ways.

Saturday, October 27, 2018
Time after Pentecost

Mark 8:22-26
Jesus heals a blind man

[Jesus and the disciples] came to Bethsaida. Some people brought a blind man to [Jesus] and begged him to touch him. He took the blind man by the hand and led him out of the village; and when he had put saliva on his eyes and laid his hands on him, he asked him, "Can you see anything?" And the man looked up and said, "I can see people, but they look like trees, walking." Then Jesus laid his hands on his eyes again; and he looked intently and his sight was restored, and he saw everything clearly. Then he sent him away to his home, saying, "Do not even go into the village." (Mark 8:22-26)

Psalm
Psalm 126
Sowing with tears, reaping with joy

Additional Reading
Jeremiah 29:24-32
A false prophet exposed by Jeremiah

Hymn: Amazing Grace, How Sweet the Sound, ELW 779

Merciful God, pour out your gifts of healing on your church and on this world. Raise up among us people with gifts to bind up the aches in our bodies, minds, and communities and to transform the world by your grace.

Sunday, October 28, 2018
Time after Pentecost

Simon and Jude, Apostles (transferred to October 29)

Mark 10:46-52
Christ heals blind Bartimaeus

[Jesus and the disciples] came to Jericho. As [Jesus] and his disciples and a large crowd were leaving Jericho, Bartimaeus son of Timaeus, a blind beggar, was sitting by the roadside. When he heard that it was Jesus of Nazareth, he began to shout out and say, "Jesus, Son of David, have mercy on me!" Many sternly ordered him to be quiet, but he cried out even more loudly, "Son of David, have mercy on me!" Jesus stood still and said, "Call him here." And they called the blind man, saying to him, "Take heart; get up, he is calling you." So throwing off his cloak, he sprang up and came to Jesus. Then Jesus said to him, "What do you want me to do for you?" The blind man said to him, "My teacher, let me see again." Jesus said to him, "Go; your faith has made you well." Immediately he regained his sight and followed him on the way. (Mark 10:46-52)

Psalm

Psalm 126
Sowing with tears, reaping with joy

Additional Readings

Jeremiah 31:7-9
The remnant of Israel is gathered

Hebrews 7:23-28
Christ, the merciful high priest

Hymn: Rise, Shine, You People! ELW 665

Eternal light, shine in our hearts. Eternal wisdom, scatter the darkness of our ignorance. Eternal compassion, have mercy on us. Turn us to seek your face, and enable us to reflect your goodness, through Jesus Christ, our Savior and Lord.

Monday, October 29, 2018
Simon and Jude, Apostles (transferred)

John 14:21-27

Those who love Jesus will keep his word

[Jesus said,] "They who have my commandments and keep them are
those who love me; and those who love me will be loved by my Father,
and I will love them and reveal myself to them." Judas (not Iscariot)
said to him, "Lord, how is it that you will reveal yourself to us, and not
to the world?" Jesus answered him, "Those who love me will keep my
word, and my Father will love them, and we will come to them and
make our home with them. Whoever does not love me does not keep my
words; and the word that you hear is not mine, but is from the Father
who sent me." (John 14:21-24)

Psalm

Psalm 11
Take refuge in God

Additional Readings

**Jeremiah 26:[1-6]
7-16**
*Jeremiah promises the
judgment of God*

1 John 4:1-6
*Do not believe every spirit of
this world*

Hymn: Rejoice in God's Saints, ELW 418

*O God, we thank you for the glorious company of the apostles, and especially
on this day for Simon and Jude. We pray that, as they were faithful and
zealous in your mission, so we may with ardent devotion make known the
love and mercy of our Savior, Jesus Christ, who lives and reigns with you
and the Holy Spirit, one God, now and forever.*

Tuesday, October 30, 2018
Time after Pentecost

Psalm 119:17-24
Open my eyes

Deal bountifully with your servant,
    so that I may live and observe your word.
Open my eyes, so that I may behold
    wondrous things out of your law.
I live as an alien in the land;
    do not hide your commandments from me.
My soul is consumed with longing
    for your ordinances at all times. (Ps. 119:17-20)

Additional Readings
2 Kings 6:8-23
Elisha has power over sight

Acts 9:32-35
The healing of Aeneas

Hymn: Healer of Our Every Ill, ELW 612

*God of living waters, through the gift of baptism you draw new people
of faith into your body. Grant that the small seeds of faith being planted
throughout the church would yield great fruit among us in years to come.*

Wednesday, October 31, 2018
Reformation Day

Romans 3:19-28
Justified by God's grace as a gift

But now, apart from law, the righteousness of God has been disclosed, and is attested by the law and the prophets, the righteousness of God through faith in Jesus Christ for all who believe. For there is no distinction, since all have sinned and fall short of the glory of God; they are now justified by his grace as a gift, through the redemption that is in Christ Jesus, whom God put forward as a sacrifice of atonement by his blood, effective through faith. He did this to show his righteousness, because in his divine forbearance he had passed over the sins previously committed; it was to prove at the present time that he himself is righteous and that he justifies the one who has faith in Jesus. (Rom. 3:21-26)

Psalm

Psalm 46
The God of Jacob is our stronghold

Additional Readings

Jeremiah 31:31-34
I will write my law in their hearts

John 8:31-36
The truth will set you free

Hymn: The Church of Christ, in Every Age, ELW 729

Almighty God, gracious Lord, we thank you that your Holy Spirit renews the church in every age. Pour out your Holy Spirit on your faithful people. Keep them steadfast in your word, protect and comfort them in times of trial, defend them against all enemies of the gospel, and bestow on the church your saving peace, through Jesus Christ, our Savior and Lord, who lives and reigns with you and the Holy Spirit, one God, now and forever.

Prayer List for November

_____

_____

_____

_____

_____

_____

_____

_____

_____

_____

Time after Pentecost
November

The month of November is unique in that it begins with All Saints Day (November 1) and ends with the feast of Christ the King (often the last Sunday of November). The Sunday and daily readings seem to extend the harvest, but in a new way: they speak of God's harvest of human beings into their heavenly home.

Perhaps it is no coincidence that November's scriptural emphasis on the consummation of all things in Christ is reflected in the landscape and the chilling temperatures. Yet in the midst of this turning of the seasons and the reminders of death's presence, Christians hold forth the central feast of the year: the death and resurrection of Christ present in baptism and the holy supper. In these last days of the church's year, Christians are invited to celebrate the reign of Christ, whose death on the cross has transformed our deaths into the gate of everlasting life.

Table Prayer for November

Stay with us, God of life,
as we share the bounty of this food and drink.
We give you thanks for those who have gone before us in faith.
Bring us, with them, to the harvest of everlasting life,
where all people will feast forever at your abundant table.
We ask this through Christ our Lord. Amen.

Remembering Those Who Have Died

Use this prayer in the home or at the grave.

O God, our help in ages past and our hope for years to come:
We give you thanks for all your faithful people
who have followed the light of your word throughout the centuries
into our time and place.

Here individual names may be spoken.

As we remember these people,
strengthen us to follow Christ through this world
until we are carried into the harvest of eternal life,
where suffering and death will be no more.
Hear our prayer in the name of the good and gracious shepherd,
Jesus Christ, our Savior and Lord. Amen.

or

With reverence and affection we remember before you,
O everlasting God,
all our departed friends and relatives.
Keep us in union with them here
through faith and love toward you,
that hereafter we may enter into your presence
and be numbered with those who serve you
and look upon your face in glory everlasting,
through your Son, Jesus Christ our Lord. Amen.

Thursday, November 1, 2018
All Saints Day

John 11:32-44
The raising of Lazarus

So they took away the stone. And Jesus looked upward and said, "Father, I thank you for having heard me. I knew that you always hear me, but I have said this for the sake of the crowd standing here, so that they may believe that you sent me." When he had said this, he cried with a loud voice, "Lazarus, come out!" The dead man came out, his hands and feet bound with strips of cloth, and his face wrapped in a cloth. Jesus said to them, "Unbind him, and let him go." (John 11:41-44)

Psalm

Psalm 24
They shall receive a blessing from God

Additional Readings

Isaiah 25:6-9
A feast of rich foods

Revelation 21:1-6a
A new heaven and a new earth

Hymn: Behold the Host Arrayed in White, ELW 425

Almighty God, you have knit your people together in one communion in the mystical body of your Son, Jesus Christ our Lord. Grant us grace to follow your blessed saints in lives of faith and commitment, and to know the inexpressible joys you have prepared for those who love you, through Jesus Christ, our Savior and Lord, who lives and reigns with you and the Holy Spirit, one God, now and forever.

Friday, November 2, 2018
Time after Pentecost

Psalm 119:1-8

Seeking God with all our hearts

Happy are those whose way is blameless,
  who walk in the law of the LORD.
Happy are those who keep his decrees,
  who seek him with their whole heart,
who also do no wrong,
  but walk in his ways. (Ps. 119:1-3)

Additional Readings

Leviticus 19:32-37
Aliens to be treated as fellow citizens

Romans 3:21-31
Atonement through Christ's blood

Hymn: When the Poor Ones, ELW 725

O God, you teach us to love you and each other, not for salvation, but for the joy of walking in your ways. Inspire us to grow in faith. Ignite our passion to serve for justice. Increase our thankfulness.

Saturday, November 3, 2018
Time after Pentecost

Martín de Porres, renewer of society, died 1639

Numbers 9:9-14
The same statute for all

The LORD spoke to Moses, saying: Speak to the Israelites, saying: Anyone of you or your descendants who is unclean through touching a corpse, or is away on a journey, shall still keep the passover to the LORD. In the second month on the fourteenth day, at twilight, they shall keep it; they shall eat it with unleavened bread and bitter herbs. They shall leave none of it until morning, nor break a bone of it; according to all the statute for the passover they shall keep it. But anyone who is clean and is not on a journey, and yet refrains from keeping the passover, shall be cut off from the people for not presenting the LORD's offering at its appointed time; such a one shall bear the consequences for the sin. Any alien residing among you who wishes to keep the passover to the LORD shall do so according to the statute of the passover and according to its regulation; you shall have one statute for both the resident alien and the native. (Num. 9:9-14)

Psalm
Psalm 119:1-8
Seeking God with all our hearts

Additional Reading
Luke 10:25-37
Who is my neighbor?

Hymn: In Christ There Is No East or West, ELW 650

God of all, under the cross of your Son, Jesus Christ, all are equal; there is no "us" and "them." Forgive our miserly devotion to you and territorial self-centeredness toward others. Expand the maps of our hearts with abundant love.

Sunday, November 4, 2018
Time after Pentecost

Mark 12:28-34

Two commandments: love God and neighbor

One of the scribes came near and heard some Sadducees disputing with one another, and seeing that [Jesus] answered them well, he asked him, "Which commandment is the first of all?" Jesus answered, "The first is, 'Hear, O Israel: the Lord our God, the Lord is one; you shall love the Lord your God with all your heart, and with all your soul, and with all your mind, and with all your strength.' The second is this, 'You shall love your neighbor as yourself.' There is no other commandment greater than these." (Mark 12:28-31)

Psalm

Psalm 119:1-8
Seeking God with all our hearts

Additional Readings

Deuteronomy 6:1-9
Keeping the words of God

Hebrews 9:11-14
Redeemed through Christ's blood

Hymn: Lord, Thee I Love with All My Heart, ELW 750

Almighty God, you have taught us in your Son that love fulfills the law. Inspire us to love you with all our heart, our soul, our mind, and our strength, and teach us how to love our neighbor as ourselves, through Jesus Christ, our Savior and Lord.

Monday, November 5, 2018
Time after Pentecost

Psalm 51
A contrite heart

Have mercy on me, O God,
>   according to your steadfast love;
according to your abundant mercy
>   blot out my transgressions.
Wash me thoroughly from my iniquity,
>   and cleanse me from my sin.

For I know my transgressions,
>   and my sin is ever before me.
Against you, you alone, have I sinned,
>   and done what is evil in your sight,
so that you are justified in your sentence
>   and blameless when you pass judgment.
Indeed, I was born guilty,
>   a sinner when my mother conceived me. (Ps. 51:1-5)

Additional Readings
Deuteronomy 6:10-25
Keeping the commandments

Romans 12:17-21; 13:8-10
Love does no wrong to a neighbor

Hymn: Lord Jesus Christ, Be Present Now, ELW 527

O God, we come to you humbled and ashamed. We confess our sinful actions and inactions, how we cause pain and break trust. We beg for your mercy and forgiveness. Help us turn around and right our ways.

Tuesday, November 6, 2018
Time after Pentecost

Deuteronomy 28:58—29:1
Warnings against disobedience

If you do not diligently observe all the words of this law that are written in this book, fearing this glorious and awesome name, the LORD your God, then the LORD will overwhelm both you and your offspring with severe and lasting afflictions and grievous and lasting maladies. He will bring back upon you all the diseases of Egypt, of which you were in dread, and they shall cling to you. Every other malady and affliction, even though not recorded in the book of this law, the LORD will inflict on you until you are destroyed. Although once you were as numerous as the stars in heaven, you shall be left few in number, because you did not obey the LORD your God. (Deut. 28:58-62)

Psalm
Psalm 51
A contrite heart

Additional Reading
Acts 7:17-29
Moses becomes a resident alien

Hymn: Jesus Loves Me! ELW 595

Mighty and merciful God, the brokenness in our lives can seem beyond repair and you can seem far away. Undeserving, we still dare to trust in your unfailing love and pray for renewed hope and restored relationships.

Wednesday, November 7, 2018
Time after Pentecost

John Christian Frederick Heyer, died 1873; Bartholomaeus Ziegenbalg, died 1719;
Ludwig Nommensen, died 1918; missionaries

Micah 6:1-8
Do justice

"With what shall I come before the LORD,
  and bow myself before God on high?
Shall I come before him with burnt offerings,
  with calves a year old?
Will the LORD be pleased with thousands of rams,
  with ten thousands of rivers of oil?
Shall I give my firstborn for my transgression,
  the fruit of my body for the sin of my soul?"
He has told you, O mortal, what is good;
  and what does the LORD require of you
but to do justice, and to love kindness,
  and to walk humbly with your God? (Micah 6:6-8)

Psalm
Psalm 51
A contrite heart

Additional Reading
John 13:31-35
Commandment to love one another

Hymn: Rise Up, O Saints of God! ELW 669

*Glory to you, O God! With our salvation secured by your Son, Jesus Christ,
we are freed to focus on what is good just for the joy of it: doing justice,
loving kindness, and walking humbly with you.*

Thursday, November 8, 2018
Time after Pentecost

Psalm 146
God lifts those bowed down

The LORD sets the prisoners free;
    the LORD opens the eyes of the blind.
The LORD lifts up those who are bowed down;
    the LORD loves the righteous.
The LORD watches over the strangers;
    he upholds the orphan and the widow,
    but the way of the wicked he brings to ruin.

The LORD will reign forever,
    your God, O Zion, for all generations.
Praise the LORD! (Ps. 146:7c-10)

Additional Readings
Numbers 36:1-13
Women spared from poverty

Romans 5:6-11
Justified by Christ's blood

Hymn: When Our Song Says Peace, ELW 709

God of love and justice, you call us to your holy mission: lift those brought low, protect the vulnerable, and free the oppressed. Bless us with the faithful courage and compassion to live into your heavenly kingdom on earth.

Friday, November 9, 2018
Time after Pentecost

Deuteronomy 15:1-11
Open your hand to the poor

If there is among you anyone in need, a member of your community in any of your towns within the land that the LORD your God is giving you, do not be hard-hearted or tight-fisted toward your needy neighbor. You should rather open your hand, willingly lending enough to meet the need, whatever it may be. Be careful that you do not entertain a mean thought, thinking, "The seventh year, the year of remission, is near," and therefore view your needy neighbor with hostility and give nothing; your neighbor might cry to the LORD against you, and you would incur guilt. Give liberally and be ungrudging when you do so, for on this account the LORD your God will bless you in all your work and in all that you undertake. Since there will never cease to be some in need on the earth, I therefore command you, "Open your hand to the poor and needy neighbor in your land." (Deut. 15:7-11)

Psalm
Psalm 146
God lifts those bowed down

Additional Reading
Hebrews 9:15-24
The blood of the old covenant

Hymn: Hear I Am, Lord, ELW 574

Abundant God, the source of all we enjoy, free us from our selfish and self-righteous stinginess. Open our hearts and hands to generously, liberally, and ungrudgingly see and meet the needs of neighbors known and unknown.

Saturday, November 10, 2018
Time after Pentecost

Mark 11:12-14, 20-24
Condemnation and blessing

In the morning as [Jesus and the disciples] passed by, they saw the fig tree withered away to its roots. Then Peter remembered and said to him, "Rabbi, look! The fig tree that you cursed has withered." Jesus answered them, "Have faith in God. Truly I tell you, if you say to this mountain, 'Be taken up and thrown into the sea,' and if you do not doubt in your heart, but believe that what you say will come to pass, it will be done for you. So I tell you, whatever you ask for in prayer, believe that you have received it, and it will be yours." (Mark 11:20-24)

Psalm
Psalm 146
God lifts those bowed down

Additional Reading
Deuteronomy 24:17-22
Laws concerning the poor

Hymn: What a Friend We Have in Jesus, ELW 742

O God, you promise to hear and answer prayer. When we are too scared or sad to pray, you send your Spirit to intercede for us. Help us draw closer to you with prayers of adoration, confession, thanksgiving, and supplication.

Sunday, November 11, 2018
Time after Pentecost

Martin, Bishop of Tours, died 397
Søren Aabye Kierkegaard, teacher, died 1855

Mark 12:38-44

A widow's generosity

[Jesus] sat down opposite the treasury, and watched the crowd putting money into the treasury. Many rich people put in large sums. A poor widow came and put in two small copper coins, which are worth a penny. Then he called his disciples and said to them, "Truly I tell you, this poor widow has put in more than all those who are contributing to the treasury. For all of them have contributed out of their abundance; but she out of her poverty has put in everything she had, all she had to live on." (Mark 12:41-44)

Psalm

Psalm 146
God lifts those bowed down

Additional Readings

1 Kings 17:8-16
God feeds Elijah and the widow

Hebrews 9:24-28
The sacrifice of Christ

Hymn: Take My Life, That I May Be, ELW 583/685

O God, you show forth your almighty power chiefly by reaching out to us in mercy. Grant us the fullness of your grace, strengthen our trust in your promises, and bring all the world to share in the treasures that come through your Son, Jesus Christ, our Savior and Lord.

Monday, November 12, 2018
Time after Pentecost

Psalm 94
God will vindicate the righteous

Happy are those whom you discipline, O Lord,
　　and whom you teach out of your law,
giving them respite from days of trouble,
　　until a pit is dug for the wicked.
For the Lord will not forsake his people;
　　he will not abandon his heritage;
for justice will return to the righteous,
　　and all the upright in heart will follow it. (Ps. 94:12-15)

Additional Readings
Ruth 1:1-22
The widow's poverty

1 Timothy 5:1-8
Widows set their hope on God

Hymn: Let Justice Flow like Streams, ELW 717

God of the weary and weak, we know you are with us. You bless us with a passion for justice. When might continually triumphs over right, and when our efforts seem fruitless, grant us faith, courage, and patience.

Tuesday, November 13, 2018
Time after Pentecost

1 Timothy 5:9-16
The church assists widows

Let a widow be put on the list if she is not less than sixty years old and
has been married only once; she must be well attested for her good
works, as one who has brought up children, shown hospitality, washed
the saints' feet, helped the afflicted, and devoted herself to doing good
in every way. But refuse to put younger widows on the list; for when
their sensual desires alienate them from Christ, they want to marry,
and so they incur condemnation for having violated their first pledge.
Besides that, they learn to be idle, gadding about from house to house;
and they are not merely idle, but also gossips and busybodies, saying
what they should not say. So I would have younger widows marry, bear
children, and manage their households, so as to give the adversary
no occasion to revile us. For some have already turned away to follow
Satan. If any believing woman has relatives who are really widows, let
her assist them; let the church not be burdened, so that it can assist
those who are real widows. (1 Tim. 5:9-16)

Psalm
Psalm 94
God will vindicate the righteous

Additional Reading
Ruth 3:14—4:6
The widow's next of kin receive her

Hymn: Will You Let Me Be Your Servant, ELW 659

*Abundant God, you bless us to generously give as we are able, and to
graciously receive as we need. Thank you for the faithful community that
bears one another's burdens and shares each other's joys.*

Wednesday, November 14, 2018
Time after Pentecost

Luke 4:16-30
Jesus praises a foreign widow

And [Jesus] said, "Truly I tell you, no prophet is accepted in the prophet's hometown. But the truth is, there were many widows in Israel in the time of Elijah, when the heaven was shut up three years and six months, and there was a severe famine over all the land; yet Elijah was sent to none of them except to a widow at Zarephath in Sidon. There were also many lepers in Israel in the time of the prophet Elisha, and none of them was cleansed except Naaman the Syrian." (Luke 4:24-27)

Psalm
Psalm 94
God will vindicate the righteous

Additional Reading
Ruth 4:7-22
The widow's life restored

Hymn: In Christ There Is No East or West, ELW 650

Forgive our holier-than-the-other arrogance, Almighty God, and bless us with the humble, grateful awareness of unmerited grace. When preaching and teaching makes us uncomfortable, open us to your good news. Help us understand and faithfully respond.

Thursday, November 15, 2018
Time after Pentecost

Psalm 16
My heart is glad

I bless the LORD who gives me counsel;
>   in the night also my heart instructs me.
I keep the LORD always before me;
>   because he is at my right hand, I shall not be moved.

Therefore my heart is glad, and my soul rejoices;
>   my body also rests secure.
For you do not give me up to Sheol,
>   or let your faithful one see the Pit. (Ps. 16:7-10)

Additional Readings
Daniel 4:4-18
Nebuchadnezzar's dream

1 Timothy 6:11-21
Life that really is life

Hymn: Sing Praise to God, the Highest Good, ELW 871

We adore you, O God, source of abundant and eternal life. We thank you for the comfort, counsel, and courage of your Holy Spirit. We joyfully claim our inheritance as your beloved, freed by grace to boldly love and serve.

Friday, November 16, 2018
Time after Pentecost

Daniel 4:19-27
Nebuchadnezzar's dream interpreted

"You shall be driven away from human society, and your dwelling shall be with the wild animals. You shall be made to eat grass like oxen, you shall be bathed with the dew of heaven, and seven times shall pass over you, until you have learned that the Most High has sovereignty over the kingdom of mortals, and gives it to whom he will. As it was commanded to leave the stump and roots of the tree, your kingdom shall be re-established for you from the time that you learn that Heaven is sovereign. Therefore, O king, may my counsel be acceptable to you: atone for your sins with righteousness, and your iniquities with mercy to the oppressed, so that your prosperity may be prolonged." (Dan. 4:25-27)

Psalm
Psalm 16
My heart is glad

Additional Reading
Colossians 2:6-15
Christ, the head of every ruler and authority

Hymn: Rise, O Sun of Righteousness, ELW 657

Sovereign God, when we are tempted by the vain glories of this world's power and prestige, trouble our consciences to care for creation and people in need. Bless us to understand that you, and you alone, are God.

Saturday, November 17, 2018
Time after Pentecost

Elizabeth of Hungary, renewer of society, died 1231

Mark 12:1-12

The stone which the builders rejected

Jesus said, "Have you not read this scripture:
'The stone that the builders rejected
  has become the cornerstone;
this was the Lord's doing,
  and it is amazing in our eyes'?"

When they realized that he had told this parable against them, they wanted to arrest him, but they feared the crowd. So they left him and went away. (Mark 12:10-12)

Psalm

Psalm 16
My heart is glad

Additional Reading

Daniel 4:28-37
Nebuchadnezzar praises God

Hymn: Christ Is Made the Sure Foundation, ELW 645

God of power and might, we approach your throne with confidence and fear, awed by your amazing work in the world. Thank you for the gift of your Son, Jesus Christ, the cornerstone and foundation of our faith.

Sunday, November 18, 2018
Time after Pentecost

Mark 13:1-8
The end and the coming of the Son

As [Jesus] came out of the temple, one of his disciples said to him, "Look, Teacher, what large stones and what large buildings!" Then Jesus asked him, "Do you see these great buildings? Not one stone will be left here upon another; all will be thrown down."

When he was sitting on the Mount of Olives opposite the temple, Peter, James, John, and Andrew asked him privately, "Tell us, when will this be, and what will be the sign that all these things are about to be accomplished?" Then Jesus began to say to them, "Beware that no one leads you astray. Many will come in my name and say, 'I am he!' and they will lead many astray. When you hear of wars and rumors of wars, do not be alarmed; this must take place, but the end is still to come. For nation will rise against nation, and kingdom against kingdom; there will be earthquakes in various places; there will be famines. This is but the beginning of the birth pangs." (Mark 13:1-8)

Psalm
Psalm 16
My heart is glad

Additional Readings
Daniel 12:1-3
God will deliver the people

Hebrews 10:11-14
[15-18] 19-25
The way to God through Christ

Hymn: Through the Night of Doubt and Sorrow, ELW 327

Almighty God, your sovereign purpose brings salvation to birth. Give us faith to be steadfast amid the tumults of this world, trusting that your kingdom comes and your will is done through your Son, Jesus Christ, our Savior and Lord.

Monday, November 19, 2018
Time after Pentecost

Psalm 13
Prayer for salvation

Consider and answer me, O LORD my God!
>   Give light to my eyes, or I will sleep the sleep of death,
and my enemy will say, "I have prevailed";
>   my foes will rejoice because I am shaken.

But I trusted in your steadfast love;
>   my heart shall rejoice in your salvation.
I will sing to the LORD,
>   because he has dealt bountifully with me. (Ps. 13:3-6)

Additional Readings
Daniel 8:1-14
A vision of destructive power

Hebrews 10:26-31
Falling into the hands of the living God

Hymn: You Servants of God, ELW 825

O God, you are big enough to hear our laments, even when we shake our fists in prayer, demand attention, and ask, "Why?" Have compassion on us when we are weak and hurting. Help us feel your loving presence.

Tuesday, November 20, 2018
Time after Pentecost

Hebrews 10:32-39
Call for endurance

But recall those earlier days when, after you had been enlightened, you endured a hard struggle with sufferings, sometimes being publicly exposed to abuse and persecution, and sometimes being partners with those so treated. For you had compassion for those who were in prison, and you cheerfully accepted the plundering of your possessions, knowing that you yourselves possessed something better and more lasting. Do not, therefore, abandon that confidence of yours; it brings a great reward. For you need endurance, so that when you have done the will of God, you may receive what was promised. (Heb. 10:32-36)

Psalm
Psalm 13
Prayer for salvation

Additional Reading
Daniel 8:15-27
Signs of the end times

Hymn: How Firm a Foundation, ELW 796

God of all, you love us as we are. You see our flashes of faithful confidence and hear our whispers of faithful doubt. For the encouragement of Christian community, for the witness of generations of believers, thank you.

Wednesday, November 21, 2018
Time after Pentecost

Zechariah 12:1—13:1
The future of Jerusalem

And the Lord will give victory to the tents of Judah first, that the glory of the house of David and the glory of the inhabitants of Jerusalem may not be exalted over that of Judah. On that day the Lord will shield the inhabitants of Jerusalem so that the feeblest among them on that day shall be like David, and the house of David shall be like God, like the angel of the Lord, at their head. And on that day I will seek to destroy all the nations that come against Jerusalem. (Zech. 12:7-9)

Psalm
Psalm 13
Prayer for salvation

Additional Reading
Mark 13:9-23
The coming sufferings

Hymn: Jerusalem, My Happy Home, ELW 628

Forever God, we live and die and live again in you. Give comfort and courage to those who suffer, those who long for your heavenly kingdom, and those who live into your heavenly kingdom here on earth.

Blessing of the Household for Thanksgiving Day

We gather this day to give thanks to God for the gifts of this land and its people, for God has been generous to us. As we ask God's blessing upon this food we share, may we be mindful of the lonely and the hungry.

As we prepare to offer thanks to God, let us listen to the words of scripture:

I give thanks to my God always for you because of the grace of God that has been given you in Christ Jesus, for in every way you have been enriched in him, in speech and knowledge of every kind—just as the testimony of Christ has been strengthened among you—so that you are not lacking in any spiritual gift as you wait for the revealing of our Lord Jesus Christ. He will also strengthen you to the end, so that you may be blameless on the day of our Lord Jesus Christ. (1 Cor. 1:4-8)

Let us pray.
God most provident, we join all creation in offering you praise through Jesus Christ. For generations the people of this land have sung of your bounty. With them, we offer you thanksgiving for the rich harvest we have received at your hands. Bless us and this food that we share with grateful hearts. Continue to make our land fruitful and let our love for you be seen in our pursuit of justice and peace and in our generous response to those in need. We ask this through Christ our Lord. Amen.

May Christ, the living bread, bring us to the feast of eternal life. Amen.

Thursday, November 22, 2018
Time after Pentecost

Day of Thanksgiving (U.S.A.)

Psalm 93

Your throne has been established

The LORD is king, he is robed in majesty;
> the LORD is robed, he is girded with strength.
He has established the world; it shall never be moved;
> your throne is established from of old;
> you are from everlasting.

The floods have lifted up, O LORD,
> the floods have lifted up their voice;
> the floods lift up their roaring.
More majestic than the thunders of mighty waters,
> more majestic than the waves of the sea,
> majestic on high is the LORD!

Your decrees are very sure;
> holiness befits your house,
> O LORD, forevermore. (Ps. 93:1-5)

Additional Readings

Ezekiel 28:1-10
A king pretends to be God

Acts 7:54—8:1a
The Son at God's right hand

Hymn: Blessing and Honor, ELW 854

Sovereign God, ruler of heaven and earth, we are awed by your power and humbled by your love. With joyful worship and service, we praise you. With generous offerings of our time, talent, and treasure, we thank you.

Friday, November 23, 2018
Time after Pentecost

Clement, Bishop of Rome, died around 100
Miguel Agustín Pro, martyr, died 1927

1 Corinthians 15:20-28
That God may be all in all

Then comes the end, when he hands over the kingdom to God the
Father, after he has destroyed every ruler and every authority and
power. For he must reign until he has put all his enemies under his feet.
The last enemy to be destroyed is death. For "God has put all things
in subjection under his feet." But when it says, "All things are put in
subjection," it is plain that this does not include the one who put all
things in subjection under him. When all things are subjected to him,
then the Son himself will also be subjected to the one who put all things
in subjection under him, so that God may be all in all. (1 Cor. 15:24-28)

Psalm
Psalm 93
Your throne has been established

Additional Reading
Ezekiel 28:20-26
Israel will be safe

Hymn: Jesus Lives, My Sure Defense, ELW 621

*All-powerful God, Christ's resurrection defeated death, bringing us eternal
life. Though with the confidence of faith we do not fear death, we admit that
we fear dying. Come close during our last days on earth. Comfort those who
grieve.*

Saturday, November 24, 2018
Time after Pentecost

Justus Falckner, died 1723; Jehu Jones, died 1852; William Passavant, died 1894;
pastors in North America

John 3:31-36

The one who comes from above

The one who comes from above is above all; the one who is of the earth belongs to the earth and speaks about earthly things. The one who comes from heaven is above all. He testifies to what he has seen and heard, yet no one accepts his testimony. Whoever has accepted his testimony has certified this, that God is true. He whom God has sent speaks the words of God, for he gives the Spirit without measure. The Father loves the Son and has placed all things in his hands. Whoever believes in the Son has eternal life; whoever disobeys the Son will not see life, but must endure God's wrath. (John 3:31-36)

Psalm
Psalm 93
Your throne has been established

Additional Reading
Daniel 7:1-8, 15-18
Daniel's vision of four beasts

Hymn: All Who Believe and Are Baptized, ELW 442

Ever-living God, while waiting for Jesus to come again and fully establish your reign on earth as it is in heaven, bless us with urgent patience and passion as we work for justice and share your good news.

Sunday, November 25, 2018
Christ the King

Isaac Watts, hymnwriter, died 1748

John 18:33-37

The kingdom of Christ

Then Pilate entered the headquarters again, summoned Jesus, and asked him, "Are you the King of the Jews?" Jesus answered, "Do you ask this on your own, or did others tell you about me?" Pilate replied, "I am not a Jew, am I? Your own nation and the chief priests have handed you over to me. What have you done?" Jesus answered, "My kingdom is not from this world. If my kingdom were from this world, my followers would be fighting to keep me from being handed over to the Jews. But as it is, my kingdom is not from here." Pilate asked him, "So you are a king?" Jesus answered, "You say that I am a king. For this I was born, and for this I came into the world, to testify to the truth. Everyone who belongs to the truth listens to my voice." (John 18:33-37)

Psalm

Psalm 93
Your throne has been established

Additional Readings

Daniel 7:9-10, 13-14
The coming one rules over all

Revelation 1:4b-8
Christ, the ruler of the earth

Hymn: Jesus Shall Reign, ELW 434

Almighty and ever-living God, you anointed your beloved Son to be priest and sovereign forever. Grant that all the people of the earth, now divided by the power of sin, may be united by the glorious and gentle rule of Jesus Christ, our Savior and Lord, who lives and reigns with you and the Holy Spirit, one God, now and forever.

Monday, November 26, 2018
Time after Pentecost

Psalm 76
God is victorious

In Judah God is known,
    his name is great in Israel.
His abode has been established in Salem,
    his dwelling place in Zion.
There he broke the flashing arrows,
    the shield, the sword, and the weapons of war. (Ps. 76:1-3)

Additional Readings
Daniel 7:19-27
The holy ones receive the kingdom

Revelation 11:1-14
The dead are filled with the breath of life

Hymn: A Mighty Fortress Is Our God, ELW 503/504/505

Mighty God, through his death and resurrection, your son, Jesus Christ, conquered sin, evil, and death. The war is over. Now, with the courage of victors and motivated by love, we are freed to battle injustice and hatred in our world today.

Tuesday, November 27, 2018
Time after Pentecost

Revelation 11:15-19

God's reign at the end of time

Then the twenty-four elders who sit on their thrones before God fell on their faces and worshiped God, singing,

> "We give you thanks, Lord God Almighty,
>> who are and who were,
>
> for you have taken your great power
>> and begun to reign.
>
> The nations raged,
>> but your wrath has come,
>> and the time for judging the dead,
>
> for rewarding your servants, the prophets
>> and saints and all who fear your name,
>> both small and great,
>
> and for destroying those who destroy the earth." (Rev. 11:16-18)

Psalm

Psalm 76
God is victorious

Additional Reading

Ezekiel 29:1-12
Prophecy against Pharaoh

Hymn: Lo! He Comes with Clouds Descending, ELW 435

Victorious God, when Jesus comes again in glory you promise a new heaven on earth. Right wins over might. Creation is restored and corruption destroyed. Those who love you and serve others are vindicated. Alleluia!

Wednesday, November 28, 2018
Time after Pentecost

Ezekiel 30:20-26
I am the Lord

Therefore thus says the Lord God: I am against Pharaoh king of Egypt, and will break his arms, both the strong arm and the one that was broken; and I will make the sword fall from his hand. I will scatter the Egyptians among the nations, and disperse them throughout the lands. I will strengthen the arms of the king of Babylon, and put my sword in his hand; but I will break the arms of Pharaoh, and he will groan before him with the groans of one mortally wounded. I will strengthen the arms of the king of Babylon, but the arms of Pharaoh shall fall. And they shall know that I am the Lord, when I put my sword into the hand of the king of Babylon. He shall stretch it out against the land of Egypt, and I will scatter the Egyptians among the nations and disperse them throughout the countries. Then they shall know that I am the Lord. (Ezek. 30:22-26)

Psalm
Psalm 76
God is victorious

Additional Reading
John 16:25-33
I have conquered the world

Hymn: Lead On, O King Eternal! ELW 805

Eternal God, you are great and good. Pour out your Holy Spirit on us so we might be bold witnesses. Make us eager to share the gospel story of saving grace so all may know you are the Lord.

Thursday, November 29, 2018
Time after Pentecost

Psalm 25:1-10
To you I lift up my soul

To you, O LORD, I lift up my soul.
O my God, in you I trust;
> do not let me be put to shame;
> do not let my enemies exult over me.
Do not let those who wait for you be put to shame;
> let them be ashamed who are wantonly treacherous. (Ps. 25:1-3)

Additional Readings
Nehemiah 9:6-15
Remembering the exodus

1 Thessalonians 5:1-11
Keep awake

Hymn: O God of Love, O King of Peace, ELW 749

Steadfast and trustworthy God, we are your grateful people. Look with favor on us and bless us with peace. Shield us from the shaming of others and release us from the shame we place on ourselves.

Friday, November 30, 2018
Andrew, Apostle

John 1:35-42
Jesus calls Andrew

One of the two who heard John speak and followed him was Andrew, Simon Peter's brother. He first found his brother Simon and said to him, "We have found the Messiah" (which is translated Anointed). He brought Simon to Jesus, who looked at him and said, "You are Simon son of John. You are to be called Cephas" (which is translated Peter). (John 1:40-42)

Psalm

Psalm 19:1-6
The heavens declare God's glory

Additional Readings

Ezekiel 3:16-21
A sentinel for the house of Israel

Romans 10:10-18
Faith comes from the word of Christ

Hymn: Jesus Calls Us; o'er the Tumult, ELW 696

Almighty God, you gave your apostle Andrew the grace to obey the call of your Son and to bring his brother to Jesus. Give us also, who are called by your holy word, grace to follow Jesus without delay and to bring into his presence those who are near to us, for he lives and reigns with you and the Holy Spirit, one God, now and forever.

Prayer List for December

_____

_____

_____

_____

_____

_____

_____

_____

_____

_____

Saturday, December 1, 2018
Time after Pentecost

Luke 21:20-24
A messianic warning

Jesus said, "When you see Jerusalem surrounded by armies, then know that its desolation has come near. Then those in Judea must flee to the mountains, and those inside the city must leave it, and those out in the country must not enter it; for these are days of vengeance, as a fulfillment of all that is written. Woe to those who are pregnant and to those who are nursing infants in those days! For there will be great distress on the earth and wrath against this people; they will fall by the edge of the sword and be taken away as captives among all nations; and Jerusalem will be trampled on by the Gentiles, until the times of the Gentiles are fulfilled." (Luke 21:20-24)

Psalm
Psalm 25:1-10
To you I lift up my soul

Additional Reading
Nehemiah 9:26-31
Remembering deliverance from exile

Hymn: Hark! A Thrilling Voice Is Sounding! ELW 246

Tragedy and destruction are constant potentials at our doors, yet you are a constant reality in our lives during all things, O God. Fulfill in us your desire for peace, gentleness, and an end to violence.

Advent

In the days of Advent, Christians prepare to celebrate the presence of God's Word among us in our own day. During these four weeks, we pray that the reign of God, which Jesus preached and lived, would come among us. We pray that God's justice would flourish in our land, that the people of the earth would live in peace, that the weak and the sick and the hungry would be strengthened, healed, and fed with God's merciful presence.

During the last days of Advent, Christians welcome Christ with names inspired by the prophets: wisdom, liberator of slaves, mighty power, radiant dawn and sun of justice, the keystone of the arch of humanity, and Emmanuel—God with us.

The Advent Wreath

One of the best-known customs for the season is the Advent wreath. The wreath and winter candle-lighting in the midst of growing darkness strengthen some of the Advent images found in the Bible. The unbroken circle of greens is clearly an image of everlasting life, a victory wreath, the crown of Christ, or the wheel of time itself. Christians use the wreath as a sign that Christ reaches into our time to lead us to the light of everlasting life. The four candles mark the progress of the four weeks of Advent and the growth of light. Sometimes the wreath is embellished with natural dried flowers or fruit. Its evergreen branches lead the household and the congregation to the evergreen Christmas tree. In many homes, the family gathers for prayer around the wreath.

An Evening Service of Light for Advent

This brief order may be used on any evening during the season of Advent. If the household has an Advent wreath (one candle for each of the four weeks of Advent), it may be lighted during this service. Alternatively, one simple candle (perhaps a votive candle) may be lighted instead.

Lighting the Advent Wreath

May this candle/these candles be a sign of the coming light of Christ.

One or more candles may be lighted. Use this blessing when lighting the first candle.

Blessed are you, O Lord our God, ruler of the universe.
You call all nations to walk in your light
and to seek your ways of justice and peace,
for the night is past, and the dawn of your coming is near.
Bless us as we light the first candle of this wreath.
Rouse us from sleep,
that we may be ready to greet our Lord when he comes
and welcome him into our hearts and homes,
for he is our light and our salvation.
Blessed be God forever.
Amen.

Blessings for the second, third, and fourth weeks of Advent are provided on pages 379, 387, and 395, respectively.

Reading

Read one or more of the scripture passages appointed for the day in the dated pages that follow.

Hymn

One of the following, or the hymn suggested for the day, may be sung. The hymn might be accompanied by small finger cymbals.

Light One Candle to Watch for Messiah, ELW 240
People, Look East, ELW 248
Savior of the Nations, Come, ELW 263

During the final seven days of the Advent season (beginning on December 17), the hymn "O Come, O Come, Emmanuel" (ELW 257) is particularly appropriate. The stanzas of that hymn are also referred to as the "O Antiphons." The first stanza of the hymn could be sung each day during the final days before Christmas in addition to the stanza that is specifically appointed for the day.

First stanza
O come, O come, Emmanuel,
and ransom captive Israel,
that mourns in lonely exile here
until the Son of God appear.
Refrain   Rejoice! Rejoice! Emmanuel shall come to you, O Israel.

December 17
O come, O Wisdom from on high,
embracing all things far and nigh:
in strength and beauty come and stay;
teach us your will and guide our way.   *Refrain*

December 18
O come, O come, O Lord of might,
as to your tribes on Sinai's height
in ancient times you gave the law
in cloud, and majesty, and awe.   *Refrain*

December 19
O come, O Branch of Jesse, free
your own from Satan's tyranny;
from depths of hell your people save,
and give them vict'ry o'er the grave.   *Refrain*

December 20

O come, O Key of David, come,
and open wide our heav'nly home;
make safe the way that leads on high,
and close the path to misery.   *Refrain*

December 21

O come, O Dayspring, come and cheer;
O Sun of justice, now draw near.
Disperse the gloomy clouds of night,
and death's dark shadow put to flight.   *Refrain*

December 22

O come, O King of nations, come,
O Cornerstone that binds in one:
refresh the hearts that long for you;
restore the broken, make us new.   *Refrain*

December 23

O come, O come, Emmanuel,
and ransom captive Israel,
that mourns in lonely exile here
until the Son of God appear.   *Refrain*

Text: Psalteriolum Cantionum Catholicarum, Köln, 1710; tr. composite
Text sts. 2, 6, 7 © 1997 Augsburg Fortress

Table Prayer for Advent

For use when a meal follows.

Blessed are you, O Lord our God,
the one who is, who was, and who is to come.
At this table you fill us with good things.
May these gifts strengthen us
to share with the hungry and all those in need,
as we wait and watch for your coming among us
in Jesus Christ our Lord. Amen.

Candles may be extinguished now or after the meal, if one is to follow.

Sunday, December 2, 2018
First Sunday of Advent

Luke 21:25-36

Watch for the coming of the Son of Man

[Jesus said,] "There will be signs in the sun, the moon, and the stars, and on the earth distress among nations confused by the roaring of the sea and the waves. People will faint from fear and foreboding of what is coming upon the world, for the powers of the heavens will be shaken. Then they will see 'the Son of Man coming in a cloud' with power and great glory. Now when these things begin to take place, stand up and raise your heads, because your redemption is drawing near." (Luke 21:25-28)

Psalm

Psalm 25:1-10
To you I lift up my soul

Additional Readings

Jeremiah 33:14-16
A righteous branch springs from David

1 Thessalonians 3:9-13
Strengthen hearts of holiness

Hymn: Wake, Awake, for Night Is Flying, ELW 436

Stir up your power, Lord Christ, and come. By your merciful protection alert us to the threatening dangers of our sins, and redeem us for your life of justice, for you live and reign with the Father and the Holy Spirit, one God, now and forever.

Monday, December 3, 2018
Week of Advent 1

Francis Xavier, missionary to Asia, died 1552

Psalm 90
Prayer for life from God

Lord, you have been our dwelling place
  in all generations.
Before the mountains were brought forth,
  or ever you had formed the earth and the world,
  from everlasting to everlasting you are God.

You turn us back to dust,
  and say, "Turn back, you mortals."
For a thousand years in your sight
  are like yesterday when it is past,
  or like a watch in the night. (Ps. 90:1-4)

Additional Readings
Numbers 17:1-11
The budding of Aaron's rod

2 Peter 3:1-18
Growing in grace

Hymn: O God, Our Help in Ages Past, ELW 632

We are mortal and nothing but dust compared to you, O God. But you do not compare us. You confirm our worth and give value to our lives. Show forth in us your everlasting grace and be our eternal home.

Tuesday, December 4, 2018
Week of Advent 1

John of Damascus, theologian and hymnwriter, died around 749

Revelation 22:12-16

Jesus as the fulfillment of David's line

"See, I am coming soon; my reward is with me, to repay according to everyone's work. I am the Alpha and the Omega, the first and the last, the beginning and the end."

Blessed are those who wash their robes, so that they will have the right to the tree of life and may enter the city by the gates. Outside are the dogs and sorcerers and fornicators and murderers and idolaters, and everyone who loves and practices falsehood.

"It is I, Jesus, who sent my angel to you with this testimony for the churches. I am the root and the descendant of David, the bright morning star." (Rev. 22:12-16)

Psalm

Psalm 90
Prayer for life from God

Additional Reading

2 Samuel 7:18-29
The flowering of David's line

Hymn: The King Shall Come, ELW 260

Eternal God, our actions do not always match our desire to enter your kingdom, but you wash away our sin and grant us access to life eternal. Fulfill in us the promises of baptism and make us testimonies of your saving grace.

Wednesday, December 5, 2018
Week of Advent 1

Luke 11:29-32
The coming of the Son of Man

When the crowds were increasing, [Jesus] began to say, "This generation is an evil generation; it asks for a sign, but no sign will be given to it except the sign of Jonah. For just as Jonah became a sign to the people of Nineveh, so the Son of Man will be to this generation. The queen of the South will rise at the judgment with the people of this generation and condemn them, because she came from the ends of the earth to listen to the wisdom of Solomon, and see, something greater than Solomon is here! The people of Nineveh will rise up at the judgment with this generation and condemn it, because they repented at the proclamation of Jonah, and see, something greater than Jonah is here!" (Luke 11:29-32)

Psalm
Psalm 90
Prayer for life from God

Additional Reading
Isaiah 1:24-31
Warning not to wither

Hymn: Mine Eyes Have Seen the Glory, ELW 890

Faithful God, we constantly look for signs in our lives to prove our worth and to justify our actions, but you determine our merit and you alone render judgment. Fulfill in us your desire for grace and forgiveness.

Thursday, December 6, 2018
Week of Advent 1

Nicholas, Bishop of Myra, died around 342

Luke 1:68-79

God's tender compassion

[Zechariah prophesied about John,]
"...you, child, will be called the prophet of the Most High;
    for you will go before the Lord to prepare his ways,
to give knowledge of salvation to his people
    by the forgiveness of their sins.
By the tender mercy of our God,
    the dawn from on high will break upon us,
to give light to those who sit in darkness and in the shadow
        of death,
    to guide our feet into the way of peace." (Luke 1:76-79)

Additional Readings

Malachi 3:5-12
Return to me

Philippians 1:12-18a
Proclaiming Christ

Hymn: Blessed Be the God of Israel, ELW 250

Directing God, we don't always follow the way that you have set before us. We find ourselves lost in darkness. May your presence give us light and guide our feet. Fulfill in us the knowledge of your mercy.

Friday, December 7, 2018
Week of Advent 1

Ambrose, Bishop of Milan, died 397

Malachi 3:13-18

Those who serve God

You have spoken harsh words against me, says the LORD. Yet you say, "How have we spoken against you?" You have said, "It is vain to serve God. What do we profit by keeping his command or by going about as mourners before the LORD of hosts? Now we count the arrogant happy; evildoers not only prosper, but when they put God to the test they escape."

Then those who revered the LORD spoke with one another. The LORD took note and listened, and a book of remembrance was written before him of those who revered the LORD and thought on his name. They shall be mine, says the LORD of hosts, my special possession on the day when I act, and I will spare them as parents spare their children who serve them. Then once more you shall see the difference between the righteous and the wicked, between one who serves God and one who does not serve him. (Mal. 3:13-18)

Psalm

Luke 1:68-79
God's tender compassion

Additional Reading

Philippians 1:18b-26
Paul rejoices though imprisoned

Hymn: Savior of the Nations, Come, ELW 263

The world has ways to make us feel as though we are nothing. Yet, O God, you take note of us. You see our struggles to follow your commandments and you are moved by them. Fulfill in us your righteousness and justice.

Luke 9:1-6

The mission of the Twelve

Then Jesus called the twelve together and gave them power and authority over all demons and to cure diseases, and he sent them out to proclaim the kingdom of God and to heal. He said to them, "Take nothing for your journey, no staff, nor bag, nor bread, nor money—not even an extra tunic. Whatever house you enter, stay there, and leave from there. Wherever they do not welcome you, as you are leaving that town shake the dust off your feet as a testimony against them." They departed and went through the villages, bringing the good news and curing diseases everywhere. (Luke 9:1-6)

Psalm

Luke 1:68-79
God's tender compassion

Additional Reading

Malachi 4:1-6
The sun of righteousness shall rise

Hymn: The Son of God, Our Christ, ELW 584

God, we are often overwhelmed by the desire and belief that we need to have more, but you provide all the resources we need to live each day. Fulfill in us the abundance that faith in you provides.

Lighting the Advent Wreath

Use this blessing when lighting the first two candles.

Blessed are you, O Lord our God, ruler of the universe.
John the Baptist calls all people to prepare the Lord's way
for the kingdom of heaven is near.
Bless us as we light the candles on this wreath.
Baptize us with the fire of your Spirit,
that we may be a light shining in the darkness
welcoming others as Christ has welcomed us,
for he is our light and our salvation.
Blessed be God forever.
Amen.

Sunday, December 9, 2018
Second Sunday of Advent

Luke 3:1-6

Prepare the way of the Lord

[John the Baptist] went into all the region around the Jordan, proclaiming a baptism of repentance for the forgiveness of sins, as it is written in the book of the words of the prophet Isaiah,

"The voice of one crying out in the wilderness:
'Prepare the way of the Lord,
 make his paths straight.
Every valley shall be filled,
 and every mountain and hill shall be made low,
and the crooked shall be made straight,
 and the rough ways made smooth;
and all flesh shall see the salvation of God.'" (Luke 3:3-6)

Psalm

Luke 1:68-79
God's tender compassion

Additional Readings

Malachi 3:1-4
The messenger refines and purifies

Philippians 1:3-11
A harvest of righteousness

Hymn: On Jordan's Bank the Baptist's Cry, ELW 249

Stir up our hearts, Lord God, to prepare the way of your only Son. By his coming give to all the people of the world knowledge of your salvation; through Jesus Christ, our Savior and Lord, who lives and reigns with you and the Holy Spirit, one God, now and forever.

Monday, December 10, 2018
Week of Advent 2

Psalm 126
Prayer for restoration

Restore our fortunes, O LORD,
    like the watercourses in the Negeb.
May those who sow in tears
    reap with shouts of joy.
Those who go out weeping,
    bearing the seed for sowing,
shall come home with shouts of joy,
        carrying their sheaves. (Ps. 126:4-6)

Additional Readings

Isaiah 40:1-11
The earth prepares for God

Romans 8:22-25
All creation waits

Hymn: Oh, That I Had a Thousand Voices, ELW 833

Sorrow over the losses in our lives can strip us bare and leave us believing we are powerless. Nevertheless, O God, you restore our hearts and give us perseverance. Fulfill in us the joy of your purpose.

Tuesday, December 11, 2018
Week of Advent 2

Isaiah 19:18-25
All nations shall praise God

On that day there will be an altar to the LORD in the center of the land of Egypt, and a pillar to the LORD at its border. It will be a sign and a witness to the LORD of hosts in the land of Egypt; when they cry to the LORD because of oppressors, he will send them a savior, and will defend and deliver them. The LORD will make himself known to the Egyptians; and the Egyptians will know the LORD on that day, and will worship with sacrifice and burnt offering, and they will make vows to the LORD and perform them. The LORD will strike Egypt, striking and healing; they will return to the LORD, and he will listen to their supplications and heal them.

On that day there will be a highway from Egypt to Assyria, and the Assyrian will come into Egypt, and the Egyptian into Assyria, and the Egyptians will worship with the Assyrians. (Isa. 19:19-23)

Psalm
Psalm 126
Prayer for restoration

Additional Reading
2 Peter 1:2-15
Living God's call

Hymn: Prepare the Royal Highway, ELW 264

God, we have known oppressors throughout all of time, those who rise to power only to use us for their own benefit. Yet you deliver us from oppression. Fulfill in us the joy of freedom in you.

Wednesday, December 12, 2018
Week of Advent 2

Isaiah 35:3-7

God's advent will change everything

Then the eyes of the blind shall be opened,
    and the ears of the deaf unstopped;
then the lame shall leap like a deer,
    and the tongue of the speechless sing for joy.
For waters shall break forth in the wilderness,
    and streams in the desert;
the burning sand shall become a pool,
    and the thirsty ground springs of water;
the haunt of jackals shall become a swamp,
    the grass shall become reeds and rushes. (Isa. 35:5-7)

Psalm

Psalm 126
Prayer for restoration

Additional Reading

Luke 7:18-30
John the Baptist questions Jesus

Hymn: Awake! Awake, and Greet the New Morn, ELW 242

*Each of us carries a weakness, something that prevents us from living fully.
But you, O God, can turn weakness into strength and curses into blessings.
Fulfill in us wholeness of mind, body, and spirit.*

Thursday, December 13, 2018
Week of Advent 2

Lucy, martyr, died 304

Isaiah 12:2-6
In your midst is the Holy One of Israel

And you will say in that day:
>Give thanks to the LORD,
>>call on his name;
>make known his deeds among the nations;
>>proclaim that his name is exalted.

>Sing praises to the LORD, for he has done gloriously;
>>let this be known in all the earth.
>Shout aloud and sing for joy, O royal Zion,
>>for great in your midst is the Holy One of Israel. (Isa. 12:4-6)

Additional Readings
Amos 6:1-8
Punishment for self-indulgence

2 Corinthians 8:1-15
Encouragement to be generous

Hymn: Rejoice, Rejoice, Believers, ELW 244

God, we wait for the day to sing praises for all that you have done, yet you call us to praise your name each day. Fulfill in us the knowledge of your glory and open our mouths to sing songs of joy.

Friday, December 14, 2018
Week of Advent 2

John of the Cross, renewer of the church, died 1591

Amos 8:4-12

Do not trample the needy

Hear this, you that trample on the needy,
    and bring to ruin the poor of the land,
saying, "When will the new moon be over
    so that we may sell grain;
and the sabbath,
    so that we may offer wheat for sale?
We will make the ephah small and the shekel great,
    and practice deceit with false balances,
buying the poor for silver
    and the needy for a pair of sandals,
    and selling the sweepings of the wheat."

The LORD has sworn by the pride of Jacob:
Surely I will never forget any of their deeds. (Amos 8:4-7)

Psalm
Isaiah 12:2-6
In your midst is the Holy One of Israel

Additional Reading
2 Corinthians 9:1-15
Generous giving bears fruit

Hymn: Hark, the Glad Sound! ELW 239

We tend to think of ourselves first and believe we are entitled to what others have and more, and yet, God, you provide enough for everyone to have what they need. Fulfill in us a desire to be generous and your will to share with others.

Saturday, December 15, 2018
Week of Advent 2

Amos 9:8-15
God will set things right

The time is surely coming, says the LORD,
>   when the one who plows shall overtake the one who reaps,
>   and the treader of grapes the one who sows the seed;
the mountains shall drip sweet wine,
>   and all the hills shall flow with it.
I will restore the fortunes of my people Israel,
>   and they shall rebuild the ruined cities and inhabit them;
they shall plant vineyards and drink their wine,
>   and they shall make gardens and eat their fruit.
I will plant them upon their land,
>   and they shall never again be plucked up
>   out of the land that I have given them,
>   says the LORD your God. (Amos 9:13-15)

Psalm
Isaiah 12:2-6
In your midst is the Holy One of Israel

Additional Reading
Luke 1:57-66
The birth of John the Baptist

Hymn: People, Look East, ELW 248

God, there's so much wrong with the world we live in and too often we allow bad news to destroy our hope that goodness is possible. Help us to join your tireless work to bring about restoration. Fulfill in us the good news of your promises.

Lighting the Advent Wreath

Use this blessing when lighting three candles.

Blessed are you, O Lord our God, ruler of the universe.
Your prophets spoke of a day when the desert would blossom
and waters would break forth in the wilderness.
Bless us as we light the candles on this wreath.
Strengthen our hearts
as we prepare for the coming of the Lord.
May he give water to all who thirst,
for he is our light and our salvation.
Blessed be God forever.
Amen.

Sunday, December 16, 2018
Third Sunday of Advent

Luke 3:7-18
One more powerful is coming

As the people were filled with expectation, and all were questioning in their hearts concerning John, whether he might be the Messiah, John answered all of them by saying, "I baptize you with water; but one who is more powerful than I is coming; I am not worthy to untie the thong of his sandals. He will baptize you with the Holy Spirit and fire. His winnowing fork is in his hand, to clear his threshing floor and to gather the wheat into his granary; but the chaff he will burn with unquenchable fire."

So, with many other exhortations, he proclaimed the good news to the people. (Luke 3:15-18)

Psalm
Isaiah 12:2-6
In your midst is the Holy One of Israel

Additional Readings
Zephaniah 3:14-20
Rejoice in God

Philippians 4:4-7
Rejoice, the Lord is near

Hymn: O Lord, How Shall I Meet You, ELW 241

Stir up the wills of your faithful people, Lord God, and open our ears to the preaching of John, that, rejoicing in your salvation, we may bring forth the fruits of repentance; through Jesus Christ, our Savior and Lord, who lives and reigns with you and the Holy Spirit, one God, now and forever.

Monday, December 17, 2018
Week of Advent 3

Isaiah 11:1-9

A ruler brings justice and peace

A shoot shall come out from the stump of Jesse,
    and a branch shall grow out of his roots.
The spirit of the LORD shall rest on him,
    the spirit of wisdom and understanding,
    the spirit of counsel and might,
    the spirit of knowledge and the fear of the LORD.
His delight shall be in the fear of the LORD.

He shall not judge by what his eyes see,
    or decide by what his ears hear;
but with righteousness he shall judge the poor,
    and decide with equity for the meek of the earth;
he shall strike the earth with the rod of his mouth,
    and with the breath of his lips he shall kill the wicked.
Righteousness shall be the belt around his waist,
    and faithfulness the belt around his loins. (Isa. 11:1-5)

Additional Readings

Numbers 16:1-19
Korah's company rebels

Hebrews 13:7-17
Respect your leaders

Hymn: O Holy Spirit, Enter In, ELW 786

Not all who lead us do so to bring about justice. But you, O God, sent your Son to guide us with your Spirit. Fulfill in us your wisdom, understanding, council, and might, and fill our leaders with knowledge of righteousness and equity.

Tuesday, December 18, 2018
Week of Advent 3

Numbers 16:20-35
God destroys Korah's company

As soon as [Moses] finished speaking all these words, the ground under them was split apart. The earth opened its mouth and swallowed them up, along with their households—everyone who belonged to Korah and all their goods. So they with all that belonged to them went down alive into Sheol; the earth closed over them, and they perished from the midst of the assembly. All Israel around them fled at their outcry, for they said, "The earth will swallow us too!" And fire came out from the LORD and consumed the two hundred fifty men offering the incense. (Num. 16:31-35)

Psalm
Isaiah 11:1-9
A ruler brings justice and peace

Additional Reading
Acts 28:23-31
Paul preaches in Rome

Hymn: Lost in the Night, ELW 243

There are times when what we desire most is vengeance on those who have wronged us. But you, O God, crave justice. Your wrath is horrifying. Your mercy is great. Fulfill in us your judgment of mercy and spare us from condemnation.

Wednesday, December 19, 2018
Week of Advent 3

Luke 7:31-35
The Messiah and John the Baptist

[Jesus said,] "To what then will I compare the people of this generation, and what are they like? They are like children sitting in the marketplace and calling to one another,

'We played the flute for you, and you did not dance;
we wailed, and you did not weep.'

For John the Baptist has come eating no bread and drinking no wine, and you say, 'He has a demon'; the Son of Man has come eating and drinking, and you say, 'Look, a glutton and a drunkard, a friend of tax collectors and sinners!' Nevertheless, wisdom is vindicated by all her children." (Luke 7:31-35)

Psalm
Isaiah 11:1-9
A ruler brings justice and peace

Additional Reading
Micah 4:8-13
God will thresh out the people

Hymn: There's a Voice in the Wilderness, ELW 255

We don't always notice you in our daily lives. We neglect to look or we ignore you. But you, O God, are constantly waiting patiently for us to notice. Give us wisdom to recognize you and the ability to point you out to others.

Thursday, December 20, 2018
Week of Advent 3

Katharina von Bora Luther, renewer of the church, died 1552

Psalm 80:1-7

Show the light of your countenance

Give ear, O Shepherd of Israel,
>   you who lead Joseph like a flock!
You who are enthroned upon the cherubim, shine forth
>   before Ephraim and Benjamin and Manasseh.
Stir up your might,
>   and come to save us!

Restore us, O God;
>   let your face shine, that we may be saved. (Ps. 80:1-3)

Additional Readings

Jeremiah 31:31-34
A new covenant written on the heart

Hebrews 10:10-18
New priest, new sacrifice once for all

Hymn: Come, Thou Long-Expected Jesus, ELW 254

No matter how strong or smart, skilled or talented we are, we can't save ourselves. But you, O God, are mighty and you hear us when we call to you. Fulfill in us the light of your salvation and restore us.

Friday, December 21, 2018
Week of Advent 3

Hebrews 10:32-39
Confidence that rewards

But recall those earlier days when, after you had been enlightened, you endured a hard struggle with sufferings, sometimes being publicly exposed to abuse and persecution, and sometimes being partners with those so treated. For you had compassion for those who were in prison, and you cheerfully accepted the plundering of your possessions, knowing that you yourselves possessed something better and more lasting. Do not, therefore, abandon that confidence of yours; it brings a great reward. For you need endurance, so that when you have done the will of God, you may receive what was promised. (Heb. 10:32-36)

Psalm
Psalm 80:1-7
Show the light of your countenance

Additional Reading
Isaiah 42:10-18
Sing to God a new song

Hymn: All Earth Is Hopeful, ELW 266

Fighting for your justice has harsh consequences. It requires making sacrifices and placing ourselves in dangerous positions. But you, O God, give us confidence that what we do is not in vain. Fulfill in us the reward of your righteousness.

Saturday, December 22, 2018
Week of Advent 3

Isaiah 66:7-11

God as a nursing mother

Before she was in labor
>she gave birth;
before her pain came upon her
>she delivered a son....

Shall I open the womb and not deliver?
>says the LORD;
shall I, the one who delivers, shut the womb?
>says your God.

Rejoice with Jerusalem, and be glad for her,
>all you who love her;
rejoice with her in joy,
>all you who mourn over her—
that you may nurse and be satisfied
>from her consoling breast;
that you may drink deeply with delight
>from her glorious bosom. (Isa. 66:7, 9-11)

Psalm
Psalm 80:1-7
Show the light of your countenance

Additional Reading
Luke 13:31-35
Jesus as mother hen laments over Jerusalem

Hymn: Love Divine, All Loves Excelling, ELW 631

Not all parents are loving; even the best mothers and fathers fail their children in some regard. But you, O God, gather us into your arms and offer your breast for us to nurse. Fulfill in us the contentment your nourishment provides.

Lighting the Advent Wreath

Use this blessing when lighting all four candles.

Blessed are you, O Lord our God, ruler of the universe.
In your Son, Emmanuel,
you have shown us your light
and saved us from the power of sin.
Bless us as we light the candles on this wreath.
Increase our longing for your presence,
that at the celebration of your Son's birth
his Spirit might dwell anew in our midst,
for he is our light and our salvation.
Blessed be God forever.
Amen.

Sunday, December 23, 2018
Fourth Sunday of Advent

Luke 1:39-45 [46-55]

Blessed are you among women

In those days Mary set out and went with haste to a Judean town in the hill country, where she entered the house of Zechariah and greeted Elizabeth. When Elizabeth heard Mary's greeting, the child leaped in her womb. And Elizabeth was filled with the Holy Spirit and exclaimed with a loud cry, "Blessed are you among women, and blessed is the fruit of your womb. And why has this happened to me, that the mother of my Lord comes to me? For as soon as I heard the sound of your greeting, the child in my womb leaped for joy. And blessed is she who believed that there would be a fulfillment of what was spoken to her by the Lord." (Luke 1:39-45)

Psalm
Luke 1:46b-55
My soul magnifies the Lord

Additional Readings
Micah 5:2-5a
From Bethlehem comes a ruler

Hebrews 10:5-10
I have come to do your will

Hymn: O Come, O Come, Emmanuel, ELW 257

Stir up your power, Lord Christ, and come. With your abundant grace and might, free us from the sin that binds us, that we may receive you in joy and serve you always, for you live and reign with the Father and the Holy Spirit, one God, now and forever.

Christmas

Over the centuries, various customs have developed which focus the household on welcoming the light of Christ: the daily or weekly lighting of the Advent wreath, the blessing of the lighted Christmas tree, the candle-lit procession of Las Posadas, the flickering lights of the luminaria, the Christ candle at Christmas.

The Christian household not only welcomes the light of Christ at Christmas but celebrates the presence of that light throughout the Twelve Days, from Christmas until the Epiphany, January 6. In the Christmas season, Christians welcome the light of Christ that is already with us through faith. In word and gesture, prayer and song, in the many customs of diverse cultures, Christians celebrate this life-giving Word and ask that it dwell more deeply in the rhythm of daily life.

Table Prayer for the Twelve Days of Christmas

With joy and gladness we feast upon your love, O God.
You have come among us in Jesus, your Son,
and your presence now graces this table.
May Christ dwell in us that we might bear his love to all the world,
for he is Lord forever and ever. Amen.

Lighting the Christmas Tree

Use this prayer when you first illumine the tree or when you gather at the tree.

Holy God,
we praise you as we light this tree.
It gives light to this place
as you shine light into darkness through Jesus,
the light of the world.

God of all,
we thank you for your love,
the love that has come to us in Jesus.
Be with us now as we remember that gift of love
and help us to share that love with a yearning world.

Creator God,
you made the stars in the heavens.
Thank you for the light that shines on us in Jesus,
the bright morning star.
Amen.

Blessing of the Nativity Scene

This blessing may be used when figures are added to the nativity scene and throughout the days of Christmas.

Bless us, O God, as we remember a humble birth. With each angel and shepherd we place here before you, show us the wonder found in a stable. In song and prayer, silence and awe, we adore your gift of love, Christ Jesus our Savior.
Amen.

Monday, December 24, 2018

Nativity of Our Lord
Christmas Eve

Luke 2:1-14 [15-20]

God with us

In those days a decree went out from Emperor Augustus that all the world should be registered. This was the first registration and was taken while Quirinius was governor of Syria. All went to their own towns to be registered. Joseph also went from the town of Nazareth in Galilee to Judea, to the city of David called Bethlehem, because he was descended from the house and family of David. He went to be registered with Mary, to whom he was engaged and who was expecting a child. While they were there, the time came for her to deliver her child. And she gave birth to her firstborn son and wrapped him in bands of cloth, and laid him in a manger, because there was no place for them in the inn. (Luke 2:1-7)

Psalm	Additional Readings	
Psalm 96	**Isaiah 9:2-7**	**Titus 2:11-14**
Let the earth be glad	*A child is born for us*	*The grace of God has appeared*

Hymn: O Little Town of Bethlehem, ELW 279

Almighty God, you made this holy night shine with the brightness of the true Light. Grant that here on earth we may walk in the light of Jesus' presence and in the last day wake to the brightness of his glory; through your Son, Jesus Christ our Lord, who lives and reigns with you and the Holy Spirit, one God, now and forever.

Tuesday, December 25, 2018
Nativity of Our Lord
Christmas Day

John 1:1-14

The Word became flesh

In the beginning was the Word, and the Word was with God, and the Word was God. He was in the beginning with God. All things came into being through him, and without him not one thing came into being. What has come into being in him was life, and the life was the light of all people. The light shines in the darkness, and the darkness did not overcome it.

And the Word became flesh and lived among us, and we have seen his glory, the glory as of a father's only son, full of grace and truth. (John 1:1-5, 14)

Psalm

Psalm 98
The victory of our God

Additional Readings

Isaiah 52:7-10
Heralds announce God's salvation

Hebrews 1:1-4 [5-12]
God has spoken by a Son

Hymn: Let All Together Praise Our God, ELW 287

Almighty God, you gave us your only Son to take on our human nature and to illumine the world with your light. By your grace adopt us as your children and enlighten us with your Spirit, through Jesus Christ, our Redeemer and Lord, who lives and reigns with you and the Holy Spirit, one God, now and forever.

Wednesday, December 26, 2018
Stephen, Deacon and Martyr

Matthew 23:34-39
Jesus laments that Jerusalem kills her prophets

[Jesus said,]"Therefore I send you prophets, sages, and scribes, some of whom you will kill and crucify, and some you will flog in your synagogues and pursue from town to town, so that upon you may come all the righteous blood shed on earth, from the blood of righteous Abel to the blood of Zechariah son of Barachiah, whom you murdered between the sanctuary and the altar. Truly I tell you, all this will come upon this generation.

"Jerusalem, Jerusalem, the city that kills the prophets and stones those who are sent to it! How often have I desired to gather your children together as a hen gathers her brood under her wings, and you were not willing! See, your house is left to you, desolate. For I tell you, you will not see me again until you say, 'Blessed is the one who comes in the name of the Lord.'" (Matt. 23:34-39)

Psalm
Psalm 17:1-9, 15
I call upon you, O God

Additional Readings
2 Chronicles 24:17-22
Zechariah is stoned to death

Acts 6:8—7:2a, 51-60
Stephen is stoned to death

Hymn: What Child Is This, ELW 296

We give you thanks, O Lord of glory, for the example of Stephen the first martyr, who looked to heaven and prayed for his persecutors. Grant that we also may pray for our enemies and seek forgiveness for those who hurt us, through Jesus Christ, our Savior and Lord, who lives and reigns with you and the Holy Spirit, one God, now and forever.

Thursday, December 27, 2018
John, Apostle and Evangelist

John 21:20-25
The beloved disciple remains with Jesus

Peter turned and saw the disciple whom Jesus loved following them; he was the one who had reclined next to Jesus at the supper and had said, "Lord, who is it that is going to betray you?" When Peter saw him, he said to Jesus, "Lord, what about him?" Jesus said to him, "If it is my will that he remain until I come, what is that to you? Follow me!" So the rumor spread in the community that this disciple would not die. Yet Jesus did not say to him that he would not die, but, "If it is my will that he remain until I come, what is that to you?"

This is the disciple who is testifying to these things and has written them, and we know that his testimony is true. But there are also many other things that Jesus did; if every one of them were written down, I suppose that the world itself could not contain the books that would be written. (John 21:20-25)

Psalm
Psalm 116:12-19
The death of faithful servants

Additional Readings
Genesis 1:1-5, 26-31
Humankind is created by God

1 John 1:1—2:2
Jesus, the Word of life

Hymn: Love Has Come, ELW 292

Merciful God, through John the apostle and evangelist you have revealed the mysteries of your Word made flesh. Let the brightness of your light shine on your church, so that all your people, instructed in the holy gospel, may walk in the light of your truth and attain eternal life, through Jesus Christ, our Savior and Lord, who lives and reigns with you and the Holy Spirit, one God, now and forever.

Friday, December 28, 2018
The Holy Innocents, Martyrs

Matthew 2:13-18

Herod kills innocent children

Now after [the wise men] had left, an angel of the Lord appeared to Joseph in a dream and said, "Get up, take the child and his mother, and flee to Egypt, and remain there until I tell you; for Herod is about to search for the child, to destroy him." Then Joseph got up, took the child and his mother by night, and went to Egypt, and remained there until the death of Herod. This was to fulfill what had been spoken by the Lord through the prophet, "Out of Egypt I have called my son."

When Herod saw that he had been tricked by the wise men, he was infuriated, and he sent and killed all the children in and around Bethlehem who were two years old or under, according to the time that he had learned from the wise men. (Matt. 2:13-16)

Psalm

Psalm 124
We have escaped like a bird

Additional Readings

Jeremiah 31:15-17
Rachel weeps for her children

1 Peter 4:12-19
Continue to do good while suffering

Hymn: Lo, How a Rose E'er Blooming, ELW 272

We remember today, O God, the slaughter of the innocent children of Bethlehem by order of King Herod. Receive into the arms of your mercy all innocent victims. By your great might frustrate the designs of evil tyrants and establish your rule of justice, love, and peace, through Jesus Christ, our Savior and Lord, who lives and reigns with you and the Holy Spirit, one God, now and forever.

Saturday, December 29, 2018
Fifth Day of Christmas

1 Chronicles 28:1-10
Solomon will build the temple

[David said:] "And of all my sons, for the LORD has given me many, he has chosen my son Solomon to sit upon the throne of the kingdom of the LORD over Israel. He said to me, 'It is your son Solomon who shall build my house and my courts, for I have chosen him to be a son to me, and I will be a father to him. I will establish his kingdom forever if he continues resolute in keeping my commandments and my ordinances, as he is today.' Now therefore in the sight of all Israel, the assembly of the LORD, and in the hearing of our God, observe and search out all the commandments of the LORD your God; that you may possess this good land, and leave it for an inheritance to your children after you forever." (1 Chron. 28:5-8)

Psalm
Psalm 147:12-20
Praise God in Zion

Additional Reading
1 Corinthians 3:10-17
The temple of the Spirit

Hymn: Let Our Gladness Have No End, ELW 291

God, we don't always act for the benefit of our children. We use and misuse the fruits of your creation. You gave us instructions so our children will have an inheritance. Fulfill your commandments in us so that they will possess goodness.

Sunday, December 30, 2018
First Sunday of Christmas

Luke 2:41-52

Jesus increased in favor with all

When [Jesus'] parents saw him they were astonished; and his mother said to him, "Child, why have you treated us like this? Look, your father and I have been searching for you in great anxiety." He said to them, "Why were you searching for me? Did you not know that I must be in my Father's house?" But they did not understand what he said to them. Then he went down with them and came to Nazareth, and was obedient to them. His mother treasured all these things in her heart.

And Jesus increased in wisdom and in years, and in divine and human favor. (Luke 2:48-52)

Psalm

Psalm 148
God's splendor is over earth and heaven

Additional Readings

1 Samuel 2:18-20, 26
Samuel grew in favor with all

Colossians 3:12-17
Clothe yourselves in love

Hymn: Once in Royal David's City, ELW 269

Shine into our hearts the light of your wisdom, O God, and open our minds to the knowledge of your word, that in all things we may think and act according to your good will and may live continually in the light of your Son, Jesus Christ, who lives and reigns with you and the Holy Spirit, one God, now and forever.

405

Monday, December 31, 2018
Week of Christmas 1

Psalm 147:12-20
Praise God in Zion

Praise the LORD, O Jerusalem!
　　Praise your God, O Zion!
For he strengthens the bars of your gates;
　　he blesses your children within you.
He grants peace within your borders;
　　he fills you with the finest of wheat.
He sends out his command to the earth;
　　his word runs swiftly.
He gives snow like wool;
　　he scatters frost like ashes. (Ps. 147:12-16)

Additional Readings
1 Kings 3:5-14
God grants a discerning mind

John 8:12-19
I am the light

Hymn: Cold December Flies Away, ELW 299

The feelings of fear and anxiety threaten our sense of certainty and our need for control. But you, O God, are always in control and we can be certain of this. Fulfill in us firmness of faith and confidence in your love of us.

Lesser Festivals and Commemorations

Interested in enriching your prayer life further and in learning more about the people included among the festivals and commemorations? See Gail Ramshaw's *More Days for Praise: Festivals and Commemorations in Evangelical Lutheran Worship.* Each day's entry includes a brief chronology of the person's life; a summary of why the person is remembered by the church; an image of, or related to, the commemoration; a quote from the person, where possible; and devotional hymn and prayer suggestions for the day (Augsburg Fortress, 2016; 320 pages; ISBN 9781451496215).

January 1—Name of Jesus Every Jewish boy was circumcised and formally named on the eighth day of his life. Already in his infancy, Jesus bore the mark of a covenant that he made new through the shedding of his blood on the cross.

January 2—Johann Konrad Wilhelm Loehe Wilhelm Loehe was a pastor in nineteenth-century Germany. From the small town of Neuendettelsau he sent pastors to North America, Australia, New Guinea, Brazil, and the Ukraine.

January 15—Martin Luther King Jr. Martin Luther King Jr. is remembered as an American prophet of justice among races and nations. Many churches hold commemorations near Dr. King's birth date of January 15, in conjunction with the American civil holiday honoring him.

January 17—Antony of Egypt Antony was one of the earliest Egyptian desert fathers. He became the head of a group of monks who lived in a cluster of huts and devoted themselves to communal prayer, worship, and manual labor.

January 17—Pachomius Another of the desert fathers, Pachomius was born in Egypt about 290. He organized hermits into a religious community in which the members prayed together and held their goods in common.

January 18—Confession of Peter; *Week of Prayer for Christian Unity begins* The Week of Prayer for Christian Unity is framed by two commemorations, the Confession of Peter and the Conversion of Paul. On this day the church remembers that Peter was led by God's grace to acknowledge Jesus as "the Christ, the Son of the living God" (Matt. 16:16).

January 19—Henry When Erik, king of Sweden, determined to invade Finland for the purpose of converting the people there to Christianity, Henry went with him. Henry is recognized as the patron saint of Finland.

January 21—Agnes Agnes was a girl of about thirteen living in Rome, who had chosen a life of service to Christ as a virgin, despite the Roman emperor Diocletian's ruling that had outlawed all Christian activity. She gave witness to her faith and was put to death as a result.

January 25—Conversion of Paul; *Week of Prayer for Christian Unity ends* As the Week of Prayer for Christian Unity comes to an end, the church remembers how a man of Tarsus named Saul, a former persecutor of the early Christian church, was led to become one of its chief preachers.

January 26—Timothy, Titus, Silas On the two days following the celebration of the Conversion of Paul, his companions are remembered. Timothy, Titus, and Silas were missionary coworkers with Paul.

January 27—Lydia, Dorcas, Phoebe On this day the church remembers three women who were companions in Paul's ministry.

January 28—Thomas Aquinas Thomas Aquinas was a brilliant and creative theologian who immersed himself in the thought of Aristotle and worked to explain Christian beliefs in the philosophical culture of the day.

February 2—Presentation of Our Lord Forty days after the birth of Christ, the church marks the day Mary and Joseph presented him in the temple in accordance with Jewish law. Simeon greeted Mary and Joseph, responding with the canticle that begins "Now, Lord, you let your servant go in peace."

February 3—Ansgar Ansgar was a monk who led a mission to Denmark and later to Sweden. His work ran into difficulties with the rulers of the day, and he was forced to withdraw into Germany, where he served as a bishop in Hamburg.

February 5—The Martyrs of Japan In the sixteenth century, Jesuit missionaries, followed by Franciscans, introduced the Christian faith in Japan. By 1630, Christianity was driven underground. This day commemorates the first martyrs of Japan, twenty-six missionaries and converts, who were killed by crucifixion.

February 14—Cyril, Methodius These brothers from a noble family in Thessalonika in northeastern Greece were priests who are regarded as the founders of Slavic literature. Their work in preaching and worshiping in the language of the people is honored by Christians in both East and West.

February 18—Martin Luther On this day Luther died at the age of sixty-two. For a time, he was an Augustinian monk, but it is primarily for his work as a biblical scholar, translator of the Bible, reformer of the liturgy, theologian, educator, and father of German vernacular literature that he is remembered.

February 23—Polycarp Polycarp was bishop of Smyrna and a link between the apostolic age and the church at the end of the second century. At the age of eighty-six he was martyred for his faith.

February 25—Elizabeth Fedde Fedde was born in Norway and trained as a deaconess. Among her notable achievements is the establishment of the Deaconess House in Brooklyn and the Deaconess House and Hospital of the Lutheran Free Church in Minneapolis.

March 1—George Herbert Herbert was ordained a priest in 1630 and served the little parish of St. Andrew Bremerton until

his death. He is best remembered, however, as a writer of poems and hymns, such as "Come, My Way, My Truth, My Life" and "The King of Love My Shepherd Is."

March 2—John Wesley, Charles Wesley The Wesleys were leaders of a revival in the Church of England. Their spiritual methods of frequent communion, fasting, and advocacy for the poor earned them the name "Methodists."

March 7—Perpetua, Felicity In the year 202 the emperor Septimius Severus forbade conversions to Christianity. Perpetua, a noblewoman; Felicity, a slave; and other companions were all catechumens at Carthage in North Africa, where they were imprisoned and sentenced to death.

March 10—Harriet Tubman, Sojourner Truth Harriet Tubman helped about three hundred slaves to escape via the Underground Railroad until slavery was abolished in the United States. After slavery was abolished in New York in 1827, Sojourner Truth became deeply involved in Christianity, and in later life she was a popular speaker against slavery and for women's rights.

March 12—Gregory the Great Gregory held political office and at another time lived as a monk, all before he was elected to the papacy. He also established a school to train church musicians; thus Gregorian chant is named in his honor.

March 17—Patrick Patrick went to Ireland from Britain to serve as a bishop and missionary. He made his base in the north of Ireland and from there made many missionary journeys, with much success.

March 19—Joseph The Gospel of Luke shows Joseph acting in accordance with both civil and religious law by returning to Bethlehem for the census and by presenting the child Jesus in the temple on the fortieth day after his birth.

March 21—Thomas Cranmer Cranmer's lasting achievement is contributing to and overseeing the creation of the Book of Common Prayer, which remains (in revised form) the worship book of the Anglican Communion. He was burned at the stake under Queen Mary for his support of the Protestant Reformation.

March 22—Jonathan Edwards Edwards was a minister in Connecticut and has been described as the greatest of the New England Puritan preachers. Edwards carried out mission work among the Housatonic

Indians of Massachusetts and became president of the College of New Jersey, later to be known as Princeton University.

March 24—Oscar Arnulfo Romero Romero is remembered for his advocacy on behalf of the poor in El Salvador, though it was not a characteristic of his early priesthood. After several years of threats to his life, Romero was assassinated while presiding at the eucharist.

March 25—Annunciation of Our Lord Nine months before Christmas, the church celebrates the annunciation. In Luke the angel Gabriel announces to Mary that she will give birth to the Son of God, and she responds, "Here am I, the servant of the Lord."

March 29—Hans Nielsen Hauge Hans Nielsen Hauge was a layperson who began preaching in Norway and Denmark after a mystical experience that he believed called him to share the assurance of salvation with others. At the time, itinerant preaching and religious gatherings held without the supervision of a pastor were illegal, and Hauge was arrested several times.

March 31—John Donne This priest of the Church of England is commemorated for his poetry and spiritual writing. Most of his poetry was written before his ordination and is sacred and secular, intellectual and sensuous.

April 4—Benedict the African Although Benedict was illiterate, his fame as a confessor brought many visitors to him, and he was eventually named superior of a Franciscan community. A patron saint of African Americans, Benedict is remembered for his patience and understanding when confronted with racial prejudice and taunts.

April 6—Albrecht Dürer, Matthias Grünewald, Lucas Cranach These great artists revealed through their work the mystery of salvation and the wonder of creation. Though Dürer remained a Roman Catholic, at his death Martin Luther wrote to a friend, "Affection bids us mourn for one who was the best." Several religious works are included in Grünewald's small surviving corpus, the most famous being the Isenheim Altarpiece. Lucas Cranach was widely known for his woodcuts, some of which illustrated the first German printing of the New Testament.

April 9—Dietrich Bonhoeffer In 1933, and with Hitler's rise to power, Bonhoeffer became a leading spokesman for the Confessing Church, a resistance movement against the Nazis. After leading a worship service on April 8, 1945, at Schönberg prison, he was taken away to be hanged the next day.

April 10—Mikael Agricola Agricola began a reform of the Finnish church along Lutheran lines. He translated the New Testament, the prayer book, hymns, and the mass into Finnish and through this work set the rules of orthography that are the basis of modern Finnish spelling.

April 19—Olavus Petri, Laurentius Petri These two brothers are commemorated for their introduction of the Lutheran movement to the Church of Sweden after studying at the University of Wittenberg. Together the brothers published a complete Bible in Swedish and a revised liturgy in 1541.

April 21—Anselm This eleventh-century Benedictine monk stands out as one of the greatest theologians between Augustine and Thomas Aquinas. He is perhaps best known for his "satisfaction" theory of atonement, in which God takes on human nature in Jesus Christ in order to make the perfect payment for sin.

April 23—Toyohiko Kagawa Toyohiko Kagawa's vocation to help the poor led him to live among them. He was arrested for his efforts to reconcile Japan and China after the Japanese attack of 1940.

April 25—Mark Though Mark himself was not an apostle, it is likely that he was a member of one of the early Christian communities. The gospel attributed to him is brief and direct and is considered by many to be the earliest gospel.

April 29—Catherine of Siena Catherine of Siena was a member of the Order of Preachers (Dominicans), and among Roman Catholics she was the first woman to receive the title Doctor of the Church. She also advised popes and any uncertain persons who told her their problems.

May 1—Philip, James Philip and James are commemorated together because the remains of these two saints were placed in the Church of the Apostles in Rome on this day in 561.

May 2—Athanasius At the Council of Nicea in 325 and when he himself served as bishop of Alexandria, Athanasius defended the full divinity of Christ against the Arian position held by emperors, magistrates, and theologians.

May 4—Monica Almost everything known about Monica comes from Augustine's *Confessions*, his autobiography. Her dying wish was that her son remember her at the altar of the Lord, wherever he was.

May 8—Julian of Norwich Julian was most likely a Benedictine nun living in an isolated cell attached to the Carrow Priory in Norwich, England. When she was about thirty years old, she reported visions that she later compiled into a book, *Sixteen Revelations of Divine Love*, which is a classic of medieval mysticism.

May 9—Nicolaus Ludwig von Zinzendorf Drawn from an overly intellectual Lutheran faith to Pietism, at the age of twenty-two Count Zinzendorf permitted a group of Moravians to live on his lands. Zinzendorf participated in worldwide missions emanating from this community and is also remembered for writing hymns characteristic of his Pietistic faith.

May 14—Matthias After Christ's ascension, the apostles met in Jerusalem to choose a replacement for Judas. Though little is known about him, Matthias had traveled among the disciples from the time of Jesus' baptism until his ascension.

May 18—Erik Erik, long considered the patron saint of Sweden, ruled there from 1150 to 1160. He is honored for efforts to bring peace to the nearby pagan kingdoms and for his crusades to spread the Christian faith in Scandinavia.

May 21—Helena Helena was the mother of Constantine, a man who later became the Roman emperor. Helena is remembered for traveling through Palestine and building churches on the sites she believed to be where Jesus was born, where he was buried, and from which he ascended.

May 24—Nicolaus Copernicus, Leonhard Euler Copernicus formally studied astronomy, mathematics, Greek, Plato, law, medicine, and canon law and is chiefly remembered for his work as an astronomer and his idea that the sun, not the earth, is the center of the solar system. Euler is regarded as one of the founders of the science of pure mathematics and made important contributions to mechanics, hydrodynamics, astronomy, optics, and acoustics.

May 27—John Calvin Having embraced the views of the Reformation by his mid-twenties, John Calvin was a preacher in Geneva, was banished once, and later returned to reform the city with a rigid, theocratic discipline. Calvin is considered the father of the Reformed churches.

May 29—Jiří Tranovský Jiří Tranovský is considered the "Luther of the Slavs" and the father of Slovak hymnody. He produced a translation of the Augsburg Confession and published his hymn collection *Cithara Sanctorum* (Lyre of the Saints), also known as the Tranoscius, which is the foundation of Slovak Lutheran hymnody.

May 31—Visit of Mary to Elizabeth Sometime after the annunciation, Mary visited her cousin Elizabeth, who greeted Mary with the words, "Blessed are you among women," and Mary responded with her famous song, the Magnificat.

June 1—Justin Justin was a teacher of philosophy and engaged in debates about the truth of Christian faith. Having been arrested and jailed for practicing an unauthorized religion, he refused to renounce his faith, and he and six of his students were beheaded.

June 3—The Martyrs of Uganda King Mwanga of Uganda was angered by Christian members of the court whose first allegiance was not to him but to Christ. On this date in 1886, thirty-two young men were burned to death for refusing to renounce Christianity. Their persecution led to a much stronger Christian presence in the country.

June 3—John XXIII Despite the expectation upon his election that the seventy-seven-year-old John XXIII would be a transitional pope, he had great energy and spirit. He convened the Second Vatican Council in order to open the windows of the church. The council brought about great changes in Roman Catholic worship and ecumenical relationships.

June 5—Boniface Boniface led large numbers of Benedictine monks and nuns in establishing churches, schools, and seminaries. Boniface was preparing a group for confirmation on the eve of Pentecost when he and others were killed by a band of pagans.

June 7—Seattle The city of Seattle was named after Noah Seattle against his wishes. After Chief Seattle became a Roman Catholic, he began the practice of morning and evening prayer in the tribe, a practice that continued after his death.

June 9—Columba, Aidan, Bede These three monks from the British Isles were pillars among those who kept alive the light of learning and devotion during the Middle

Ages. Columba founded three monasteries, including one on the island of Iona, off the coast of Scotland. Aidan, who helped bring Christianity to the Northumbria area of England, was known for his pastoral style and ability to stir people to charity and good works. Bede was a Bible translator and scripture scholar who wrote a history of the English church and was the first historian to date events anno Domini (AD), the "year of our Lord."

June 11—Barnabas Though he was not among the Twelve mentioned in the gospels, the book of Acts gives Barnabas the title of apostle. When Paul came to Jerusalem after his conversion, Barnabas took him in over the fears of the other apostles who doubted Paul's discipleship.

June 14—Basil the Great, Gregory of Nyssa, Gregory of Nazianzus, Macrina The three men in this group are known as the Cappadocian fathers; all three explored the mystery of the Holy Trinity. Basil's Longer Rule and Shorter Rule for monastic life are the basis for Eastern monasticism to this day, and express a preference for communal monastic life over that of hermits. Gregory of Nazianzus defended Orthodox trinitarian and christological doctrine, and his preaching won over the city of Constantinople. Gregory of Nyssa is remembered as a writer on spiritual life and the contemplation of God in worship and sacraments. Macrina was the older sister of Basil and Gregory of Nyssa, and her teaching was influential within the early church.

June 21—Onesimos Nesib Onesimos, an Ethiopian, was captured by slave traders and taken from his homeland to Eritrea, where he was bought, freed, and educated by Swedish missionaries. He translated the Bible into Oromo and returned to his homeland to preach the gospel there.

June 24—John the Baptist The birth of John the Baptist is celebrated exactly six months before Christmas Eve. For Christians in the Northern Hemisphere, these two dates are deeply symbolic, since John said that he must decrease as Jesus increased. John was born as the days are longest and then steadily decrease, while Jesus was born as the days are shortest and then steadily increase.

June 25—Presentation of the Augsburg Confession On this day in 1530 the German and Latin editions of the Augsburg Confession were presented to Emperor Charles of the Holy Roman Empire. The Augsburg Confession was written by Philipp Melanchthon and endorsed by Martin Luther and consists of a brief summary of points in which the reformers saw their teaching as either agreeing with or differing from that of the Roman Catholic Church of the time.

June 25—Philipp Melanchthon Though he died on April 19, Philipp Melanchthon is commemorated today in connection with the Augsburg Confession. Colleague and co-reformer with Martin Luther, Melanchthon was a brilliant scholar, known as "the teacher of Germany."

June 27—Cyril Remembered as an outstanding theologian, Cyril defended the Orthodox teachings about the person of Christ against Nestorius, who was at that time bishop of Constantinople. Eventually it was decided that Cyril's interpretation, that Christ's person included both divine and human natures, was correct.

June 28—Irenaeus Irenaeus believed that only Matthew, Mark, Luke, and John were trustworthy gospels. As a result of his battles with the Gnostics, he was one of the first to speak of the church as "catholic," meaning that congregations did not exist by themselves but were linked to one another throughout the whole church.

June 29—Peter, Paul One of the things that unites Peter and Paul is the tradition that says they were martyred together on this date in AD 67 or 68. What unites them even more closely is their common confession of Jesus Christ.

July 1—Catherine Winkworth, John Mason Neale Many of the most beloved hymns in the English language are the work of these gifted poets. Catherine Winkworth devoted herself to the translation of German hymns into English, while John Mason Neale specialized in translating many ancient Latin and Greek hymns.

July 3—Thomas Alongside the doubt for which Thomas is famous, the Gospel according to John shows Thomas moving from doubt to deep faith. Thomas makes one of the strongest confessions of faith in the New Testament, "My Lord and my God!" (John 20:28).

July 6—Jan Hus Jan Hus was a Bohemian priest who spoke against abuses in the church of his day in many of the same ways Luther would a century later. The followers of Jan Hus became known as the Czech Brethren and later became the Moravian Church.

July 11—Benedict of Nursia Benedict is known as the father of Western monasticism. Benedict encouraged a generous spirit of hospitality. Visitors to Benedictine communities are to be welcomed as Christ himself.

July 12—Nathan Söderblom In 1930 this Swedish theologian, ecumenist, and social activist received the Nobel Prize for peace. Söderblom organized the Universal Christian Council on Life and Work, which was one of the organizations that in 1948 came together to form the World Council of Churches.

July 17—Bartolomé de Las Casas Bartolomé de Las Casas was a Spanish priest and a missionary in the Western Hemisphere. Throughout the Caribbean and Central America, he worked to stop the enslavement of native people, to halt the brutal treatment of women by military forces, and to promote laws that humanized the process of colonization.

July 22—Mary Magdalene The gospels report Mary Magdalene was one of the women of Galilee who followed Jesus. As the first person to whom the risen Lord appeared, she returned to the disciples with the news and has been called "the apostle to the apostles" for her proclamation of the resurrection.

July 23—Birgitta of Sweden Birgitta's devotional commitments led her to give to the poor and needy all that she owned while she began to live a more ascetic life. She founded an order of monks and nuns, the Order of the Holy Savior (Birgittines), whose superior was a woman.

July 25—James James was one of the sons of Zebedee and is counted as one of the twelve disciples. James was the first of the Twelve to suffer martyrdom and is the only apostle whose martyrdom is recorded in scripture.

July 28—Johann Sebastian Bach, Heinrich Schütz, George Frederick Handel These three composers did much to enrich the worship life of the church. Johann Sebastian Bach drew on the Lutheran tradition of hymnody and wrote about two hundred cantatas, including at least two for each Sunday and festival day in the Lutheran calendar of his day. George Frederick Handel was not primarily a church musician, but his great work *Messiah* is a musical proclamation of the scriptures. Heinrich Schütz wrote choral settings of biblical texts and paid special attention to ways his composition would underscore the meaning of the words.

July 29—Mary, Martha, Lazarus of Bethany Mary and Martha are remembered for the hospitality and refreshment they offered Jesus in their home. Following the characterization drawn by Luke, Martha represents the active life, and Mary, the contemplative.

July 29—Olaf Olaf is considered the patron saint of Norway. While at war in the Baltic and in Normandy, he became a Christian; then he returned to Norway and declared himself king, and from then on Christianity was the dominant religion of the realm.

August 8—Dominic Dominic believed that a stumbling block to restoring heretics to the church was the wealth of clergy, so he formed an itinerant religious order, the Order of Preachers (Dominicans), who lived in poverty, studied philosophy and theology, and preached against heresy.

August 10—Lawrence Lawrence was one of seven deacons of the congregation at Rome and, like the deacons appointed in Acts, was responsible for financial matters in the church and for the care of the poor.

August 11—Clare At age eighteen, Clare of Assisi heard Francis preach a sermon. With Francis's help she and a growing number of companions established a women's Franciscan community called the Order of Poor Ladies, or Poor Clares.

August 13—Florence Nightingale, Clara Maass Nightingale led a group of thirty-eight nurses to serve in the Crimean War, where they worked in appalling conditions. She returned to London as a hero and there resumed her work for hospital reform. Clara Maass was born in New Jersey and served as a nurse in the Spanish-American War, where she encountered the horrors of yellow fever. Later responding to a call for subjects in research on yellow fever, Maass contracted the disease and died.

August 14—Maximilian Kolbe, Kaj Munk Confined in Auschwitz, Father Kolbe was a Franciscan priest who gave generously of his meager resources and finally volunteered to be starved to death in place of another man who was a husband and father. Kaj Munk, a Danish Lutheran pastor and playwright, was an outspoken critic of the Nazis. His plays frequently highlighted the eventual victory of the Christian faith despite the church's weak and ineffective witness.

August 15—Mary, Mother of Our Lord The honor paid to Mary as mother of our Lord goes back to biblical times, when Mary herself sang, "From now on all generations will call me blessed" (Luke 1:48). Mary's song speaks of reversals in the reign of God: the mighty are cast down, the lowly are lifted up, the hungry are fed, and the rich are sent away empty-handed.

August 20—Bernard of Clairvaux Bernard was a Cistercian monk who became an abbot of great spiritual depth. Through translation his several devotional writings and hymns are still read and sung today.

August 24—Bartholomew Bartholomew is mentioned as one of Jesus' disciples in Matthew, Mark, and Luke. Except for his name on these lists of the Twelve, little is known.

August 28—Augustine As an adult, Augustine came to see Christianity as a religion appropriate for a philosopher. Augustine was baptized by Ambrose at the Easter Vigil in 387, was made bishop of Hippo in 396, and was one of the greatest theologians of the Western church.

August 28—Moses the Black A man of great strength and rough character, Moses the Black was converted to Christian faith toward the close of the fourth century. The change in his heart and life had a profound impact on his native Ethiopia.

September 2—Nikolai Frederik Severin Grundtvig Grundtvig was a prominent Danish theologian of the nineteenth century. From his university days, he was convinced that poetry spoke to the human spirit better than prose, and he wrote more than a thousand hymns.

September 9—Peter Claver Peter Claver was born into Spanish nobility and was persuaded to become a Jesuit missionary. He served in Cartagena (in what is now Colombia) by teaching and caring for the slaves.

September 13—John Chrysostom John was a priest in Antioch and an outstanding preacher. His eloquence earned him the nickname Chrysostom ("golden mouth"), but he also preached against corruption among the royal court, whereupon the empress sent him into exile.

September 14—Holy Cross Day The celebration of Holy Cross Day commemorates the dedication of the Church of the Resurrection in 335 on the location believed to have been where Christ was buried.

September 16—Cyprian During Cyprian's time as bishop, many people had denied the faith under duress. In contrast to some who held the belief that the church should not receive these people back, Cyprian believed they ought to be welcomed into full communion after a period of penance.

September 17—Hildegard, Abbess of Bingen Hildegard lived virtually her entire life in convents yet was widely influential. She advised and reproved kings and popes, wrote poems and hymns, and produced treatises in medicine, theology, and natural history.

September 18—Dag Hammarskjöld Dag Hammarskjöld was a Swedish diplomat and humanitarian who served as secretary general of the United Nations. The depth of Hammarskjöld's Christian faith was unknown until his private journal, *Markings*, was published following his death.

September 21—Matthew Matthew was a tax collector, an occupation that was distrusted, since tax collectors were frequently dishonest and worked as agents for the Roman occupying government; yet it was these outcasts to whom Jesus showed his love. Since the second century, tradition has attributed the first gospel to him.

September 29—Michael and All Angels The scriptures speak of angels who worship God in heaven, and in both testaments angels are God's messengers on earth. Michael is an angel whose name appears in Daniel as the heavenly being who leads the faithful dead to God's throne on the day of resurrection, while in the book of Revelation, Michael fights in a cosmic battle against Satan.

September 30—Jerome Jerome translated the scriptures into the Latin that was spoken and written by the majority of people in his day. His translation is known as the Vulgate, which comes from the Latin word for "common."

October 4—Francis of Assisi Francis renounced wealth and future inheritance and devoted himself to serving the poor. Since Francis had a spirit of gratitude for all of God's creation, this commemoration has been a traditional time to bless pets and animals, creatures Francis called his brothers and sisters.

October 4—Theodor Fliedner Fliedner's work was instrumental in the revival of the ministry of deaconesses among Lutherans. Fliedner's deaconess motherhouse in Kaiserswerth, Germany, inspired Lutherans all over the world to commission deaconesses to serve in parishes, schools, prisons, and hospitals.

October 6—William Tyndale Tyndale's plan to translate the scriptures into English met opposition from Henry VIII. Though Tyndale completed work on the New Testament in 1525 and worked on a portion of the Old Testament, he was tried for heresy and burned at the stake.

October 7—Henry Melchior Muhlenberg Muhlenberg was prominent in setting the course for Lutheranism in the United States by helping Lutheran churches make the transition from the state churches of Europe to independent churches of America. Among other things, he established the first Lutheran synod in America and developed an American Lutheran liturgy.

October 15—Teresa of Avila Teresa of Avila (also known as Teresa de Jesús) chose the life of a Carmelite nun after reading the letters of Jerome. Teresa's writings on devotional life are widely read by members of various denominations.

October 17—Ignatius Ignatius was the second bishop of Antioch in Syria. When his own martyrdom approached, he wrote in one of his letters, "I prefer death in Christ Jesus to power over the farthest limits of the earth.... Do not stand in the way of my birth to real life."

October 18—Luke Luke, as author of both Luke and Acts, was careful to place the events of Jesus' life in both their social and religious contexts. Some of the most loved parables and canticles are found only in this gospel.

October 23—James of Jerusalem James is described in the New Testament as the brother of Jesus, and the secular historian Josephus called James, the brother of Jesus, "the so-called Christ." Little is known about James, but Josephus reported that the Pharisees respected James for his piety and observance of the law.

October 26—Philipp Nicolai, Johann Heermann, Paul Gerhardt These three outstanding hymnwriters all worked in Germany in the seventeenth century during times of war and plague. Philipp Nicolai's hymns "Wake, Awake, for Night Is Flying" and "O Morning Star, How Fair and Bright!" were included in a series of meditations he wrote to comfort his parishioners during the plague. The style of Johann Heermann's hymns (including "Ah, Holy Jesus") moved away from the more objective style of Reformation hymnody toward expressing the emotions of faith. Paul Gerhardt, whom some have called the greatest of Lutheran

hymnwriters, lost a preaching position at St. Nicholas's Church in Berlin because he refused to sign a document stating he would not make theological arguments in his sermons.

October 28—Simon, Jude Little is known about Simon and Jude. In New Testament lists of the apostles, Simon the "zealot" or Cananaean is mentioned, but he is never mentioned apart from these lists. Jude, sometimes called Thaddaeus, is also mentioned in lists of the Twelve.

October 31—Reformation Day By the end of the seventeenth century, many Lutheran churches celebrated a festival commemorating Martin Luther's posting of the 95 Theses, a summary of abuses in the church of his time. At the heart of the reform movement was the gospel, the good news that it is by grace through faith that we are justified and set free.

November 1—All Saints Day The custom of commemorating all of the saints of the church on a single day goes back at least to the third century. All Saints Day celebrates the baptized people of God, living and dead, who make up the body of Christ.

November 3—Martín de Porres Martín was a lay brother in the Order of Preachers (Dominicans) and engaged in many charitable works. He is recognized as an advocate for Christian charity and interracial justice.

November 7—John Christian Frederick Heyer, Bartholomaeus Ziegenbalg, Ludwig Nommensen Heyer was the first missionary sent out by American Lutherans, and he became a missionary in the Andhra region of India. Ziegenbalg was a missionary to the Tamils of Tranquebar on the southeast coast of India. Nommensen worked among the Batak people, who had previously not seen Christian missionaries.

November 11—Martin of Tours In 371 Martin was elected bishop of Tours. As bishop he developed a reputation for intervening on behalf of prisoners and heretics who had been sentenced to death.

November 11—Søren Aabye Kierkegaard Kierkegaard, a nineteenth-century Danish theologian whose writings reflect his Lutheran heritage, was the founder of modern existentialism. Kierkegaard's work attacked the established church of his day—its complacency, its tendency to intellectualize faith, and its desire to be accepted by polite society.

November 17—Elizabeth of Hungary This Hungarian princess gave away large sums of money, including her dowry, for relief of the poor and sick. She founded hospitals, cared for 392 orphans, and used the royal food supplies to feed the hungry.

November 23—Clement Clement is best remembered for a letter he wrote to the Corinthian congregation still having difficulty with divisions in spite of Paul's canonical letters. Clement's letter is also a witness to early understandings of church government and the way each office in the church works for the good of the whole.

November 23—Miguel Agustín Pro Miguel Agustín Pro grew up among oppression in Mexico and worked on behalf of the poor and homeless. Miguel and his two brothers were arrested, falsely accused of throwing a bomb at the car of a government official, and executed by a firing squad.

November 24—Justus Falckner, Jehu Jones, William Passavant Not only was Falckner the first Lutheran pastor to be ordained in North America, but he published a catechism that was the first Lutheran book published on the continent. Jones was the Lutheran Church's first African American pastor and carried out missionary work in Philadelphia, which led to the formation there of the first African American Lutheran congregation (St. Paul's). William Passavant helped to establish hospitals and orphanages in a number of cities and was the first to introduce deaconesses to the work of hospitals in the United States.

November 25—Isaac Watts Watts wrote about six hundred hymns, many of them in a two-year period beginning when he was twenty years old. When criticized for writing hymns not taken from scripture, he responded that if we can pray prayers that are not from scripture but written by us, then surely we can sing hymns that we have made up ourselves.

November 30—Andrew Andrew was the first of the Twelve. As a part of his calling, he brought other people, including Simon Peter, to meet Jesus.

December 3—Francis Xavier Francis Xavier became a missionary to India, Southeast Asia, Japan, and the Philippines. Together with Ignatius Loyola and five others, Francis formed the Society of Jesus (Jesuits).

December 4—John of Damascus John left a career in finance and government to become a monk in an abbey near Jerusalem. He wrote many hymns as well as theological works, including *The Fount of Wisdom*, a work that touches on philosophy, heresy, and the orthodox faith.

December 6—Nicholas Nicholas was a bishop in what is now Turkey. Legends that surround Nicholas tell of his love for God and neighbor, especially the poor.

December 7—Ambrose Ambrose was baptized, ordained, and consecrated a bishop all on the same day. While bishop he gave away his wealth and lived in simplicity.

December 13—Lucy Lucy was a young Christian of Sicily who was martyred during the persecutions under Emperor Diocletian. Her celebration became particularly important in Sweden and Norway, perhaps because the feast of Lucia (whose name means "light") originally fell on the shortest day of the year.

December 14—John of the Cross John was a monk of the Carmelite religious order who met Teresa of Avila when she was working to reform the Carmelite Order and return it to a stricter observance of its rules. His writings, like Teresa's, reflect a deep interest in mystical thought and meditation.

December 20—Katharina von Bora Luther Katharina took vows as a nun, but around age twenty-four she and several other nuns who were influenced by the writings of Martin Luther left the convent. When she later became Luther's wife, she proved herself a gifted household manager and became a trusted partner.

December 26—Stephen Stephen, a deacon and the first martyr of the church, was one of those seven upon whom the apostles laid hands after they had been chosen to serve widows and others in need. Later, Stephen's preaching angered the temple authorities, and they ordered him to be put to death by stoning.

December 27—John John, the son of Zebedee, was a fisherman and one of the Twelve. Tradition has attributed authorship of the gospel and the three epistles bearing his name to the apostle John.

December 28—The Holy Innocents The infant martyrs commemorated on this day were the children of Bethlehem, two years old and younger, who were killed by Herod, who worried that his reign was threatened by the birth of a new king named Jesus.

Anniversary of Baptism (abbreviated)

This order is intended for use in the home. It may be adapted for use in another context, such as a Christian education setting. When used in the home, a parent or sponsor may be the leader. A more expanded version of this order appears in *Evangelical Lutheran Worship Pastoral Care* (pp. 128–135).

A bowl of water may be placed in the midst of those who are present.

Gathering

A baptismal hymn or acclamation (see Evangelical Lutheran Worship #209–217, 442–459) may be sung.

The sign of the cross may be made by all in remembrance of their baptism as the leader begins.

In the name of the Father, and of the + Son, and of the Holy Spirit.
Amen.

The candle received at baptism or another candle may be used. As it is lighted, the leader may say:

Jesus said, I am the light of the world.
Whoever follows me will have the light of life.

Reading

One or more scripture readings follow. Those present may share in reading.

A reading from Mark: People were bringing little children to Jesus in order that he might touch them; and the disciples spoke sternly to them. But when Jesus saw this, he was indignant and said, "Let the little children come to me; do not stop them; for it is to such as these that the kingdom of God belongs." And he took them up in his arms, laid his hands on them, and blessed them. *(Mark 10:13-14, 16)*

A reading from Second Corinthians: If anyone is in Christ, there is a new creation: everything old has passed away; see, everything has become new! *(2 Corinthians 5:17)*

A reading from First John: Beloved, let us love one another, because love is from God; everyone who loves is born of God and knows God. *(1 John 4:7)*

Those present may share experiences related to baptism and their lives as baptized children of God. A portion of the Small Catechism (Evangelical Lutheran Worship, pp. 1160–1167) may be read as part of this conversation.

A baptismal hymn or acclamation may be sung.

Baptismal Remembrance

A parent or sponsor may trace a cross on the forehead of the person celebrating a baptismal anniversary. Water from a bowl placed in the midst of those present may be used. These or similar words may be said.

Name, when you were baptized, you were marked with the cross of Christ forever.
Remember your baptism with thanksgiving and joy.

Prayers

Prayers may include the following or other appropriate prayers. Others who are present may place a hand on the head or shoulder of the one who is celebrating the anniversary.

Let us pray.
Gracious God, we thank you for the new life you give us through holy baptism. Especially, we ask you to bless *name* on the anniversary of *her/his* baptism. Continue to strengthen *name* with the Holy Spirit, and increase in *her/him* your gifts of grace: the spirit of wisdom and understanding, the spirit of counsel and might, the spirit of knowledge and the fear of the Lord, the spirit of joy in your presence; through Jesus Christ, our Savior and Lord.
Amen.

Other prayers may be added. Those present may offer petitions and thanksgivings.

The prayers may conclude with the Lord's Prayer.

Our Father in heaven,
   hallowed be your name, your kingdom come,
   your will be done, on earth as in heaven.
Give us today our daily bread.
Forgive us our sins
   as we forgive those who sin against us.
Save us from the time of trial and deliver us from evil.
For the kingdom, the power, and the glory are yours,
   now and forever. Amen.

Blessing

The order may conclude with this or another suitable blessing.

Almighty God, who gives us a new birth by water and the Holy Spirit and forgives us all our sins, strengthen us in all goodness and by the power of the Holy Spirit keep us in eternal life through Jesus Christ our Lord.
Amen.

The greeting of peace may be shared by all.

Other suggested readings for this service:
John 3:1-8: *Born again from above*
Romans 6:3-11: *Raised with Christ in baptism*
Galatians 3:26-28: *All are one in Christ*
Ephesians 4:1-6: *There is one body and one Spirit*
Colossians 1:11-13: *Claimed by Christ, heirs of light*
1 Peter 2:2-3: *Long for spiritual food*
1 Peter 2:9: *Chosen in baptism to tell about God*
Revelation 22:1-2: *The river of the water of life*

Prayers for Various Situations

A prayer to begin the work day

May the graciousness of the Lord our God be upon us;
prosper the work of our hands. (Ps. 90:17, *ELW*)
Generous God, you call us to lives of service.
In my words and actions this day, move me to serve in Christ's name.
When I lack energy, inspire me. When I lack courage, strengthen me.
When I lack compassion, be merciful to me.
You may make the sign of the cross.

In all things, O God, you are our way, our truth and our life. Reveal through me
your life-giving work, that I love my neighbors as myself. I ask this in Jesus'
name. Amen.

A prayer to begin the school day

Show me your ways, O Lord, and teach me your paths. (Ps. 25:4, *ELW*)
Christ be with me: in you I am never alone.
Christ within me: your Spirit is at work in me.
Christ behind me: reassure me when I struggle.
Christ before me: lead me when I am uncertain.
Christ beneath me: support me when I am weak.
Christ above me: encourage me to do my best.
Christ in quiet: I listen for the sound of your voice.
Christ in danger: I will not fear, for you are with me.
You may make the sign of the cross.

In all things, O God, you are our way, our truth, and our life.
Teach me to love you and my neighbors as myself.
I ask this in Jesus' name. Amen.
(Based on the Prayer of St. Patrick)

Time of conflict, crisis, disaster

O God, where hearts are fearful and constricted, grant courage and hope.
Where anxiety is infectious and widening, grant peace and reassurance.

Where impossibilities close every door and window, grant imagination and resistance. Where distrust twists our thinking, grant healing and illumination. Where spirits are daunted and weakened, grant soaring wings and strengthened dreams. All these things we ask in the name of Jesus Christ, our Savior and Lord. Amen.

The care of children

Almighty God, with a mother's love and a father's care you have blessed us with the joy and responsibility of children. As we bring them up, give us gracious love, calm strength, and patient wisdom, that we may teach them to love whatever is just and true and good, following the example of Jesus Christ, our Savior. Amen.

Health of body and soul

By your power, great God, our Lord Jesus healed the sick and gave new hope to the hopeless. Though we cannot command or possess your power, we pray for those who want to be healed. Mend their wounds, soothe fevered brows, and make broken people whole again. Help us to welcome every healing as a sign that, though death is against us, you are for us, and have promised renewed and risen life in Jesus Christ the Lord. Amen.

Those in affliction

Lord Christ, you came into the world as one of us, and suffered as we do. As we go through the trials of life, help us to realize that you are with us at all times and in all things; that we have no secrets from you; and that your loving grace enfolds us for eternity. In the security of your embrace we pray. Amen.

Those in emotional distress

Merciful God, you give us the grace that helps in time of need. Surround *name* with your steadfast love and lighten *her/his* burden. By the power of your Spirit, free *her/him* from distress and give *her/him* a new mind and heart made whole in the name of the risen Christ. Amen.

Those who suffer abuse and violence

Holy One, you do not distance yourself from the pain of your people, but in Jesus you bear that pain with all who suffer at others' hands. With your cleansing love bring healing and strength to *name*; and by your justice, lift *her/him* up, that in body, mind, and spirit, *she/he* may again rejoice. In Jesus' name we pray. Amen.

Those in trouble or bereavement

Almighty God, your love never fails, and you can turn the shadow of death into daybreak. Help us to receive your word with believing hearts, so that, confident in your promises, we may have hope and be lifted out of sorrow into the joy and peace of your presence; through Jesus Christ our Savior and Lord. Amen.

Those suffering from addiction

O blessed Jesus, you ministered to all who came to you. Look with compassion upon all who through addiction have lost their health and freedom. Restore to them the assurance of your unfailing mercy; remove the fears that attack them; strengthen those who are engaged in the work of recovery; and to those who care for them, give honesty, understanding, and persevering love; for your mercy's sake. Amen.

The chronically ill and those who support them

Loving God, your heart overflows with compassion for your whole creation. Pour out your Spirit on all people living with illness for which there is no cure, as well as their families and loved ones. Help them to know that you claim them as your own and deliver them from fear and pain; for the sake of Jesus Christ, our healer and Lord. Amen.

Caregivers and others who support the sick

God, our refuge and strength, our present help in time of trouble, care for those who tend the needs of *name*. Strengthen them in body and spirit. Refresh them when weary; console them when anxious; comfort them in grief; and hearten them in discouragement. Be with us all, and give us peace at all times and in every way; through Christ our peace. Amen.

Recovery from sickness

Almighty and merciful God, you are the only source of health and healing; you alone can bring calmness and peace. Grant to us, your children, an awareness of your presence and a strong confidence in you. In our pain, our weariness, and our anxiety, surround us with your care, protect us by your loving might, and permit us once more to enjoy health and strength and peace; through Jesus Christ, our Savior and Lord. Amen.

A prayer attributed to Francis of Assisi

Lord, make us instruments of your peace. Where there is hatred, let us sow love; where there is injury, pardon; where there is discord, union; where there is doubt, faith; where there is despair, hope; where there is darkness, light; where there is sadness, joy. Grant that we may not so much seek to be consoled as to console; to be understood as to understand; to be loved as to love. For it is in giving that we receive; it is in pardoning that we are pardoned; and it is in dying that we are born to eternal life. Amen.

A prayer of Catherine of Siena

Power of the eternal Father, help me. Wisdom of the Son, enlighten the eye of my understanding. Tender mercy of the Holy Spirit, unite my heart to yourself. Eternal God, restore health to the sick and life to the dead. Give us a voice, your own voice, to cry out to you for mercy for the world. You, light, give us light. You, wisdom, give us wisdom. You, supreme strength, strengthen us. Amen.

A prayer of Julian of Norwich

In you, Father all-mighty, we have our preservation and our bliss. In you, Christ, we have our restoring and our saving. You are our mother, brother, and savior. In you, our Lord the Holy Spirit, is marvelous and plenteous grace. You are our clothing; for love you wrap us and embrace us. You are our maker, our lover, our keeper. Teach us to believe that by your grace all shall be well, and all shall be well, and all manner of things shall be well. Amen.

A prayer of Martin Luther

Behold, Lord, an empty vessel that needs to be filled. My Lord, fill it. I am weak in the faith; strengthen me. I am cold in love; warm me and make me fervent, that my love may go out to my neighbor. I do not have a strong and firm faith; at times I doubt and am unable to trust you altogether. O Lord, help me. Strengthen my faith and trust in you. In you I have sealed the treasure of all I have. I am poor; you are rich and came to be merciful to the poor. I am a sinner; you are upright. With me, there is an abundance of sin; in you is the fullness of righteousness. Therefore I will remain with you, of whom I can receive, but to whom I may not give. Amen.

Prayers on pages 419–422 from *Evangelical Lutheran Worship.*

Morning Blessing

You may make the sign of the cross.

I am a beloved child of God, marked with the cross of Christ forever.

Your mercies are new every morning. *(Based on Lam. 3:23)*

Thank you, gracious God, for the gift of this new day.
Awaken me to your abiding presence;
open my eyes to your creation;
open my ears to your promises;
open my heart to the needs of others.
Fill me with your Spirit and guide me this day
in works of kindness, justice, and mercy.
I ask this in the name of Jesus, the light and life of the world.
Amen.

A Simplified Form for Morning Prayer

Opening

O Lord, open my lips,
and my mouth shall proclaim your praise.
Glory to the Father, and to the Son,
and to the Holy Spirit:
as it was in the beginning, is now,
and will be forever. Amen.

The alleluia is omitted during Lent.

[Alleluia.]

Psalmody

The psalmody may begin with Psalm 63, Psalm 67, Psalm 95, Psalm 100, or another psalm appropriate for morning. Psalms provided in this book for each week may be used instead of or in addition to the psalms mentioned.

A time of silence follows.

A hymn may follow (see the suggested hymn for each day).

Readings

One or more readings for each day may be selected from those provided in this book. The reading of scripture may be followed by silence for reflection.

The reflection may conclude with these or similar words.

Long ago God spoke to our ancestors
in many and various ways by the prophets,
but in these last days God has spoken to us by the Son.

Gospel Canticle

The song of Zechariah may be sung or said.

Blessed are you, Lord, the God of Israel,
you have come to your people and set them free.
You have raised up for us a mighty Savior,
born of the house of your servant David.
Through your holy prophets, you promised of old
to save us from our enemies,
from the hands of all who hate us,
to show mercy to our forebears,
and to remember your holy covenant.
This was the oath you swore to our father Abraham:
to set us free from the hands of our enemies,
free to worship you without fear,
holy and righteous before you, all the days of our life.
And you, child, shall be called the prophet of the Most High,
for you will go before the Lord to prepare the way,
to give God's people knowledge of salvation
by the forgiveness of their sins.
In the tender compassion of our God
the dawn from on high shall break upon us,
to shine on those who dwell in darkness and the shadow of death,
and to guide our feet into the way of peace.

Prayers

Various intercessions may be spoken at this time. The prayer provided in this book for each day may also be used.

The following prayer is especially appropriate for morning.

Almighty and everlasting God,
you have brought us in safety to this new day.
Preserve us with your mighty power,
that we may not fall into sin
nor be overcome in adversity.

In all we do, direct us to the fulfilling of your purpose;
through Jesus Christ our Lord.
Amen.

The Lord's Prayer

Our Father in heaven,
  hallowed be your name,
  your kingdom come,
  your will be done, on earth as in heaven.
Give us today our daily bread.
Forgive us our sins
  as we forgive those who sin against us.
Save us from the time of trial
  and deliver us from evil.
For the kingdom, the power, and the glory are yours,
  now and forever. Amen.

Blessing

Let us bless the Lord.
Thanks be to God.

Almighty God,
the Father, + the Son, and the Holy Spirit,
bless and preserve us.
Amen.

Additional materials for daily prayer are available in Evangelical Lutheran Worship
(pp. 295–331) and may supplement this simple order.

A Simplified Form for Evening Prayer

Opening
Jesus Christ is the light of the world,
the light no darkness can overcome.
Stay with us, Lord, for it is evening,
and the day is almost over.
Let your light scatter the darkness
and illumine your church.

Psalmody
The psalmody may begin with Psalm 141, Psalm 121, or another psalm appropriate for evening. Psalms provided in this book for each week may be used instead of or in addition to the psalms mentioned.

A time of silence follows.

A hymn may follow (see the suggested hymn for each day).

Readings
One or more readings for each day may be selected from those provided in this book. The reading of scripture may be followed by silence for reflection.

The reflection may conclude with these or similar words.

Jesus said, I am the light of the world.
Whoever follows me will never walk in darkness.

Gospel Canticle

The song of Mary may be sung or said.

My soul proclaims the greatness of the Lord,
my spirit rejoices in God my Savior,
for you, Lord, have looked with favor on your lowly servant.
From this day all generations will call me blessed:
you, the Almighty, have done great things for me,
and holy is your name.
You have mercy on those who fear you,
from generation to generation.
You have shown strength with your arm
and scattered the proud in their conceit,
casting down the mighty from their thrones
and lifting up the lowly.
You have filled the hungry with good things
and sent the rich away empty.
You have come to the aid of your servant Israel,
to remember the promise of mercy,
the promise made to our forebears,
to Abraham and his children forever.

Prayers

Various intercessions may be spoken at this time. The prayer provided in this book for each day may also be used.

The following prayer is especially appropriate for evening.

We give thanks to you, heavenly Father,
through Jesus Christ your dear Son,
that you have graciously protected us today.
We ask you to forgive us all our sins, where we have done wrong,
and graciously to protect us tonight.

For into your hands we commend ourselves:
our bodies, our souls, and all that is ours.
Let your holy angels be with us,
so that the wicked foe may have no power over us.
Amen.

The Lord's Prayer

Our Father in heaven,
   hallowed be your name,
   your kingdom come,
   your will be done, on earth as in heaven.
Give us today our daily bread.
Forgive us our sins
   as we forgive those who sin against us.
Save us from the time of trial
   and deliver us from evil.
For the kingdom, the power, and the glory are yours,
   now and forever. Amen.

Blessing

Let us bless the Lord.
Thanks be to God.

The peace of God,
which surpasses all understanding,
keep our hearts and our minds in Christ Jesus.
Amen.

Additional materials for daily prayer are available in Evangelical Lutheran Worship *(pp. 295–331) and may supplement this simple order.*

Evening Blessing

You may make the sign of the cross.

I am a beloved child of God, marked with the cross of Christ forever.
Come to me, all you that are weary . . . and I will give you rest.
(Matt. 11:28).

Thank you, gracious God, for the gift of this coming night.
Restore me with your right spirit. Calm my mind. Quiet my heart.
Enfold me with your bountiful mercy.
Protect me from all harm,
that I sleep assured of the peace found in you alone.
I ask this in the name of Jesus, who gives us rest. Amen.

Night Prayers with Children

Dear Jesus, as a hen covers her chicks with her wings to keep them safe,
protect us this night under your golden wings; for your mercy's sake.
Amen.

We bless you, God, for the day just spent,
for laughter, tears, and all you've sent.
Grant us, Good Shepherd, through this night,
a peaceful sleep till morning light.

A parent or caregiver may trace the cross on the child's forehead or heart and say one of these blessings:

God the Father, Son, and Holy Spirit watch over you.
May God protect you through the night.
May the Lord Jesus keep you in his love.

Suggestions for Daily Reflection

God's word for me this day is:

God's word will shape my day by:

I will share God's word with others through:

My prayers today will include:

- The church universal, its ministry, and the mission of the gospel

- The well-being of creation

- Peace and justice in the world, the nations and those in authority, the community

- The poor, oppressed, sick, bereaved, lonely

- All who suffer in body, mind, or spirit

- Special concerns